ENGLISH FARMSTEADS, 1750–1914

ROYAL COMMISSION ON THE HISTORICAL MONUMENTS OF ENGLAND

ENGLISH FARMSTEADS, 1750-1914

P S Barnwell and Colum Giles

Drawn illustrations by A T Adams

ROYAL COMMISSION ON THE HISTORICAL MONUMENTS OF ENGLAND

Published by the Royal Commission on the Historical Monuments of England
at the National Monuments Record Centre, Kemble Drive, Swindon SN2 2GZ

Published with the aid of a grant from the Rural Development Commission

© Crown copyright 1997

Applications for reproduction should be made to the RCHME

First published 1997

ISBN 1 873592 30 2

British Library Cataloguing in Publication Data
A CIP catalogue record for this book is available from the British Library

Designed by Chuck Goodwin, 27 Artesian Road, London W2 5DA

Printed in Great Britain by Alden Press, Oxford

Contents

COMMISSIONERS

CHAIRMAN'S FOREWORD

The half-century since the Second World War has been a period of immense change in England's rural areas. Demographic trends have see-sawed. First, the increased mechanisation in agriculture contributed to a decline in the demand for labour and caused a depopulation of rural areas. Then, in the era of rising property values in the 1980s, prosperity and private transport led to the development of the countryside for new housing. In the same period, agriculture, always changing in response to markets and technology, continued to adapt to new economic circumstances and to explore its role in a European market, and new methods of production and crops were introduced.

In this era of rapid change, England's farm buildings, largely built to serve Victorian agriculture, have become increasingly redundant. Late 20th-century farming is highly mechanised and in many areas operates most efficiently on a scale larger than was common before 1900. As a result, old farm buildings and indeed whole farmsteads have fallen into disuse, or have been converted to general storage purposes. Their often tranquil settings make them attractive for conversion to dwellings, and the phenomenon of the farm village, surrounded by tarmac and littered with cars, has become a feature of the English countryside.

The threat to old farm buildings has led, rather more slowly than might have been wished, to a realisation that much of the history of English agriculture is being destroyed by demolition and conversion. The Royal Commission's survey of farmsteads, begun in 1992, was a response to this threat and to the fact that, beyond a small core of enthusiasts, the importance of this class of monument was imperfectly understood. The fate of England's countryside is inextricably linked to that of its rural buildings, for farm buildings figure prominently in people's perception of the country's varied landscape. It is hoped that the Royal Commission's survey and this publication will contribute to the continuing debate about what the nation wishes its rural areas to be, both economically and visually.

The redundancy of old farm buildings is beyond dispute, but better understanding about their evolution will be a crucial element in the devising of schemes for their reuse. Economic reuse of old buildings offers in almost all cases the best assurance of conservation. The Rural Development Commission's Redundant Building Grant Scheme, operating in a number of areas, is one initiative which seeks to assist in finding suitable new uses for farm buildings. The best conversions can demonstrate that historic buildings can provide good commercial working environments whilst still retaining much of their character and place in the landscape.

One of the purposes of this volume is to stimulate the recording of old farm buildings. The Royal Commission's work has necessarily been highly selective, and much recording remains to be done. The subject is a fascinating one, offering an insight into the rich variety of England's architectural heritage and into a way of life once so central to rural existence but now irrevocably lost. If this volume succeeds in encouraging others to make a contribution to our understanding of the national picture, then one of the main objectives underlying the Royal Commission's effort will have been achieved.

Commissioners wish to thank the authors of this book and all members of Commission staff who have helped in its production. Thanks should also be recorded to all those who, in either a professional capacity or as interested amateurs, supported the survey. Commissioners are grateful to the Rural Development Commission for financial help with the costs of publication. Gratitude is expressed to the owners and occupiers of the farmsteads examined by Commission staff; their interest in the heritage represented by their farm buildings is one of the more encouraging discoveries of the survey.

FARINGDON

ACKNOWLEDGEMENTS

Many people contributed to this publication and to the survey which lies behind it. Members of the Historic Farm Buildings Group, in particular Nigel Harvey and Dr Susanna Wade Martins, were important advisers at different stages of the work. Jeremy Lake of English Heritage has ensured that the Royal Commission has been informed of developments in the thematic listing of farmsteads. Staff from the Royal Commission on the Ancient and Historical Monuments of Scotland joined with the survey staff in a number of useful discussions relating to the two surveys of farmsteads being conducted north and south of the border; Dr Geoffrey Stell and Graham Douglas of RCAHMS, and Dr John Shaw of the National Museums of Scotland, were especially helpful. Staff of the Public Record Office, in particular William Foot, and of County Record Offices in the areas of survey were unfailingly helpful, as were Roy Brigden of the Museum of English Rural Life; Dr Stafford Linsley of the University of Newcastle; Kenneth Major; and Rodney Cousins of the Museum of Lincolnshire Life.

Major contributions have been made by present and past Commissioners and staff of RCHME. Dr Malcolm Airs, Professor Gwyn Meirion-Jones, Dr Marilyn Palmer and Anne Riches commented on the text and gave useful advice throughout. Professor Charles Thomas gave valuable advice regarding Cornwall. Dr John Bold and Hugh Richmond guided the survey through its different stages; Stephen Croad helped in the formulation of the project; Janet Atterbury provided the setting for the selection of areas through her work on the Survey of Surveys; maps were supplied by National Monuments Record Staff, co-ordinated by David Esplin; aerial photographs were taken by Roger Featherstone, Pete Horne and Dave MacLeod; other photography was provided by Keith Buck, Keith Findlater, James Davies, Mike Hesketh-Roberts and Peter Williams; editorial assistance from Kate Owen, Dr Robin Taylor, Hilary Walford, Dr Diane Williams and Russell Walton; and administrative support by Davina Turner, Joanne Hodgson, Jean Craven and Mary Glass. The index was prepared by Ann Hudson.

The final acknowledgement must be to the owners and occupiers of the farmsteads recorded in the course of the survey. They generously provided access to their farm buildings, and often showed a keen interest in the history of the farms, frequently in the same family hands for many generations. Without their help, the production of this volume would not have been possible.

ILLUSTRATION CREDITS

EDITORIAL NOTES

Block plans are reproduced at scales between 1:1500 and 1:2500. Plans of individual buildings and farmsteads are at various scales, from 1:500 to 1:300. Sections are mostly at 1:150, though there are exceptions to this: Fig 2.18a (1:300); Fig 7.9 (1:400) and Fig 7.15 (1:200). Bird's-eye views are mostly at 1:600, the exceptions being Figs 2.31c, 3.23a, 4.34a,b, 5.7d, 5.15e(ii), 5.15f(ii) (1:200); Figs 2.29a, 3.22a-d, 4.18c, 5.15a-d, 5.17c, 6.22c,d, 6.24b (1:300); Figs 5.3f, 6.3 (1:400) and Fig 7.8a-c (1:800).

Drawings without scale bars are not drawn to scale, though perspective cutaway views are based on a fairly uniform perspective grid allowing a degree of comparability.

LIST OF ILLUSTRATIONS

ABBREVIATIONS

CBA   Council for British Archaeology
JRASE   *Journal of the Royal Agricultural Society of England*
OD   Ordnance Datum
MAFF   Ministry of Agriculture, Fisheries and Food
PRO   Public Record Office

PREFACE

There is no generally accepted definition of 'historic' or 'old' farm buildings. Some historians have defined them as those built before 1880, which saw the beginning of the long agricultural depression and the end of more than a century's impressive farm-building development; some, with less agricultural relevance, as those built before 1900, 1914 and 1939. There is even a case to be made for a terminal date of 1950, which combines chronological convenience with the beginnings of the post-war farm-buildings reconstruction that initiated a period of substantial change. This, however, is in advance of the general perception of what is historic, and in this volume the terminal date is taken to be c1914.

It should always be remembered, however, that the basic unit of historical concern is not the individual farm building. It is the farmstead. Farmsteads consist of groups of interdependent buildings, each designed to play its particular part in agricultural production. It is only when the origins and functions of individual buildings are known and assessed in relation to the other buildings of the farmstead that the purpose and working of the farmstead and of the individual building can be fully understood. Only old buildings which are the sole survivors of vanished farmsteads should receive individual study.

Every farmstead is or was a working, changing unit composed of buildings of different functions, types and ages and, since farm needs generally change more quickly than farm buildings, subject to continuing man-made change as well as natural wear and tear. Down the generations, therefore, obsolescence and modernisation, adaptation and conversion, maintenance and repair, have played their irregular parts and left their varied evidences.

The historical importance and interest of farmsteads are considerable and varied. As features of the landscape, farmsteads record by their siting much of the pattern of rural settlement and the making of the farmlands by reclamation and enclosure. In the lowlands, a farmstead might, for instance, have been founded by a pioneering medieval peasant, a Tudor reclaimer, or a Hanoverian landowner planning his newly enclosed holding; in the higher lands, it may mark the conversion of one of the ancient summering houses to a permanent settlement. As structures, farmsteads show building materials and methods from the days when 'all things were made by hand, and one at a time' using local materials, to the days when canal, railway and lorry brought the products of the industrial system to the farm. They also show the skill with which farmers have reused materials, including those of their own farm buildings which they have demolished – a point of some importance for those who are dating old farm buildings.

Above all, as tools of the farming trade, farm buildings record the systems, methods and processes of the past. To take a few examples, corn barns preserve the memory of the flailers just as the wheelhouse, the occasional chimney and silent indoor shafting record the development of farmstead mechanisation; yards and fattening sheds bear witness to one of this country's major achievements, the development of cattle breeds, notably the beef breeds, whose descendants still populate huge areas of the prairies and pampas to which their ancestors were exported; and traditional cow houses recall the drastic change in our farming industry when overseas imports overwhelmed much of the inherited system.

More generally, the scale and degree of complexity of farm buildings tell us much about the people who built them and used them. In particular, the familiar courtyard pattern of so many traditional farmsteads reflects the rationalising energies of the landowners and land agents of the Agricultural Revolution and their Victorian successors. They also remind us that farm buildings are one of the few classes of structure which have been little influenced by formal architecture.

Most of the old buildings we now see date from between the mid 18th and the late 19th century, when the landlord-and-tenant system dominated the agricultural economy. Under this system, the landowner was responsible for the provision and maintenance of all buildings on the farms which he leased to his tenants. On the larger estates, it was the normal practice of landlords to make their agents responsible for the design of new buildings and the supervision of their construction either by the estate yard or else by a private contractor. The use of architects for farm buildings was exceptional and generally confined to buildings where prestige was important, notably the steadings of home farms. Nineteenth-century England produced many farm buildings, but it is difficult to think of any specialised agricultural architects apart from Chancellor, Wilkinson and Dean – and the latter also described himself as 'engineer'.

There are no up-to-date national figures on the numbers, types and ages of old farm buildings now existing. The only estimate available, which was based on a collation of survey evidence, was published by the Ministry of Agriculture, Fisheries and Food in 1985. This concluded that there were then in England and Wales rather over 600,000 farm buildings built before 1900. Pre-1500 survivals were few. Nearly all were barns or dovecotes and most of them survived as individual buildings. Barns predominated among farm buildings of the 16th, 17th and mid 18th centuries, though the proportion of other buildings, notably livestock buildings, increased as the years passed. Survivals from the late 18th century onwards were very much more plentiful; they included an increasingly representative variety of types of building and so provided examples of most of the working buildings of their period. Further, these later survivals were sufficiently numerous and well preserved to provide evidence not merely on individual types of building but on the design and construction of contemporary farmsteads.

So existing farm buildings give limited but increasing information on certain types of building from the later Middle Ages to Stuart times. They give considerably more and better information from the mid 18th century onwards. In particular, they give good coverage of the buildings of the Agricultural Revolution of the Hanoverian period and of the High Farming which followed it, both of them in their time the most advanced farm buildings in the world serving the most advanced farming system in the world.

Appreciation of the historical importance of this rural legacy is, however, very recent, and stems principally from the remarkable expansion of academic agrarian history in the post-war years. The 1940s and 1950s produced the forerunners, among them the first history of farm buildings, which was published in the National Federation of Young Farmer's Clubs booklet series in 1953, and such books as Grigson's *An English Farmhouse* and Rees's *Life in the Welsh Countryside*, which foreshadowed the future importance of local studies of farm buildings in their agricultural context. The 1960s saw more definite progress, the first academic conference on farm-buildings history, the first recognition of their historical importance by suggestions for their conservation, and a major book on barns. It concluded in 1969 with the publication of J E C Peters's survey of existing pre-1880 farm buildings in a large area of Staffordshire, an admirably detailed and documented study which is now accepted as the foundation book of the new historical theme.

Development continued in the 1970s with the publication of the first substantial history in the field, Harvey's *History of Farm Buildings in England and Wales*, a photographic exhibition of old farm buildings served by an informative illustrated catalogue and, significantly, a conspicuous rise in the number of relevant research theses. But it was not until the early 1980s that the subject came of age with a remarkable increase in reports, articles and specialist studies and, more easily quantifiable, more books on the subject than had appeared in the previous fifteen years. It was, therefore, no accident that this decade saw institutional as well as academic advance. In 1985 the Historic Farm Buildings Group, the first group to be solely concerned with the subject of its title, was founded. So the new historical theme was soon equipped with a journal, a newsletter that sought to maintain a current list of publications and research in hand, and annual conferences with field visits which systematically continued to advance and collate the growing but fragmented subject to which it was committed.

One cause of this growth of interest was specialised academic momentum in an academically expanding environment. Another was the effect of growing public concern at the losses of old farm buildings caused by the rapid and drastic agricultural changes of this period which rendered increasing numbers of them obsolete and redundant. The resultant wide-ranging and prolonged discussions of the problems involved and the possible courses of action, notably the conversion of unwanted farm buildings to non-agricultural purposes, were inevitably in large measure political and offered limited scope to historians. But the movement focused general attention on the importance of old farm buildings and on the need to secure proper protection. It was significant that the Historic Farm Buildings Group described its objectives in its constitution as the study of old farm buildings and 'the promotion, where appropriate, of their conservation' and that at the major public conference it held in London in 1990 on 'Old Farm Buildings in a New Countryside' it emphasised and developed the historical case for such conservation.

Since the mid 1980s, therefore, general as well as historical interest in old farm buildings has increased considerably. One sign of the times was the welcome given by conservationists and historians alike to the increase in the number of such buildings given official protection by 'listing'. Another was the need for background information for the various official and private bodies which found themselves involved in various ways with the subject. This produced two valuable reference sources, Harvey's 1985 publication, *Historic Farm Buildings Study. Sources of Information*, and *Alternative Uses for Redundant Farm Buildings*, published by Pauline Wilkinson in 1987. Both have proved themselves of considerable value to contemporaries. Both will be of considerable value to future historians.

But the continuing problem remains. On the one hand, the farming industry cannot be expected to carry indefinitely more than a limited number of uneconomic and maintenance-demanding relics of the past. On the other, the countryside is steadily losing irreplaceable scenic and historical survivals and with them rich sources of pleasure and understanding. Despite the increase of 'listing', various relevant grant schemes, and private support for particular buildings, past and present experience suggests that the loss of these historical survivals is likely to continue. But further resources for historical preservation are not likely to increase, while conversions to new purposes, however admirable aesthetically, can seldom maintain the full historical structure and character of the original building.

The need to record traditional farm buildings while they are still there to be recorded is obvious. Once they are lost, something of our history is irretrievably lost with them. For many threatened farm buildings, recording and the preservation of their records at appropriate centres may well be their only form of survival. For more immediate practical purposes, too, recording can provide a major proportion of the evidence which, when collated with other relevant material, can be circulated in appropriate form to all those who, in their various capacities, determine the future of historic farm buildings. Recording offers a means of securing both a permanent archive of the past and a source of guidance for the future.

The importance of recording was recognised early in the formal study of farm-buildings history – the first advisory booklet on their recording appeared in 1967 – and a lengthy series of recordings, general and specialised, regional and local, illustrate its successes and their value. The first national conference on the subject, held in 1994 at the University of York, reviewed effectively its past development and the future possibilities which this suggested. (The Proceedings of the conference have been published as *Recording Historic Farm Buildings*, edited by C Giles and S Wade Martins.) But such fieldwork and its preparation for publication are a time-consuming and expensive process which, apart from the farm buildings included in the recordings for official 'listing', was until recently left to private individuals and local groups. Now, however, the limited labourers in these plentiful harvest fields have received major reinforcements from the Royal Commission on the Historical Monuments of England, the national body of survey and record. Its arrival is timely, welcome and very, very important for what it represents as well as for what it has achieved. This book is the first published evidence for this statement. It will surely not be the last.

Nigel Harvey
President, Historic Farm Buildings Group

INTRODUCTION

The Royal Commission's survey of farmsteads, executed over three years from late 1992, was a response to the grave threat posed to farm buildings by post-war demographic and economic trends, combined with developments in agriculture which made most old buildings redundant for their original purposes. The survey differs from others for two main reasons. First, the Commission's national remit dictated a broad-ranging assessment of a class of building found in great numbers across the whole country. This objective thus distinguishes this survey from many more detailed local studies conducted in recent years. Secondly, the Royal Commission's concern with physical evidence gave an emphasis which sets the survey apart from publications which draw their material from contemporary literature. Allowing the buildings to tell their own story provides an insight into how rapidly new ideas were adopted, and this in turn raises many interesting questions about the rate of agricultural change.

The objective of providing an assessment which was not purely local, and the resources available to conduct the survey – three field-workers for three years, with necessary support – shaped the survey methodology. Clearly, not all farm buildings in the country could be identified, let alone recorded; selection was an essential element in devising a workable approach to the material. English agriculture's intensely regional, even local, diversity within a national framework suggested that the Royal Commission's recording activity should mirror this characteristic. A national overview, therefore, was to be approached through the examination of, and comparison between, the farm buildings of different farming regions.

The identification of areas for survey was determined by an initial exercise designed to establish the distribution of past and current recording activity; the Royal Commission chose to work in regions where little or no recording had been conducted.[1] Five areas were selected, and the choice was designed to include predominantly arable regions (west Berkshire, south Lincolnshire and north Northumberland), a southern upland area dominated by livestock raising (east Cornwall) and a thoroughgoing

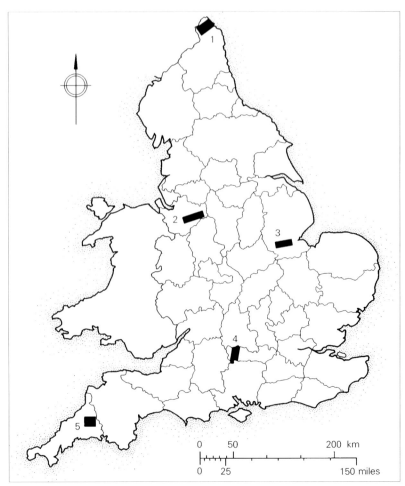

dairy area (central Cheshire) (see map). There were different emphases within the three arable regions. The coastal plain and the interior of north Northumberland, the fenlands of Lincolnshire and the rolling downs of Berkshire offered clear topographical contrasts, and the main building periods, the development of mechanised working and the importance attached to livestock gave each area a special character. The selection of areas thus covered the principal farming systems of England, ranged widely geographically and offered the chance to examine how different areas reacted to changes in agriculture.

Approximately fifty farmsteads were recorded in each of the five areas. The field

Map showing the areas selected for survey by RCHME.

Key

1 north Northumberland (chapter 4)

2 central Cheshire (chapter 6)

3 south Lincolnshire (chapter 3)

4 west Berkshire (chapter 2)

5 east Cornwall (chapter 5)

evidence was supplemented by material drawn from documentary sources; among the major classes of document were the tithe records (consulted in county Record Offices); the valuations made following the passing of the 1910 Finance Act; and the National Farm Survey, or War Record, compiled in 1941–3.[2]

This work is principally concerned with farm buildings erected between 1750 and the First World War. Some areas of the country retain substantial numbers of pre-1750 structures, but the vast majority of historic farm buildings date from the 19th century. Early buildings were recorded whenever they were encountered, but, because they tended to survive as single buildings within otherwise later complexes, it was rarely possible to gain a picture of pre-1750 farmsteads as a whole. The end date for the survey was more difficult to determine. The First World War was chosen as a rough terminal date to allow the inclusion of structures built during the Great Depression of the late 19th century. The post-1918 period – the era of the tractor, the combine harvester and electric power – must be left to a separate study.

In this volume, farmsteads are discussed as complexes designed to serve different farming systems. The form and character of individual structures are examined, but particular stress is also laid on the contribution which each building made to the working of the farmstead as a whole. The buildings of a farmstead reveal the farm's agricultural bias; changes in this bias can be revealed by alterations and additions made to a farmstead; and the relationship between the buildings indicates how processes flowed and how efficiently they worked. Farmhouses are not included as a main subject of study, since emphasis is placed on the purely agricultural activity of the farmstead rather than on the farmstead as a place of work and a place for living. Where, however, parts of the house played an important part in production, as in Cheshire, they are drawn into the discussion to show how they relate spatially and functionally to the outbuildings.

Farmsteads differ in complexity, but most share a common processing system. Good crop yields depend upon fertile land, and fertility was maintained throughout the period under review by the use of manure and of fodder crops. Grain and fodder crops enter the farmstead for processing, and some of the product, principally grain, was sold or stored. Straw was stored for use as fodder and litter, and livestock, kept within the farmstead, were fed and produced manure for use on the fields. This basic flow of process is, however, capable of different emphases, according to the relative importance locally of grain, livestock and dairy produce. The flow also becomes more complex over time, as some processes are removed from the farmstead and new products, such as artificial manures, come into use. These changes are reflected in layout and building design, and therefore architectural evidence is of major importance in providing a detailed picture of how agriculture evolved. The nature and pace of change vary from area to area, but this merely serves to emphasise that the essentially regional character of English farming is clearly revealed in its buildings.

The regional variety within, and indeed comprising, the national framework of English farming is the underlying theme of this book. This variety is examined in the chapters describing the farmsteads of the five study areas. Detailed discussion of each area is important, for it allows the intensely local character of farmsteads to be explained against a background of both national developments and regional agricultural practice. The national context is provided first in the opening chapter, which outlines the main developments in English agriculture in the post-medieval period, and also in the last chapter, which examines the relationship between the physical evidence and the national models of development derived from 19th-century documentary sources.

This book and the archive from which it has been compiled are the Royal Commission's contribution to the debate surrounding the historical importance of old farm buildings and their place in the modern world. The full national picture of development will be derived only from further locally based survey work, and it is hoped that the present work will have fitted some of the jigsaw pieces into place and will stimulate further research into this important aspect of our history.

1   ENGLISH AGRICULTURE, 1500–1914

Agriculture is an economic activity, dependent as all others on laws of supply and demand. The essential purpose of the business is to produce food to feed the population, and in the process a livelihood is provided for many and considerable wealth for a few. The link between population and agriculture is a matter of debate; on the one hand, increased population is seen as the stimulus for higher agricultural output, but a contrary view holds that it is increased output which permits population growth. The fortunes of the industry have been marked by peaks and troughs, according to whether it has been able to sell its produce at a worthwhile price, with or without the intervention of the State. However, while these basic principles have remained unaltered for centuries, the industry itself has changed beyond recognition.

The modern consensus on English agrarian development after 1500 has abandoned the idea of an agricultural revolution characterised by dramatic and far-reaching change concentrated within a short period after 1750. Instead, the process of change is now recognised to have been much more protracted, beginning earlier and continuing later than previously thought.[1] On the one hand, many new ideas are now known to have originated much earlier than once allowed, and, on the other hand, it is recognised that, for example, the gap between the development of a technique and its widespread adoption could often be significant. In addition, modern research has revealed the unevenness of change, and the picture of development is now one of immense complexity, based on intensely local and regional variations.

The broad national trend of development shows English agriculture expanding virtually continuously from the late Middle Ages to the late 19th century, with a sudden realignment after the 1870s to take account of new global conditions. The farmers of England enjoyed immense success for centuries in feeding an expanding population, which enjoyed a steadily improving standard of living, with a better and more varied diet. Farmers achieved this in a number of ways; first, by taking in more land; then by employing more efficient or intensive methods of exploitation, producing more (or more cheaply) from the same basic resource; and, finally, as external conditions changed, by adjusting to the demands of an ever-widening market, first local, later regional, then national, and, finally, global.

English Agriculture, 1500–1750

Between the early 16th century and the mid 18th century, the population of England more than doubled, from about 2.4 million in 1540 to about 6 million in 1760. Agriculture supplied the needs of this expanding population by colonising new land, sometimes former commons or wastes, and by some important innovations, or at least the more widespread application of useful techniques. Enclosure, the irrigation of water meadows, the elimination of fallow by the introduction of 'permanent tillage', the use of new root crops and grasses to maintain soil fertility, better manuring, drainage and stock breeds were all aspects of improved husbandry which developed in this period. Open-field husbandry, dominant in midland England, proved capable of raising output through the adoption of innovations such as ley farming, and communal agriculture is now regarded as less inflexible than its critics have sometimes supposed.

The strongly regional character of English agriculture by the mid 17th century, however, made many of these innovations inapplicable or insignificant within particular areas; in woodland England, for example, enclosure was already well advanced by the beginning of the 16th century. There were, too, great fluctuations of emphasis within these centuries, with the 16th-century conversion of arable land to pasture (partly based on the profits to be gained from wool) replaced later by an increased emphasis on primary food production to meet the demands of the increasing population.

One consistent trend within this period, however, was the consolidation of regional specialisation in agriculture. There was a broad distinction between the grass-growing uplands, where sheep and cattle were raised and where dairy farming was important, and the lowlands, where mixed farming predominated. Within the lowlands, farmers might concentrate on cereal production, keeping sheep and cattle mainly to ensure soil fertility by the use of their manure, or place greater emphasis on meat production. As each region developed its own particular character, it became more dependent on other regions for those products which it lacked, and 'the whole country was drawn more firmly than ever before into a dovetailed system of agricultural production'.[2] The development of a marketing system and improvements in transport allowed some areas to specialise in the production of items for consumption in England's growing towns. The provisioning of London affected agricultural practice in much of southeast England; Kent, for example, began to develop its fruit-growing in this period. The existence of rural and urban industries furthered inter-regional marketing. In the early 18th century, Defoe noted of the textile-producing dales of Yorkshire's West Riding that the population 'scarce sow corn enough for their cocks and hens'; the preoccupation of the people with the manufacture of cloth meant that corn was imported from Lincolnshire, Nottinghamshire and the East Riding, butter came from the East and North Ridings, and cheese was obtained from Cheshire.[3]

English Agriculture, 1750–1820

The next doubling of the population, from 6 million in 1760 to 12 million in 1821, placed heavy demands on English agriculture. The previously important export of cereals dwindled as grain was diverted to the growing home market, and for the first time foodstuffs were imported on a significant scale. Despite the progress made before 1750, there remained enormous scope for improvement in agricultural production. Crop strains and crop rotations were generally poor, much land required drainage, and much was underused. Efforts to increase agricultural output depended on enclosure, innovation and the distribution of land. There is no agreement among modern historians about the relative importance of these different aspects, and each one is the subject of intense debate over its causes and effects.

The period between 1750 and 1830 saw the enclosure of one-fifth of the area of England, mainly by parliamentary Act. Many contemporaries saw enclosure as a vital catalyst for wholesale improvement in agriculture, and some modern historians agree with this view, arguing that enclosed farms were important in promoting experiment and initiative. The new farms, it was held, permitted greater flexibility in the use of land and encouraged the introduction of new crops. Other historians, however, have argued against this association, pointing out that three-quarters of England was enclosed before 1750 without any revolutionary change in agriculture. Many improvements, moreover, were first introduced in open fields, demonstrating that these were not in themselves a barrier to progress. The role of enclosure in raising productivity is also open to question, for much of the land enclosed in this period was of poor quality and not best suited to intensive cultivation. The common view is that enclosure may have been prompted more by the desire of proprietors to raise rental income than by the need to improve farming, although it is also acknowledged that the farmer working an enclosed farm was in a better position to develop improved practices than his counterpart in the open-field system.

There is no doubt that many new practices, a few based for the first time on scientific principles, became widespread by the end of this period. The need to produce more from the same amount of land led to the adoption of crop rotations which replaced unproductive fallow by the use of fodder crops, which not only provided feed for livestock but also served to enrich the soil by fixing nitrogen. These rotations were known before 1750, but were only widely adopted after that date. The Norfolk four-course rotation used roots and grasses to alternate with cereals in a four-year cycle. 'Convertible' farming had a much longer cycle, and alternated between grasses, left for up to six years, and cereals, again cropped for up to six years. These rotations allowed the production of more and better manure from an increased number of better-fed livestock, and the manure kept the soil in good heart and raised crop yields. However, the importance of the new crops and rotations in raising national output is not clear. Before 1800, the rate of increase in agricultural production was very low. The benefits of the new crop rotations were evident mainly on light soils, and in many areas of the country the new rotations were of little value until large-scale drainage was undertaken.

The period after 1750 was also marked by improvements in livestock. Early 19th-century commentators frequently condemned the prevalence of traditional strains of cattle and sheep, and placed great stress on the importance of better breeding. The influence of men like Robert Bakewell of Dishley, Leicestershire, who developed cross-bred cattle and sheep, was slow to spread, but widespread interest in livestock breeds is evident in the common depiction of prize beasts in oil paintings of the period.

The provision of better tools also raised the standard of farming. There was a slow improvement in the design of ploughs, for example, with metal replacing wood, and threshing machines became well known, if not very widely used, by the early 19th century. Specialist agricultural engineers began the process of transforming machine-making into an industry based upon mass production of standardised items. One of the greatest engineering firms, Ransomes of Ipswich, was established in 1789, and Howards of Bedford set up in 1811. In addition, there slowly developed an infrastructure which provided the maintenance essential for the widespread adoption of machine-working. Although the advances of the period before 1815 were important, they represented the foundations for the later more general adoption of new machines. Mechanisation remained very restricted in this phase of the Agricultural Revolution, and production was still largely based on traditional methods using muscle power and locally made tools.

Another aspect of improved farming was the provision of better farm buildings. The literature on farming of the late 18th and early 19th centuries placed great emphasis on the importance of well-built farmsteads planned on efficient lines to minimise labour and promote the production of manure. The model farmstead of this period was based on the grouping of buildings around a yard or series of yards, and these buildings included not only barns but also shelters for livestock, the welfare of which was intimately connected to the achievement of high cereal yields. Numerous publications provided models for imitation, and, although some designs were more decorative than functional, the best show a clear understanding of the principles of integrated farming. The influence of model-farm designs is open to debate. Few were actually built, largely owing to the high capital investment required. Nevertheless, the ideas represented in the new designs were an important aspect of the contemporary discussion about improved farming, and the principles of layout and design may have had an important bearing on the form of smaller farmsteads.

A final aspect of innovation was the climate of interest in agriculture generated in this period. Agriculture was still an important element in the nation's economy, and the owners of the land were the dominant political force. Farming, therefore, was an important political issue, and during the Napoleonic Wars national survival became critically dependent on its success. Issues were aired through newly formed local agricultural societies, through the propagandising literature of men like Arthur Young and William Marshall, and even through government agencies, in particular the Board of Agriculture, founded in 1793. The image of the landowner as a responsible, sober farmer,

actively involved in the application of new ideas on agriculture, became fashionable, to the point that he became a stock figure in the literature of this and the succeeding age.

Landholding has been seen as a major influence on the performance of English agriculture. There is no doubt that the small farmer had declined in importance, to the point that, by 1830, 90 per cent of farmland was worked by tenants. Ownership became steadily more concentrated in the hands of a small *rentier* class, one which, by virtue of its position, was able to invest in many of the expensive changes needed to raise the output of English farming. Enclosure offered landowners the opportunity to create larger and supposedly more efficient farms. However, more evidence is required before the large enclosure farm can be seen as the vehicle for improved farming.

English Agriculture, 1820–1870

The doubling of the population of England and Wales between 1821 (12 million) and 1881 (26 million) stimulated further far-reaching changes to English farming. In this period, foreign foodstuffs grew in importance, with a fifth of the nation's food being imported in 1841. Home production continued, however, to be seen as the major means of satisfying demand. The solution to the problems of agriculture was sought not in a changed emphasis in output but in more intensive exploitation of the system of mixed farming that had been developed before 1815. The perceived need was for more grain, and partly for political reasons cereal prices were protected until the repeal of the Corn Laws in 1846. High Farming evolved as a means of providing increased grain yields, achieved through the thorough integration of livestock and cereal husbandry. The philosophy underpinning the system was that greater input resulted in increased output. The finite land resources were to be made more productive by the application of more and better manure, obtained from greater numbers of livestock, fed on better fodder crops. Thus the intention was to raise the whole system onto a higher plane of production, yielding not only more cereals, but also more meat and dairy products.

Many of the methods already in use to make farming more efficient were continued, sometimes with good results, sometimes with diminishing returns. Propagandising literature grew immensely in this period, led by the *Journal of the Royal Agricultural Society of England*, the first volume of which appeared in 1840. A massive programme of drainage, assisted after

1846 by government grants, led to the improvement of 4.8 million hectares (12 million acres) between 1840 and 1880, and better strains of crop and better livestock breeds were developed. Further enclosure, however, brought mainly marginal land into cultivation. Mechanisation continued to affect both large and small farms, although perceptions of the new machines underwent a transformation in this period. Before 1850, the threat posed by machinery to rural employment, and the fact that rural wages were very low in some regions, arrested progress. In the early 1830s, the Swing riots were largely directed against farmers using threshing machines. After 1850, however, the rural workforce declined in number and enjoyed higher wages. Machines were seen as less threatening, and it was in this period that they became commonplace. The land was better prepared and better maintained through the use of machines such as crushers and hoes, and sowing and harvesting were made more efficient by drills and reapers. The advent of portable steam revolutionised threshing, but had a less dramatic effect on ploughing; despite the attention focused on steam ploughing, at most only 2 per cent of the arable land in England and Wales was prepared in this way in any one year. A further feature of the period is the continued emphasis on the need for better farm buildings. In many areas, a wholesale rebuilding took place, replacing the structures of an earlier age by farmsteads suited to the needs of contemporary agriculture. This rebuilding forms the subject of the present volume.

The new emphasis within the well-established system of mixed farming was the importance attached to livestock. Greater numbers of cattle could be maintained, for they could be kept in intensive conditions and fed better-quality fodder. New foodstuffs were introduced in this period. Oil cake, at first using imported materials, became common in the middle of the 19th century, consumption rising sixfold between 1830 and 1860. The increased crop yields guaranteed that the cattle would have more straw for bedding, and this was turned into more and better manure, to be returned to the fields. Almost as an incidental side effect, meat production increased, to the point when, in the 1850s, the value of livestock in the national economy equalled that of crops for the first time. Soil fertility was also raised through the use of new types of fertiliser. Lime and bones were recommended from the early 19th century, and imports of Peruvian guano from the 1820s and Chilean nitrates from the 1840s added to the range of products available to the farmer. The first chemical fertilisers were produced in the 1840s, but their use was rare before the mid 20th century.

High Farming was not suited to all areas of the country, for in regions where the main emphasis was on stock-raising or dairying the drive to increase cereal production was of less importance. The national drive to raise production, however, succeeded in its objective. The more widespread use of fodder crops in rotations, and the application of farmyard manure and other fertilisers, allowed crop yields to rise by a half between 1830 and 1880. By the end of this period, agriculture in the grain-producing part of the country had been transformed; methods which earlier had been of limited application were then common, and great advances had been made in new areas. English farming may not have corresponded uniformly to the image created by the propagandists of the age, but for the first time it began to resemble industrial production.

English Agriculture, 1870–1914

Although High Farming succeeded, its goal slowly became inappropriate. English agriculture increasingly operated within a global economy, and from 1850 Britain began to depend increasingly on selling manufactured goods in exchange for imports of raw materials and foodstuffs. Change was in large measure forced upon the British farmer, for at this time the products of vast new territories were becoming available, undercutting the home producer. Wheat from the prairies of North America and from Australia, butter and cheese from Europe, North America and New Zealand, and, with the advent of refrigeration and better freight services, meat from the USA, Argentina, and Australia and New Zealand, were all available to the British consumer at prices the home industry could not match. By the early 20th century, Britain imported three-quarters of its wheat, the same proportion of its butter and cheese, and half its meat.

The Great Depression which set in from the 1870s was a disaster for the English farmer. The confident assumptions of Victorian High Farming were made irrelevant in a brutally short period as prices tumbled; wheat values, for example, halved between the 1860s and the 1890s, and wool prices followed suit. Severely threatened by low-priced foreign grain, meat and dairy produce, English farmers, especially those who had embraced the philosophy of High Farming, were obliged to develop new products for the market, and the production of perishable commodities, which depended on close proximity to consumers, was one area which was still safe from foreign competition. The most conspicuous change was in the shift towards liquid milk production. Rapid transport from the farm to the towns was provided by the national rail network, and from the 1860s rural producers began to replace the urban dairy as the chief source of supply. In the face of this new trade, and following a serious cattle plague in 1865, urban dairies, formerly the chief suppliers of towns, declined. There was a widespread abandonment of arable land, which by 1939 totalled only 59 per cent of the area occupied in 1875. Grassland rose in proportion, and the number of milk cows grew, the biggest rise being in the traditional arable areas of England, the south and east of the country.

Many farmers began to see the potential of supplying the urban centres with fresh fruit and vegetables, with early varieties commanding a premium. Once again the railways provided the necessary rapid and reliable transport: in 1889 the Great Western Railway carried 300 tons of strawberries, 4,500 tons of potatoes and 8,000 tons of broccoli from Devon and Cornwall to urban markets, and one Cornish farmer was able to sell fruit in Edinburgh only twenty-four hours after it had been picked.[4] In Lincolnshire, potatoes and other vegetables became major crops, and numerous light railways were built to ensure their rapid transport to railheads for dispatch to market.[5] Breeding horses for use in towns was another means by which the struggling arable farmer could diversify to meet the needs of the growing urban centres, and this led to the apparent paradox of unprecedented numbers of horses being recorded on farms in a period of depression for arable farming.[6]

The realignment did not amount to a total abandonment of the earlier system of mixed farming. Grain was still grown in large quantities, but after 1870 there was an increasing emphasis on the production of barley, much of it for fodder, at the expense of wheat. Fewer root fodder crops were grown, for livestock were increasingly raised on grain, much of it imported, or on grass, grown on former arable land. Sheep numbers declined markedly after 1880; wool prices fell, and, since less land was used for root fodder crops, sheep were no longer so important in the process of restoring fertility to the soil. Despite foreign competition, however, English livestock were still a valuable source of income. Quality meat production in particular found a specialist niche in the market.

The period after 1870 was, therefore, one which witnessed a dramatic shift in the emphasis of English agriculture. Threatened by cheap imports which forced down the prices of their traditional products, the English farmer was obliged to exploit well-established sources of income and to develop new products. Investment was not an attractive option for the landowner, for agriculture ceased to offer the sort of returns which the age of High Farming had brought. Any available capital was required for machinery or for the development of new products and markets, and large-scale investment in farm buildings declined markedly.

Postscript: 1914 to the Present Day

Since the First World War, English agriculture has experienced two more periods of revolutionary change. The first, in the middle decades of the century, saw the widespread adoption of new machines. It was in this period that the tractor began to replace the horse, and the combine harvester to take the place of the reaper. Mechanisation also affected dairy farming, with milking machines and milking parlours, the design of which was conditioned by new hygiene regulations. The machines were powered by electricity, sometimes generated on the farm but increasingly drawn from the national grid. Meat production became more intensive, with large-scale pig units, poultry houses and beef units becoming common for the first time. The second revolution, in the late 20th century, coincided with the UK's entry into the then European Economic Community. This has brought significant changes to the types of product grown on English farms – maize, linseed, rape and so on – and to the way in which production is coordinated and financed, often by remote corporations for which agriculture is just one source of income.

These changes have distanced agricultural practice ever further from that for which pre-1914 buildings were constructed. The typical grain-producing farm of eastern England, for example, carries on its work today in new sheds, where corn can be stored and dried, leaving the old barn and farm buildings empty or used for storage (Fig 1.1). The redundancy of most old farm buildings is testimony to the immense differences between agriculture today and English farming at its high point in the Victorian era.

Fig 1.1 Great Hidden Farm, Hungerford, Berkshire. This aerial view shows the older timber-framed farm buildings surrounded by large modern sheds, used for livestock-raising and grain-processing and storage.

2 WEST BERKSHIRE

The Survey Area

The landscape of west Berkshire is that of chalk downlands, broad river valleys and, between the two, undulating countryside. The chosen survey area incorporates all three types of land. It is centred on the valley of the River Kennet, between Hungerford in the west downstream to Newbury in the east (Fig 2.1). To the north, the land rises gently to a plateau, but to the south, it rises, gently first, then more steeply, up the scarp slope of the downs, to Walbury Hill, at 297 m OD (974 ft) the highest point in the county. The scenery is varied. The downlands have an open aspect with wide horizons, but on the lower land the undulations, combined with old woodlands, limit the views, and the scale of the landscape is more intimate. In the river valleys, especially in that of the Kennet, there are broad plains, still subject to seasonal flooding and giving a marshy, reedy landscape. The settlement pattern is mixed, with some major villages (Kintbury, Boxford), a number of minor villages (Upper and Lower Green in Inkpen, Wickham Green in Welford), and a large number of isolated hamlets and individual farms, many representing early piecemeal enclosure or relics of a former manorial centre.

The natural conditions are favourable to agriculture. The climate is moderate, with low rainfall (an average of 558 mm or 22 in. per year in the mid 19th century).[1] The area's soils vary, with thin loams over much of the chalk, gravels and loams with flints in the Kennet Valley, and poorer loams in the southern part of the area.[2] Climate and soils combined to make 'almost every part of Berkshire ... well adapted for wheat, and it is found to be prolific in no common degree, in this valuable grain which furnishes "the staff of life"'.[3]

The area was well served by market towns and by inland navigation. In the early 19th century, Newbury was well established as one of the largest corn markets in the region, and in the mid 19th century Hungerford built a new corn exchange.[4] Both towns were linked to the Thames river system, and thence to London, by the Kennet and Avon Canal, built in the early 18th century; wheat (including seed wheat),

barley, malt and flour were the principal agricultural exports in the early 19th century. In the same period, East Ilsley, bordering on the northern part of the survey area, was famous for sheep-dealing; there was a very important annual fair and a fortnightly market; at the fair, more than 30,000 sheep might be sold.[5] The region was overwhelmingly agricultural in its economy, and this was to have important social consequences when mechanisation began to affect the area in the early 19th century. The construction of the Great Western Railway branch line, opened in 1847, gave the area improved access to urban markets, and allowed a strong dairy industry to develop.

Landholding in Berkshire

In the 19th century and perhaps earlier, Berkshire was a county of large and medium-sized estates. The clearest index to landholding within the county is provided by the late 19th-century documentary sources, compiled at a date when most of the farmsteads examined in this survey had been at least partially built, but probably broadly reflecting the pattern of ownership at an earlier period. In 1873, Berkshire's 175,581 hectares (433,863 acres) were divided among 7,240 owners, with over half the land lying in seventy-six estates of more than 405 hectares (1,000 acres). The total of 54 per cent of land held in estates of over 405 hectares (1,000 acres) in 1883 placed Berkshire firmly in the middle of the national league table. Alongside these larger estates, however, an important role was played by owners of smaller holdings; in 1883, nearly 20 per cent of the land was held in estates of between 120 and 405 hectares (300–1,000 acres).[6]

Within the survey area, there was in the 19th century considerable variety in terms of landholding. Part of the Craven estate, at over 7,700 hectares (19,225 acres) the second largest within the county in 1873, lay within the area; the estate included the parish of Hamstead Marshall, one of the family's chief seats until a fire destroyed the house in 1718. The family was also the principal landowner in Kintbury,

Enborne, Inkpen and Speen. A group of parishes (Welford, Boxford, Peasemore) were dominated by the Archer-Houblon or Eyre family for much of the 19th and 20th centuries; unlike the Craven family, the Archer-Houblons were resident within the area, and in 1873 had an estate of 2,321 hectares (5,737 acres). There were at different times other important gentry families resident within the area; the Suttons at Benham Park, Speen; the Dundas family of Kintbury (326 hectares (806 acres) in 1873); the Cherry family of Denford, Kintbury (642 hectares (1,587 acres) in 1873); the Butlers of Kirby House, Inkpen (565 hectares (1,397 acres) in 1873), and the Slopers of West Woodhay (553 hectares (1,367 acres) in 1873). There were, in addition, smaller estates: in 1838, for example, Edward Tull owned three farms, totalling 259 hectares (641 acres), in Peasemore, and in Kintbury in 1844 there were a number of small landowners as well as large estates.[7]

Despite the existence of many large estates, an early 19th-century writer calculated that 'about one third of the whole county is occupied by the proprietors of the soil', and that 'a high spirited and independent yeomanry, actively engaged in agriculture, and each forming a circle of connection around him, is the distinguishing character of the county'. The tithe apportionments record the existence of owner-occupied farms within the survey area; in Inkpen Richard Froom had a small farm (Northcroft Farm, 24 hectares (60 acres)), and in Boxford the Revd John Wells held Wyfield Manor Farm (155 hectares (384 acres)).[8]

The tenure under which farms were held varied considerably and appears to have changed over time. In the late 18th century, leasehold tenure was not regarded as common, and its absence was seen as 'very detrimental to good husbandry, and a great check to many improvements'. In the early 19th century it was remarked that 'by far the greatest part of the land is freehold', and that this was the best type of tenure for farmers. Short, fixed-term leases, usually for seven, fourteen or twenty-one years, were common. This apparent contradiction of the picture suggested for the late 18th century may in fact reflect a genuine increase in leasing, and certainly by the middle of the 19th century leases were regarded as commonplace.[9]

Berkshire enjoyed a reputation for improving landlords, and an Agricultural Society was established in the county in 1794 to promote improvements in farming.[10] The shire was known for its pioneers, although it is not clear that the example of a few extraordinary cases was widely followed. In the 18th century,

Fig 2.1 Map of the Berkshire survey area.

Jethro Tull, the inventor of the seed drill, farmed in Shalbourne, just south of Hungerford, and in the early 19th century the Buscot farm of E L Loveden, Esquire, was cited as a model for emulation.[11] Later in the century, the vast Coleshill Farm, built for the Earl of Radnor in 1853–4, attracted wide attention, but most celebrated of all were Prince Albert's farms on the Windsor estate; these were renowned for their farm buildings, for their use of machinery, for their development of the best livestock breeds, and for the welfare of their workers.[12] Landlords of more modest means were also capable of advanced husbandry, and J Bailey Denton picked out the example of Haines Hill Farm, an owner-occupied farm of 182 hectares (450 acres) near Twyford, for its use of covered yards for livestock, and for its use of machinery.[13]

The Farming Landscape

In the 18th century, Berkshire had a landscape made up largely of open-field parishes, extensive commons and wastes, and some early enclosure. Late in the century, it was said that 'a moiety, at least, of the arable land ... is still lying in common fields', and in the early 19th century the persistence of open-field farming was regarded as an impediment to agricultural improvement; the old proverb was invoked that 'the lands that many owners share, can never know an owner's care'.[14] The process of enclosure gathered pace after 1800, however, to produce a largely enclosed landscape by the middle of the 19th century. Chaddleworth in 1809, Boxford in 1814, Welford in the same year, West Ilsley in 1825, all received enclosure awards for large parts of the parish.

The wastes comprised a separate problem for agricultural improvement. They lay mainly on the chalk downs, and in the late 18th century provided wide expanses of unenclosed grazing.[15] The wastes were seen by some as a vital resource for sheep husbandry, so important in the local economy; they were 'the very support of the farms, which every good husbandman there will acknowledge'. Others, however, saw the potential for wholesale colonisation for arable purposes, and slowly the wastes were eroded. Although the tithe surveys recorded some surviving down pastures (149 hectares (368 acres) in Inkpen, for example), and although some commons still remain – for example, in Hungerford – by the mid 19th century the downs landscape had been at least partially transformed by enclosure and by incorporation into the system of intensive arable husbandry characteristic of the area. The chief crops grown on the newly won land were turnips, grazed off by sheep, and oats, but generous applications of fertilisers and manure were required to maintain the soil in good heart. The long-term wisdom of this change to arable was questioned at the time. Ploughing the downs would, it was claimed, soon lead to soil exhaustion, and 'after the first seven years, be the utter ruin of the farms'.[16] The traditionalist's view was expressed trenchantly in a mid-century work which had one local claiming that 'God meant the downs ... for sheep walks', but that 'they are all mad for ploughing ... these blockhead farmers ... There are higher things in this world ... than indifferent oats and d–d bad turnips.'[17]

The farms within this varied landscape were most commonly of between 40 and 120 hectares (100–300 acres) in the 19th and early 20th centuries. There were many larger farms, with a considerable number of between 120 and 200 hectares (300–500 acres) and a smaller number of over 200 hectares (500 acres). The largest farms recorded by the tithe surveys included Manor Farm, Beedon (286 hectares (707 acres)), Welford Farm, Welford (254 hectares (629 acres)), and Manor Farm, Chaddleworth (226 hectares (558 acres)). Some farms had

boundaries which took in meadow, arable and downs, and this could result in farms of three, four, or more kilometres in length. In these circumstances, remote farmsteads, known as 'down farms', were sometimes built, with buildings for crop storage and processing and for livestock. The down farms reduced the haulage of both straw and manure, keeping both near to the area where they were required rather than removing them temporarily to the main farmstead.[18]

The Farming System

The history of agriculture in Berkshire between 1750 and the First World War conforms closely to the conventionally accepted picture of how English farming evolved in the modern era. At the start of the period, the county's farming served a regional market and was based on sheep and corn. Bolstered by protective tariffs, this emphasis continued through the post-Napoleonic depression, and Berkshire shows many of the characteristics of High Farming, particularly in relation to the drive towards ever higher grain yields, which were the gospel of the age. The system foundered, however, in the later decades of the 19th century, when foreign competition, especially in cheap grain, caused a major realignment towards animal husbandry and dairy farming.

SHEEP AND CORN

Before the late 19th century, the Berkshire farming system largely revolved around sheep and corn. From at least as early as the late 18th century, sheep were raised, both on the downs and elsewhere, for sale for further fattening, the meat being destined ultimately for the London market. The sheep were valued almost as much for their manure as for their meat, the system of folding the flocks on fields of roots for 'feeding off' being an essential means of maintaining soil fertility. There was little change to sheep husbandry for much of the century, the main area of improvement being in the introduction of new breeds – the Hampshire, Leicester and Cotswold – to replace the native Berkshire and its crosses.[19] A significant decline in the sheep population occurred in the late 19th century; in 1868 the figure stood at a record high of over one-third of a million, but by 1914 the numbers had been reduced by almost two-thirds. The fall was due largely to a decline in arable farming, combined with a change in the method of maintaining soil fertility, with artificial fertilisers replacing the established method of folding sheep on root crops.[20] Despite the decline, however, sheep remained important in the local economy.

Cereal production lay at the heart of Berkshire farming for much of the period under review. The principal crop in the mid 19th century was wheat (24 per cent of arable land), followed by seeds (23 per cent), turnips (18 per cent), barley (15 per cent) and oats (8 per cent).[21] Much of the experimentation in the late 18th and early 19th centuries – the introduction of four and five-course rotations (for example, wheat, barley, grasses and roots); the folding of sheep on turnips to increase soil fertility and therefore crop yields; the use of artificial grasses (clover etc) to allow more livestock producing more manure for the fields; the use of artificial fertilisers; enclosure, including that of the upland sheep pastures; draining – was connected with the drive towards raising corn output.[22]

From the onset of the Great Depression, however, arable husbandry declined. In the county as a whole, the land under the plough was reduced from about 101,000 hectares (250,000 acres) in 1866 to about 72,850 hectares (180,000 acres) in 1906.[23] Some of the decline is explained by the fall from favour of turnips as a root crop, but among the cereal crops wheat was severely affected. Within the survey area, most parishes show a significant reduction in wheat production between 1866 and 1906; in Welford, for example, 357 hectares (882 acres) were used for wheat in 1866, but only 260 hectares (644 acres) forty years later, and in Kintbury the figures were 458 hectares (1,132 acres) in 1866 and only 280 hectares (691 acres) in 1906. Barley production also fell (for example, from 319 hectares (788 acres) in Kintbury in 1866 to 150 hectares (373 acres) in 1906), but oats, used widely as a fodder crop, were grown in increasing quantities in some, but not all, parishes; Welford more than doubled the area of land used for oats, and in Boxford the area of oats increased from 98 hectares (244 acres) in 1876 to 160 hectares (395 acres) thirty years later.[24]

BEEF AND DAIRY PRODUCTION

The late 19th-century change in cereal production reflected the wider difficulties faced by English wheat-growers in what was becoming a global market. The reaction to foreign competition, in Berkshire as elsewhere, was to turn to meat production and dairying. Before the late 19th century, cattle had played a subordinate role in the county. Dairying, including cheese production, had been important in the Vale area in the north of the county (outside the survey area), and the Kennet Valley was known for its dairying in the mid 19th century, but in the early 19th century it could be said that Berkshire was, 'emphatically speaking, neither a breeding, nor a fatting county; excepting of sheep and swine'.[25] Cattle were regarded over much of the county primarily as producers of manure – that is, as an adjunct to cereal production. New feedstuffs and artificial grasses allowed more stock to be kept, increasing the supply of manure for the arable lands.[26] There was considerable interest in improving cattle breeds, but as late as 1860 it was said that 'from the small proportion of grass-land it will naturally be inferred that neither dairies nor grazing form a very prominent feature in the county'.[27]

The situation changed markedly in the last third of the 19th century. The railways allowed the region to provide London and other cities with liquid milk, and offered farmers a way of diversifying to offset the effects of the slump in demand for grain. By 1870 Berkshire was supplying London with one-quarter of its rail-borne milk, and the Lambourn and Kennet Valleys increased their dairy production thereafter. There was a 60 per cent increase in the numbers of milk cows in the county between 1871 and the outbreak of the First World War, and the amount of permanent pasture grew in roughly the same proportion. In Kintbury, there were 144 milk cows in 1866, but nearly three times that number forty years later, and a farm in the parish had been transformed from one with 109 hectares (270 acres) of arable land and 28 hectares (70 acres) of grass to the exact reverse position, with a herd of seventy cows requiring summer grazing and winter feed.[28]

The Development of Farmsteads in West Berkshire

The farm buildings of Berkshire date from many periods, from the medieval to the modern. The immense barn at Great Coxwell (formerly Berkshire, now Oxfordshire) was built for the Cistercian Beaulieu Abbey in the mid 13th century, and at Cholsey (also now Oxfordshire) was an even earlier barn, said to have been the largest in Europe.[29] At the other extreme are the great sheds erected in the modern era to serve the needs of the contemporary farmer, operating a highly mechanised business. Most farmsteads have buildings of many dates, their present form having resulted from a protracted process of piecemeal addition.

Fig 2.2 The barn at Prior's Farm, Peasemore. The earliest part of the barn was probably built in the 17th century or earlier (BB96/3698).

Opinion about Berkshire farm buildings has varied widely. In the late 18th century, one writer stated that 'the farm buildings all over the county are respectable and convenient', but a few years later it was noted that 'the farm buildings belonging to the rack renters and lifehold tenantry, and more especially such as have no leases, are generally inferior to those of the yeomanry, and the tenure may in some measure be discovered by the style of the accommodations'. The same writer deplored the 'multiplication of buildings' which he observed, stating that 'the more purposes to which the same building can be applied the better, both for landlord and tenant'. Berkshire barns also came in for criticism, and in the early 19th century it was envisaged that the introduction of powered threshing would render them redundant, thus saving the high costs of keeping them in good repair.[30] A mid 19th-century writer implied that little progress had been made, for he found the farm buildings of the county generally 'old and insufficient' for modern farming.[31]

The normal custom for the erection and maintenance of farm buildings was to divide the responsibility between landlord and tenant. The landlord was to provide a new tenant with buildings in good repair, and thereafter to find all building materials except for thatching straw.

The tenant was responsible for paying craftsmen's wages and for the transport of building materials.[32] Many landowners who were interested in improving their estates invested heavily in farm buildings; the examples of the farmsteads at Buscot, Coleshill and Windsor have already been mentioned. Caird, however, sounded a cautionary note, stating that:

> *in the erection of farm buildings ... it is important they should not be executed on a scale more expensive than is requisite for the purpose in view, as in that case the interest of the outlay becomes a permanent dead weight which can never be remunerative. And we think it also injudicious to erect costly buildings (as we have seen instances in this county) for the use of farmers who are unable, from want of capital or want of skill, to turn them to a profitable account.[33]*

As always, the crucial consideration was whether better farm buildings repaid the costs of their construction by providing a more efficient environment for the business of agriculture. Within the survey area, the judgement of most of the large estates was in the negative, for there is little evidence of widespread estate improvement on the part of the Craven family, the Archer-Houblons, or the Suttons. The

Suttons probably came closest to setting an example, for a large new farm (Bradford's Farm, Speen) was built in *c* 1860, and new stud farms were built in Marsh Benham at later dates. On a smaller scale, the almost identical barns of *c* 1800 at North and South Stanmore Farms in Beedon indicate a policy of improvement. For the rest, the estates largely employed a policy of limited expenditure, replacing old buildings when they were worn out or fell down, and adding new structures to existing complexes when a need became apparent. As a result, the area is characterised by farmsteads with piecemeal evolution, sometimes over a lengthy period, and there are few farmsteads corresponding closely to the models published in the improving literature.

The detailed evolution of Berkshire farmsteads is difficult to analyse, for, although there are many surviving buildings from the pre-1800 period, losses in the modern era mean that there are few complexes surviving in anything resembling their pre-1800 form. That farm complexes, rather than single buildings, existed in that period is known from documents; 18th-century maps, for example, show groupings of buildings making up farmsteads.

The earliest building on most farmsteads is almost invariably the barn. Dating of these structures is often problematic, overall form and carpentry techniques continuing with little change over a long period. Within the survey area, however, are barns which on structural

grounds may be dated to the early 18th century or earlier; the earliest part of the barn at Prior's Farm, Peasemore (Fig 2.2), may be 17th century in date, and Welford Farm, Welford, and Orpenham Farm, Kintbury, have barns of perhaps early 18th-century date. None of these farms has other buildings which can confidently be dated to the same era, and it is therefore impossible to assess how the farmsteads functioned as working units in this period. It may be assumed that stables and implement sheds were also present, since these would have been necessary on arable farms, but whether livestock sheds formed a part of Berkshire farmsteads in the pre-1800 era is not known.

The earliest additions to farmsteads were frequently further barns or extensions to the original barn. By the mid 19th century, Folly Farm, Eddington, Hungerford, and Manor Farm, Chaddleworth, had two barns (Fig 2.3), Easton Farm, Welford, had three, and Manor Farm, Beedon, had five. Church Farm, Enborne, had three barns in line, Hamstead Holt Farm, Hamstead Marshall, had a U-plan arrangement of barns, and the barn at Prior's Farm, Peasemore, had been extended in two stages. The evidence confirms the continuing arable emphasis in the region's farming, although it is not clear whether the additions were necessitated by higher yields of grain, farm amalgamation or an expansion in the amount of land used for cereals, perhaps involving colonisation of former wastes.

Fig 2.3 Manor Farm, Chaddleworth, has two large timber-framed barns. The nearer barn was probably built as a straw barn serving a livestock yard (BB94/14172).

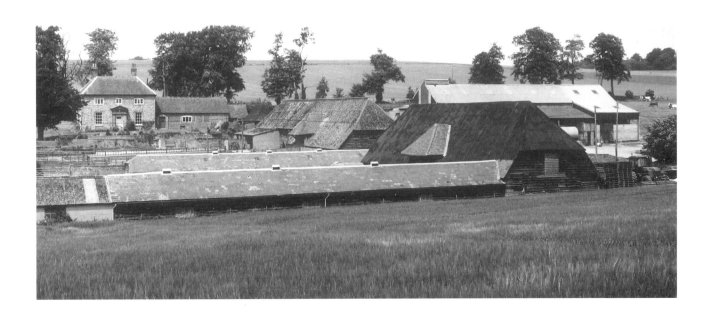

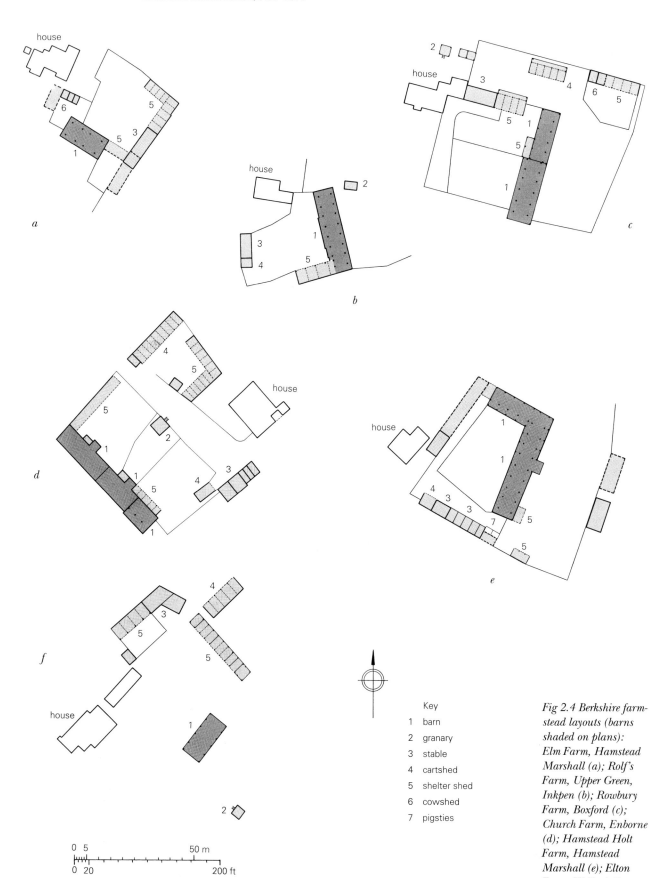

house

a

house

b

house

c

d

house

e

house

f

Key
1 barn
2 granary
3 stable
4 cartshed
5 shelter shed
6 cowshed
7 pigsties

0 5   50 m
0 20   200 ft

Fig 2.4 Berkshire farm-stead layouts (barns shaded on plans): Elm Farm, Hamstead Marshall (a); Rolf's Farm, Upper Green, Inkpen (b); Rowbury Farm, Boxford (c); Church Farm, Enborne (d); Hamstead Holt Farm, Hamstead Marshall (e); Elton Farm, Welford (f).

The layout of many farmsteads was virtually complete in its essentials by the mid 19th century. The more simple plans were often based on a layout with the main farm buildings on two sides of a yard, with a farmhouse set a little apart either in line or on a third side (Fig 2.4). The more complex plans had buildings grouped around three or four sides of a large yard, often irregular in shape.

The barn or barns were usually the dominant element within the mid 19th-century farmstead. The somewhat dispersed plans, and the wide spacing between the components of the farmstead, indicate that the typical Berkshire layout was not intended to provide the type of closely integrated arable/livestock unit such as was beginning to be common in other cereal-producing areas (for example, Northumberland) in the same period. The relatively minor role played by cattle at this time is suggested by the fact that at, for example, Kintbury Farm, Kintbury (Fig 2.5), and Elm Farm, Hamstead Marshall, shelter sheds were set a little away from the barn, implying that the small scale of cattle-raising made labour costs a minor consideration. The better layouts probably had lean-to shelters against the barn, as at Prior's Farm, Peasemore, and Church Farm, Enborne, and a few appear to have had barns, shelter sheds and yards functioning together as separate units; at Manor Farm, Chaddleworth, for example, the tithe map shows a separate yard and buildings to the south of the main barn and yard.

A common development in farmstead layout in many parts of the country in the mid and late 19th century involved the addition of livestock sheds and yards to earlier complexes. This change is characteristic of the age of High Farming, and was intended to promote large-scale manure production to maintain soil fertility; this would ensure the principal objective, high cereal yields. The benefits of this system gained a limited recognition in Berkshire, for on some farmsteads additions were made which demonstrate that cattle were drawn into the farming system in a more thoroughgoing way than before. A range of cattle shelters was added at Orpenham Farm, Kintbury, and shelters were expanded at Elm Farm, Hamstead Marshall. At Easton Farm, Welford, a new barn (probably a straw barn) was added with a range of shelter sheds, and a second range of sheds was built between two earlier barns. The plan at Easton once these additions had been made was one which indicates a relatively high degree of integration between arable farming and livestock-raising; there were three barns, two ranges of cattle shelters and extensive open yards for the collection of manure (Fig 2.6). The best

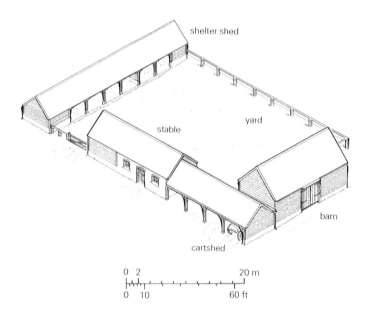

Fig 2.5 Kintbury Farm, Kintbury. This bird's-eye view shows that the mid 19th-century farmstead had the barn and shelter shed on opposite sides of the open yard, with a cartshed and stable making up the third side.

Fig 2.6 Easton Farm, Welford, shows the close association between the barn and cattle yards. There were three barns on this farmstead by the mid 19th century, and all were probably used in part as straw barns serving the adjacent yards and shelters (NMR4810/23).

example of integration, however, is provided by Bradford's Farm, Speen, rebuilt *c* 1870 as the principal farm on the Sutton estate. An earlier barn was retained in the remodelled farmstead, the core of which was a two-storey range providing cartsheds, granaries and fodder-processing areas. Abutting the range were sheds and yards for livestock, and the new buildings form a compact block with close functional links between the different parts (see Fig 2.25).

Despite this evidence for new construction, Berkshire farmsteads remained, typically, as informal groupings of buildings. Even in the late 19th century, a farmstead such as that at Elton Farm, Welford, lacked the sort of coherent planning and closely connecting building ranges characteristic of other cereal-

producing regions such as Lincolnshire and Northumberland (Fig 2.4*f*). Why this should be is a difficult question. It was certainly not for want of advice, for both the voluminous improving literature of the age, and local examples of recommended design – Coleshill, the Flemish Farm at Windsor, and Chalkpit Farm, Englefield – were available for emulation.[34] The Sutton estate did not remodel its tenant farms to conform with recommended practice; instead its main farm (Bradford's) stood as the sole example of the type. Neither did other estates embark on a policy of wholesale rebuilding along model lines. On the Archer-Houblon estate, only Easton appears to have had a fully integrated plan, and the other farmsteads, for example, Tullock Farm, had, at most, small cattle sheds, some placed remotely from the barn rather than being built in close proximity to minimise on labour.

The largely traditional, or unimproved, nature of Berkshire farmsteads may be due to a number of factors, some based on economic considerations, others on local agricultural practice. It is possible that remodelling was inhibited by the survival of so much earlier building, especially of traditional barns, redundant for contemporary agriculture but nevertheless substantial and able to be converted to numerous other uses. Adaptation and conversion, together with minor additions, were always a cheaper option than wholesale replacement, which would have required not only sheds for livestock but also the type of barn suited to the technology of the age. Estates appear generally to have been reluctant to invest in new buildings. Estate efforts to improve efficiency in this period may have been manifest more in new machinery than in buildings; steam-powered portable machines, which partially took processing out into the fields away from buildings, may have been thought to promise a better return on expenditure than bricks and mortar. It is also the case that many unimproved farmsteads were relatively small; on such farmsteads, the economies conferred by labour-saving layouts of buildings did not warrant the expenditure involved. In an area where alternative employment was restricted and where agricultural wages were low, it was cheaper to use labour than to invest in new and ostensibly more efficient buildings.[35]

Another possible explanation is that, on many farms, folded sheep rather than cattle remained, if not the principal source of manure, then at least an important supplement, thus reducing, but not eliminating, the need for large-scale cattle accommodation. The same might apply where artificial fertilisers or alternative sources of

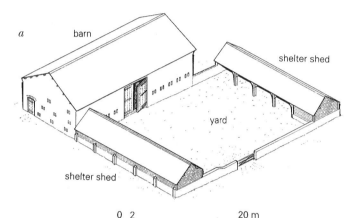

a

barn

shelter shed

yard

shelter shed

0 2   20 m

0   10   60 ft

Fig 2.7 Down farms. Bottom Barn (a) was built as an outlying farm for Clapton Farm, Kintbury, while North Stanmore Farm, Beedon (b), had three outlying down farms.

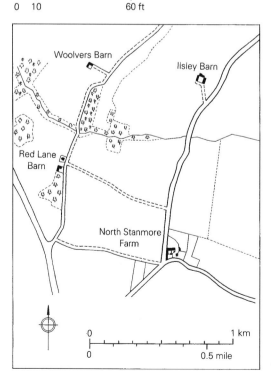

Woolvers Barn

Ilsley Barn

Red Lane Barn

North Stanmore Farm

0   1 km

0   0.5 mile

b

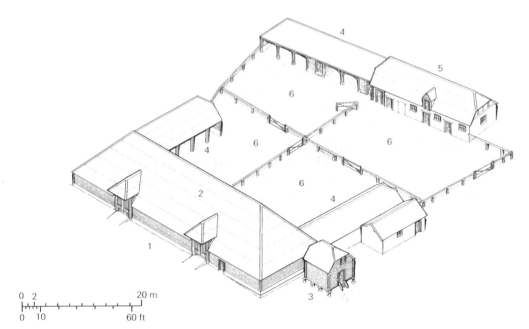

0 2   20 m

0   10   60 ft

Key

1   stack-yard
2   barn
3   granary
4   shelter shed
5   stable
6   yard

Fig 2.8 The flow of processes in a Berkshire farmstead. This reconstruction, based on Orpenham Farm, Kintbury, shows the movement of material from the stack-yard (1), through the barn (2), to the granary (3), shelter shed (4), stable (5), and yards (6).

animal manure, such as stable manure from London and from racing studs, were in widespread use, as was the case by the mid 19th century.[36] On other farms, livestock were certainly regarded as important, but were kept not in the main farmstead but in 'down farms', some distance away (Fig 2.7). Bottom Barn was built in the mid 19th century as a remote adjunct to Clapton Farm, Kintbury; the buildings included a barn, shelter sheds and cottages for labourers. By the early 20th century North Stanmore Farm, Beedon, had three outfarms, each with a barn and shelters making up steadings for the storage of crops and production of manure from cattle.[37] By the onset of the Great Depression, new buildings for cattle were intended as often for dairy herds as for manure production. The construction of the aptly named Little Farm, Hamstead Marshall, as a small dairy farmstead in the middle decades of the 19th century is indicative of a strong element in the agriculture of the area, an element which grew in importance after 1850.

Discussion of the flow of processes on the typical Berkshire farmstead centres very closely upon the barn (Fig 2.8). The predominant sheep and corn husbandry which maintained the area for so long has a very uneven expression in buildings, for, while sheep required few major or permanent structures, cereal production needed buildings, principally a barn. The arable cycle may be taken to start with the transport of cereal crops from the fields to the stack-yard (1) and the barn (2), where before the mid 19th century they were stored and processed over a long period. Out of the barn came grain

for fodder and storage, and straw for litter and chaff. The grain went to a detached granary (3), there to be stored awaiting consumption or transport to market. The straw was taken to the shelter shed (4), stable (5), and yards (6), where the working horses and cattle were kept for at least part of the year, and where it was turned into manure for the arable fields. Mid and late 19th-century changes to this flow largely involved the widespread adoption of mechanised processing; early experiments with mechanised threshing using a fixed power source appear not to have become general, and were arrested in the 1830s by opposition from labourers, but by the mid 19th century the use of portable horse machinery and steam largely removed threshing from the barn, the work being undertaken either in the stack-yard or in the fields. The grain went directly to the granary, and the straw was taken to the barn, now essentially a storage area and a space where fodder could be prepared. In addition to this principal flow were other concerns: dairy cows on some farms, pigs on many.

The Buildings of the Berkshire Farmstead

The Barn

The dating of barns in Berkshire is difficult, for traditional forms and techniques continued for an extensive period with little discernible change. Timber-framed construction remained the most common form of building well into the

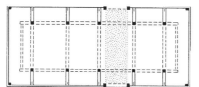

a

c

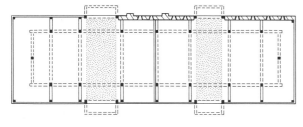

b

Fig 2.9 Aisled barns (threshing floors shaded on plans): Tullock Farm, Welford, has a double-aisled barn with a hipped roof and a single threshing floor (a; BB94/13919); the barn at Orpenham Farm, Kintbury, has two threshing floors, each with a hipped canopy over the doorway (b; BB94/14151); South Stanmore Farm, Beedon, has a large brick aisled barn with two threshing floors (c; BB94/13902); Rowles Farm, West Ilsley, has two timber-framed aisled barns built to give an overall L-plan (d; BB94/14148); Rowbury Farm, Boxford, has a large barn built in two phases, and has three threshing floors in all (e; BB94/13833).

d

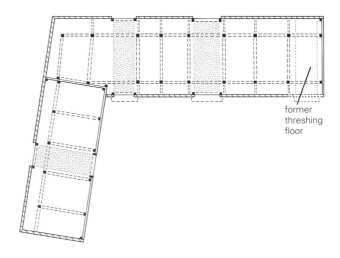

former
threshing
floor

e

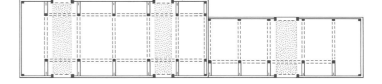

18

19th century, and the form of barns changed little between the medieval period and the age of steam threshing. The problem of dating is compounded by the common practice of reusing timbers from demolished buildings when new barns were constructed, producing a situation where many of a structure's timbers are significantly older than the building itself.

The common type of Berkshire barn was an aisled, weatherboarded building under a hipped, thatched roof (Figs 2.9, 2.10). Some

Fig 2.10 Aisled construction. The pre-1700 barn at Prior's Farm, Peasemore (a) began as an unaisled structure, but the early 18th-century barn at Orpenham Farm, Kintbury, was built as a double-aisled structure (b) with end aisles (e; BB94/14158). Typical aisled construction was employed at Rowbury Farm, Boxford (d; BB94/13835), and at Manor Farm, Chaddleworth (f; BB94/14178). The barns at Clapton Farm, Kintbury, were built in brick in the early 19th century, using aisled construction internally (g; BB94/14271). At North Stanmore Farm, Beedon, the early 19th-century brick-aisled barn has truncated principal rafter roof trusses (c).

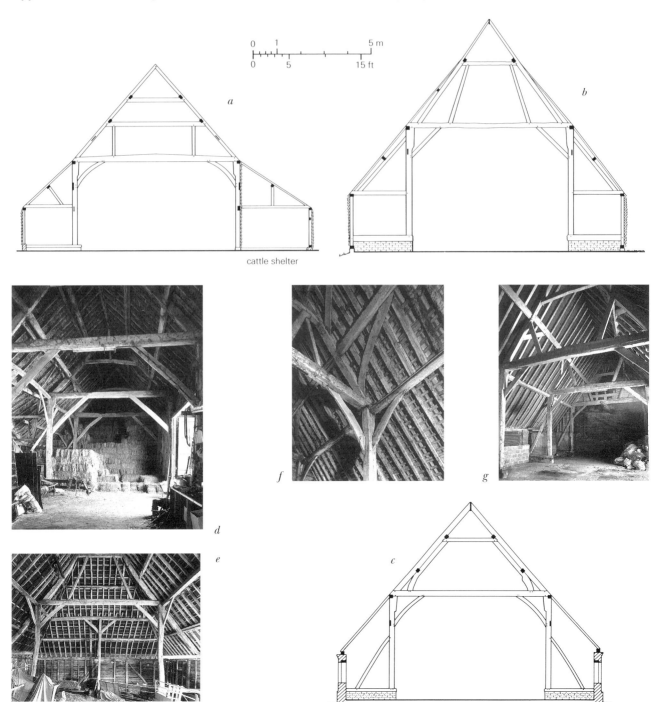

cattle shelter

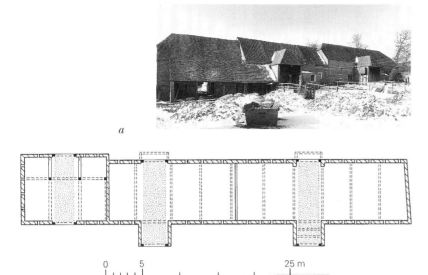

a

Fig 2.11 Unaisled barns (threshing floors shaded on plans): Church Farm, Enborne, has a linear range of three brick barns, the northern two unaisled (a; BB96/2035); Kintbury Farm, Kintbury, has a mid 19th-century timber-framed barn (b; BB94/13932); Mason's Farm, Kintbury, has a brick barn of the mid to late 19th century (c; BB94/13915).

b

c

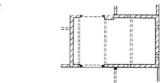

barns are single-aisled, some are double-aisled, and some also have end aisles. There is evidence that aisles were sometimes added; the double-aisled appearance of the barn at Prior's Farm, Peasemore, masks the fact that the original building, probably 17th century or earlier, was unaisled. Aisled barns were built in entirely traditional form until the early 19th century. It is known that the barn at Hunt's Green Farm, Boxford, was constructed *c* 1825, but it differs little from barns one or perhaps two centuries older. The framing of the side and end walls was usually made up of main posts pegged to the wall plate, with light studs and diagonal braces, mainly unpegged.

Aisled construction was utilised in brick as well as in timber-framed buildings, indicating that the form was not wedded to a structural medium but had a functional advantage that of providing a wider building than could be contrived using other traditional carpentry techniques. The barns of *c* 1800 at North and South Stanmore Farms have an aisled internal structure within a brick skin, as does that at Clapton Farm, Kintbury. The use of brick in these large barns suggests a desire for greater permanence than was often provided by the poor quality timber framing of the region. Brick construction was probably more expensive than timber framing, and all three barns are on large farms. Brick was also used in partial casings of earlier aisled barns, as at Elm Farm, Hamstead Marshall, and at Orpenham Farm, Kintbury.

Unaisled barns became more common in the 19th century, although, as was noted above, the earliest barn recorded in the survey (that at Prior's Farm, Peasemore) began as an unaisled structure. Both timber-framed and brick examples were recorded (Fig 2.11), and the type was particularly suited where only a small building was required; the timber-framed barn at Kintbury Farm, and the brick barn at Mason's Farm, both serve diminutive farmsteads. Not all unaisled barns were small, however; two of the range of three barns at Church Farm, Enborne, are unaisled, but they have a span comparable to that of a single-aisled building and have the extra storage capacity given by full-height side walls.

The traditional barn was built to accommodate the storage and processing of cereal crops, and these functions are revealed by its features (Fig 2.12). Full-height opposed doorways allowed access for loaded wagons, and the area between the doorways provided a threshing floor. The doorways in aisled barns were usually sheltered by hipped porches, sometimes projecting from the side walls, sometimes rising from them with an overhanging canopy. The larger barns might have more than one set of

Fig 2.12 Features of the Berkshire barn: hipped canopy over porch at South Stanmore Farm, Beedon (a; BB94/13900); planked threshing floor in the barn at Hamstead Holt Farm, Hamstead Marshall (b; BB94/14165); doors with locking bar and threshold at Hunt's Green Farm, Boxford (c; BB94/14183); the porch (d) and threshold (e) in the barn at Orpenham Farm, Kintbury; reconstruction of flail threshing (f).

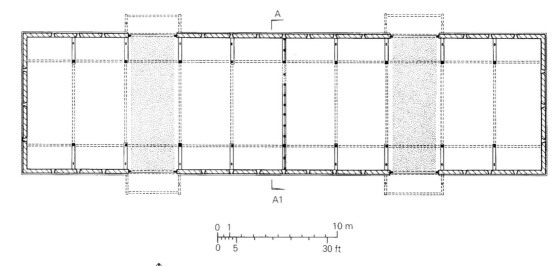

0 1   10 m
0 5   30 ft

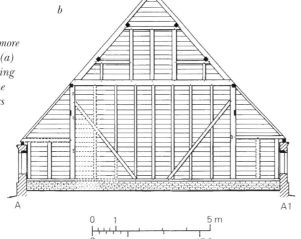

Fig 2.13 North Stanmore Farm, Beedon: plan (a) and section (b) showing central division of the barn (threshing floors shaded on plans).

0 1   5 m
0 5   15 ft

opposed doorways; the barn at Orpenham Farm, Kintbury, has two, and one barn at Rowles Farm, West Ilsley, may have had three. Whether a barn had one or more sets of opposed doorways, these openings were usually positioned to serve an interior space to either side. Thus small barns usually have a central or near central set of doorways, and larger barns have both sets of doorways symmetrically disposed so that each might serve half the barn. Departures from this rule may in some cases by explained by site evolution, a pre-existing structure preventing the optimum disposition, or perhaps by unusual (and now unknown) uses of the interior space. The threshing floors, sometimes boarded to give a better surface for processing, were provided with thresholds to prevent livestock entering the barn when the main doors were open; the thresholds took the form of planks held by runners at the foot of the doorposts. The stored crops awaiting processing, and straw after processing, required ventilation. In a timber-framed and weatherboarded barn, sufficient air

flowed through the side walls to obviate the need for vents, but these were required in brick barns, and usually took the form of slits.

On many farmsteads there was more than one barn. Two barns were common, and examples of three and even five are known. There were probably a number of reasons for this provision. Some farms undoubtedly expanded, and on others the conversion of former sheep runs to arable, together with more intensive use of older land, increased the cereal yields. In both cases, the result was that the original barn was inadequate to serve the needs of the farm, and further capacity, in the form either of an extension or of additional barns, was necessary. On other farms, it is possible that different cereal crops – wheat, barley and oats – were stored in separate buildings. That such a distinction could be provided in a single barn is indicated by the design of the two barns on the Stanmore estate in Beedon. Both barns were of ten bays, and both were divided by a timber-framed partition into two equal parts, each served by a central set of opposed doorways (Fig 2.13). The same effect was achieved in two stages at Rowbury Farm, Boxford, where the end wall of the earlier barn was retained as an internal division when a linear extension was added.

One unusual type of barn found in Berkshire and neighbouring counties is the staddle barn, which has an unaisled timber-framed structure raised on staddles, a form of construction also used for granaries. The sole recorded example within the survey area is the small barn at Holt Lodge, Kintbury (Fig 2.14). The building is of three bays, and has central opposed doorways, full height on one side only. This allowed crops to be loaded into the building from a wagon placed outside, and the form of the building indicates that it could have functioned as a conventional threshing barn

22

apart from the fact that vehicles could not enter. The use of staddles was probably an attempt to reduce problems caused by damp and vermin. The idea was not widely adopted, however, the inconvenience caused by the difficulties of access outweighing any gains conferred.

The mechanisation of barn processing

The form of the Berkshire barn reflected its functions, and, as long as these latter remained largely unaltered, so did the design of the building. An outsider's view of the suitability of the barn for mid 19th-century agriculture was expressed strongly in 1843, when landlords were encouraged

> *to find a substitute for the very expensive and very unsightly barns which encumber the farms in many parts of the southern counties, and the desire for which fills with astonishment our northern farmers, who see in them a source of needless expenditure in building and repairs, a harbour for vermin, and a great addition to the danger and destruction of fire, and a periodic robbery from the farm of part of its manure for thatching, for the purpose of perpetuating the tedious and expensive mode of threshing by hand instead of by machinery.*[38]

The statement is informed by the author's experience of managing the Greenwich Hospital estates in Northumberland, and shows a failure to understand that circumstances were different elsewhere.

Mechanisation of crop-processing affected Berkshire profoundly, but social and economic circumstances, together with the timing of the main changes, meant that the effect on farm buildings, and in particular on the barn, was minimal. The introduction of the threshing machine was the most important aspect of mechanisation, but chaff-cutters, winnowers and root-choppers also came into use in the course of the 19th century.

The arguments for the adoption of machine working stressed a number of points. The machines were held to pay for themselves by economies in labour, and it was argued also that they spared workers the crippling task of flail threshing and allowed other pressing tasks on the farm to be attended to. It was also claimed that the machines could be used to employ people when no other work was available; the same point was, however, also used to justify the retention of the flail. The use of the machine, it was maintained, allowed farmers to respond advantageously to price fluctuations in the grain markets, and permitted the secure storage of grain in a granary, thus reducing loss from

vermin. It was also recognised that the use of the machine could lead to a remodelling of the farmstead, making large and expensive barns redundant.[39]

Some of these advantages were, however, more apparent than real. Many early threshing machines were not equally efficient with all types of grain, and especially in the first years of use it was difficult to find skilled engineers to maintain them in the best working order.[40] Capital costs for the larger machines were high; some cost less than £100, but others required an investment of £400.[41] The smaller machines were less cost effective, especially when the horse power could not be used for other processes as well as threshing. Furthermore, the argument that the machines saved labour overlooked the fact that the workers either were still used on the farm, and therefore required payment, or were thrown out of work and became a burden on the parish (and the farmer) in the form of increased poor rates.[42]

The threshing machine became well known, if not common, in Berkshire in the early 19th century. Mavor speaks of 'a considerable number' of machines, some hand powered, others worked by teams of one, two, four or six horses. The early (pre-1830) use of threshing machines in Berkshire was associated closely with the colonisation of the chalk downlands, and their conversion from sheep walks to grain-producing fields.[43] Quite how many machines were in use before 1830 will never be known, but, whatever the number, the machine attracted attention for its novelty and for its potential effects on the agricultural economy of the region.

Fig 2.14 The small staddle barn at Holt Lodge, Kintbury. The timber-framed barn is raised on staddles, but the wide double doorways indicate that it was used as a barn (BB94/14261).

a

b

Fig 2.15 The horse-engine house at Folly Farm, Eddington, Hungerford, has been reconstructed in recent years but retains the form of the original (a; BB96/2039). The drawing (b) shows a portable horse wheel in use, powering a small threshing machine inside the barn.

The use of the threshing machine led in the early 1830s to the agricultural riots known collectively under the name of 'Captain Swing'. Along with other counties in the south and east of England, Berkshire was severely affected by the disturbances, which were sparked by low wage rates and perceived threats to employment.[44] One method of protest was the destruction of the threshing machines which symbolised the threat to rural labour; in Berkshire eighty-six machines were broken up. Kintbury and the neighbouring villages were the scene of agitation and machine breaking, and some of

the farmsteads recorded in the survey were visited by the rioters. The unrest was eventually quelled, but it probably inhibited the development of machine-working for some years.[45]

By the middle of the 19th century, however, circumstances had changed. Machines were much more efficient, and from the 1830s portable machines were developed, hauled and powered first by horses, later by traction engines. The contracting system grew so that the benefits of the new machinery became accessible even to small farmers, and the opposition of the labouring classes was removed because

24

rural migration had created a labour shortage in the agricultural regions of southern England.[46] As a result, threshing machines became extremely common in Berkshire after 1850, to the point where it could be written in 1860 that 'the combined steam threshing-machine has become so general as to have silenced the sound of the flail in some parts'.[47] Portable steam engines were more common in Berkshire than fixed engines, despite the fact that those model farm layouts published for emulation employed stationary engines.[48] Both types of engine, however, could be used economically to power a whole range of processes as well as threshing: chaff-cutting, milling of different types of grain, root-chopping and pulping were now commonly mechanically powered.

The effect of mechanisation on farm buildings was, even in the early years, expected to be large. Mavor believed that 'the gradual introduction of the threshing machine will render barns of the present size and number less necessary. This will be an important advantage.'[49] The slow take-up of the threshing machine before the middle of the century, however, meant that Mavor's prediction was correct only in the long term, and barns continued to be used in traditional ways for rather longer than envisaged. Even as late as 1860, some farmers preferred to thresh with the flail, especially when what was required was a steady flow of fodder for livestock rather than an instant supply of grain for sale.[50]

The first phase of mechanisation, using fixed threshing machines set up within barns, has left some evidence in buildings and documents. Folly Farm, Eddington, Hungerford, has a horse-engine house (surviving in reconstructed form) attached to the barn (Fig 2.15a), and early maps indicate the presence of similar engine houses at Manor Farm, Beedon, and Hamstead Holt Farm, Hamstead Marshall. All three installations were probably constructed in the mid 19th century. It may be assumed that the barns at all three farms had fixed threshing machines internally, although neither at these farms nor elsewhere do barns show evidence for alterations – such as the insertion of a floor – designed to house such machines. Portable installations were common for a period in the mid 19th century, especially on smaller farms. When required, the horse engine could be set up outside the barn doors, with a drive shaft or belt leading from the engine to a small thresher placed on the threshing floor (Fig 2.15b). Such an installation leaves no trace, and it is therefore impossible to estimate how commonly it was employed.

The major means of threshing after 1850 was the portable thresher hauled and powered either by horses or, increasingly commonly, by traction engine (Fig 2.16). This removed threshing from the barn entirely, and the operation was conducted either in the stack-yard or in the fields, where the crops could be stacked after harvesting. Under this system, the barn was redundant for its original purpose, and it

Fig 2.16 Reconstruction of steam-powered threshing using a mobile engine and portable threshing machine.

became a building for the storage of straw and the preparation of fodder for livestock. Some barns were converted wholly or in part to other uses. At Hamstead Holt Farm, Hamstead Marshall, one barn range was converted partly to a cow house, with corn bins for the storage of fodder, brick standings and a manure channel,

and partly to a granary, raised on an inserted floor (Fig 2.17). A similar conversion took place at Great Hidden Farm, Hungerford, and at Welford Farm, Welford, part of the barn was turned into a stable.

The redundancy of the traditional barn is expressed most strongly within the survey area at the home farm of the Sutton estate. Bradford's Farm, Speen, was rebuilt *c*1870, and, although a small traditional barn was retained, the new focus of the farmstead was a two-storey processing range (Fig 2.18,*b*,*c*). The ground floor had a number of separate rooms, the uses of which are no longer apparent, and the first floor was used for mechanically powered fodder-processing, probably including chaff-cutting, cake-breaking and grain-milling. The source of the power is not known for certain, but it is likely that one of the ground-floor rooms was used either for a fixed steam engine, or for a portable engine; guide rails in the sett floor make the latter more likely. Line shafting survives on the first floor, and pulley wheels on the shaft indicate where belt drive was taken off to different processing machines. Bradford's Farm thus corresponds closely to the model arrangements advocated by mid 19th-century writers, and exemplified in Berkshire at Haines Hill Farm (Fig 2.18*a*).

a

Fig 2.17 Berkshire barns were often turned to new uses after the middle of the 19th century. At Hamstead Holt Farm, Hamstead Marshall, a granary and corn bins were inserted in one part of a barn (a; BB94/ 14167), and the other end was converted to a cow house, revealed by the brick standings and sunken manure channel in the floor (b; BB94/ 14166).

b

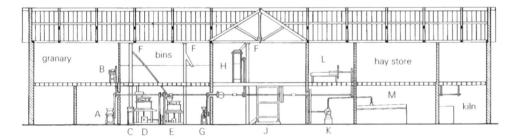

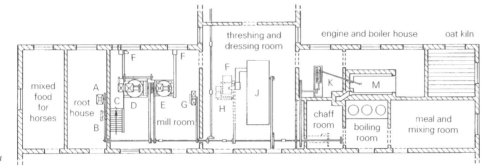

Key

A root pulper

B 'breaker' (for oil cake)

C chaff blower

D oat mill

E grinding mill

F elevators

G universal mill

H grain dresser and
   weighing machine

J threshing machine

K steam engine

L chaff cutter

M boiler

Fig 2.18 Barn processing. In the mid 19th century, Haines Hill Farm, near Twyford, was published as an example of a highly mechanised farmstead (a, redrawn from Denton 1865, pl 53). Within the survey area, the processing range at Bradford's Farm, Speen (b; BB94/14254), resembled Haines Hill in having a number of rooms on two levels, with processing machinery on the upper floor, revealed today by surviving line shafting (c; BB94/14259).

THE GRANARY

Berkshire's arable husbandry is represented most strikingly by the barn, but almost equally characteristic of the county's farmsteads is the granary. Most farms required a building to store seed corn, fodder corn and corn for sale. The granary was usually a small structure, commonly timber framed but also sometimes of brick, raised on stone staddles to reduce deterioration from damp and loss from vermin (Fig 2.19). Granary doors were often lockable to prevent theft, and the building's common proximity to the farmhouse also acted as a means of increasing security. The siting of a granary could be changed, since the building was, with a little difficulty, portable. It is likely that the granary at Orpenham Farm, Kintbury, has been moved to its present position from one closer to the house, and the same is known to be true of that at Church Farm, Enborne.

The majority of granaries appear to have been single storey, but a significant number have two storeys, with ladder access to the upper level. Traps in the floor of two-storey granaries allowed corn to be loaded and unloaded more easily.

Fig 2.19 Granaries: Halfway Farm, Welford (a; BB94/14200); Rowles Farm, West Ilsley (b; BB94/14150); Little Hidden Farm, Hungerford (c; BB94/13925); Clapton Farm, Kintbury (d; BB94/14266); cutaway view of granary at Widow's Farm, Peasemore (e); interior view of granary at Little Hidden Farm, Hungerford, showing corn bins and ladder to upper floor (f; BB94/13926); interior view of granary at Bradford's Farm, Speen, showing corn bins (g; BB94/14258); granary in roof space above cartshed at Mason's Farm, Kintbury (h; BB94/13916).

b

a

c

d

Lifting tackle may have been provided, but none survived in any granary recorded within the survey area. The inner faces of the walls were often lined with boards, and grain bins frequently divide the internal space to give storage for different kinds and grades of corn. At some farms, the granary formed a first-floor area over a cartshed. The conventional arrangement for this type is illustrated by the building at Clapton Farm, Kintbury, and at Bradford's Farm, Speen, where the granary retains a hoist mechanism to facilitate the loading of grain into and out of carts in the shed below. An unusual variant was recorded at Mason's Farm, Kintbury, where a small granary was created in the roof space over the cart bays.

Most, if not all, of the granaries recorded in the survey area date from the 19th century. It is not known whether they replace earlier granaries of similar form, although this is likely. It is possible that the larger granaries, those provided over cartsheds on large farms such as Clapton Farm, Kintbury, and Bradford's Farm, Speen, represent a mid-century response to a new demand, that of storing greater quantities of grain produced in a concentrated period by machine threshing.

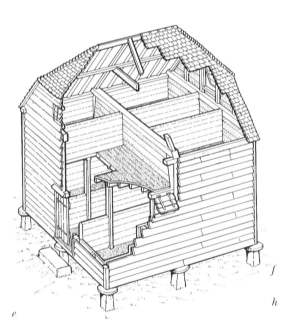

e

f

g

h

a

Fig 2.20 Stables. The stable at Tullock Farm, Welford, is typical of Berkshire, being brick built and having small windows (a; BB94/ 13920), a drop-feed system internally (b), and a hayloft with a loading door (c; BB94/ 13924). The stable at South Stanmore Farm, Beedon, is much larger (d; BB94/13907), and has a drop-feed system from a loft in the roof space (e; BB94/13911).

STABLES AND HORSE YARDS

There is some evidence that the ox was formerly in common use as a draught animal on Berkshire farms. In the early 19th century, the model farm at Buscot included a small stable, but made large-scale provision for oxen in pens, stalls and open yards, and the bailiff of the royal farms within the county advocated the use of oxen in the same period.[51] Despite this, horses were the usual source of animal power, and were important on all farms until the age of the tractor. They were used to haul wagons and carts, and also undertook an increasing amount of fieldwork in the 19th century, as machines replaced humans in such tasks as drilling and reaping.

Most stables in Berkshire date from the first half of the 19th century; whether they replace earlier stables is open to conjecture. The typical Berkshire stable was a brick building (Fig 2.20), and this may be an indication that new and better stables were seen as an important aspect of farmstead improvement, for brick buildings were warmer, drier and stronger than the sort of framed and weatherboarded structure which may have been used for stables in an earlier period. The use of brick also indicates the importance attached to providing good accommodation for horses: at Kintbury Farm, Kintbury, for example, the stable was the only

completely brick building, the barn and cattle shelters being mainly framed.

Stables were sometimes single storey, as at Kintbury Farm, but more commonly had a hayloft on the first floor. They were sometimes attached to other buildings – to the barn at Folly Farm, Eddington, Hungerford, to cattle shelters at Orpenham Farm and Mason's Farm, both in Kintbury. On other farms, the stable was a detached building. Its siting was sometimes designed to remove the horses from the main farmyard; at Kintbury Farm, Kintbury, for example, the stable faces outwards rather than into the yard, allowing the horses ready access to the adjacent implement shed and thence to the fields, as well as providing early morning light through the east-facing windows. At other farmsteads, however, the stable faced into the main yard, and the horses contended with the other traffic within this busy area. In some yards, there is a raised cobbled pathway around the perimeter leading to the stable.

The relationship between the size of the farm and that of the stable is difficult to reduce to a formula, since the size of a farm and the nature of its farming are frequently not known accurately for the period represented by the surviving accommodation for horses. Nevertheless a general correlation may be assumed, since obviously more horses were required on large arable

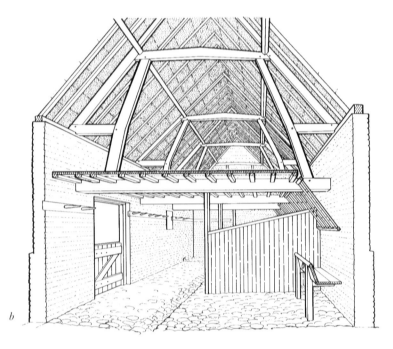

b

e

c

d

farms than on smaller enterprises. Most stables were fairly small in size, accommodating perhaps four to eight horses; the four-horse stable at Tullock Farm, Welford, served a holding of 66 hectares (163 acres) in *c* 1840. Other stables were larger – that at South Stanmore Farm, Beedon, for example, having space for as many as a dozen animals working a holding of 133 hectares (330 acres) at the same date (Fig 2.20*d*).

Quite how stables were used in Berkshire is not clear; the evidence for the existence of horse yards at some farms suggests that the horses spent considerable periods outside, going inside mainly for feeding and grooming. Access, ventilation and light were given by openings in the front wall, and the horses were usually stalled to face the rear wall. Flooring was sometimes of setts or cobbles, sloping to a drain to remove liquid manure. The stall divisions were of stout boarding, and each stall was commonly provided with a wooden manger and a hay rack, the latter supplied from the loft through a gap in the flooring. Tackle and harnesses for the horses were hung from pegs in the front wall, and a ladder rising through a small trap gave access to the hayloft. This had a loading door in either the front wall or the gable (Fig 2.20*c*). There is little evidence for the fodder rooms or chaff houses incorporated within stable ranges in some other parts of the country, the hayloft acting as a substitute. Loose boxes were sometimes built attached to the

31

Fig 2.21 (right) The horse yard and shelter at Halfway Farm, Welford (BB94/14195).

a

Fig 2.22 Stud farm at Marsh Benham, Speen. Two timber-framed ranges provided loose boxes, and hay was stored in a third (a; BB94/13823). The loose boxes were lined in stout timbers and were ventilated by louvres in the gables (b; BB94/13827).

b

stable, and in these cases were probably used for sick animals or mares with foals. At Hamstead Holt Farm, Hamstead Marshall, the principal accommodation for horses was in loose boxes rather than in a stable.

Horse yards were used on some Berkshire farms. Sited to connect with the stable, they were fenced or walled enclosures, and could be used to rest the working horses. They are shown on 19th-century Ordnance Survey maps at such farms as Orpenham Farm and Clapton Farm, Kintbury. At some farms, open-sided sheds provided shelter for the horses, and the stable, yards and shelter form an independent unit deliberately set aside from the rest of the farmstead; there are good examples at Elton Farm and Easton Farm, on the Welford estate, and at Halfway Farm, Welford (Fig 2.21). At one farmstead, Wawcott Farm, Kintbury, the horse yard included a farrier's shop with a forge and bellows, the latter in a small lean-to.

The importance of horse-breeding, especially for racing and hunting stock, grew in the 19th century. Spearing refers to racehorse stables in the middle of the century, and Berkshire, particularly the downs, became renowned for its training facilities.[52] It may be significant that, by the early 20th century, sporting tradition, an integral part of the rural gentry way of life, was considered more worthy of investment than agriculture, and within the survey area the Benham estate built two farms in Speen, one with three ranges of brick buildings on a U-plan, the other with three parallel ranges of timber-framed structures, two for loose boxes, one for fodder storage (Fig 2.22).

CATTLE ACCOMMODATION

The late 18th-century account of Berkshire agriculture indicates that cattle then formed a minor part in the regional economy, but nevertheless small numbers of cattle, whether kept for dairy purposes or for fattening, were probably present on most farms over a very long period. No certainly pre-1800 cattle shelters survive, however, suggesting that the beasts were kept either largely in the open or in makeshift shelters of impermanent construction. The shelters may have taken the form of lean-tos abutting the side of the barn, of a type represented at Prior's Farm, Peasemore (Fig 2.23*a*). The inadequacy of the provision made for cattle, and for the preservation of manure, was noted in the early 19th century, when the lack of shelter from cold winds was seen as a major defect.[53]

The greater importance attached to manure production in the age of High Farming meant that better quality cattle-housing was required. This normally took the form of a simple open-sided shelter shed connecting with a yard (Fig 2.23*b*). The sheds were most often timber framed, on a brick plinth, but completely brick examples were not uncommon, especially on larger farmsteads (Fig 2.23*c*). Some sheds have dividing walls, an indication that different types or ages of cattle were segregated from each other. A small number of sheds have mangers – of simple wooden construction at Hunt's Green Farm, Boxford, but more substantially constructed of brick with glazed earthenware troughs at the early 20th-century shed added at Halfway Farm, Welford (Fig 2.23*d*).

The absence from most Berkshire farmsteads of the mid 19th century of specialist fodder preparation buildings suggests strongly that the barn assumed this function. Closely integrated planning of the barn, sheds and yards was, however, not usual in Berkshire, and few farmsteads have the

Fig 2.23 Cattle shelter sheds. Shelter sheds were commonly built against barns, as at Prior's Farm, Peasemore (a; BB95/12213), but more extensive shelters were built on some farms. At Orpenham Farm, Kintbury (b; BB94/14153), the shelter is timber framed, and at Hunt's Green Farm, Boxford, it is of brick, with a wooden manger against the rear wall (c; BB94/14182). The shelter at Halfway Farm, Welford, has a brick manger with a glazed trough (d; BB94/14190). Some shelters, such as that at Orpenham, incorporated a fully enclosed bay, used probably as a loose box for calves or sick animals.

a

b

c

d

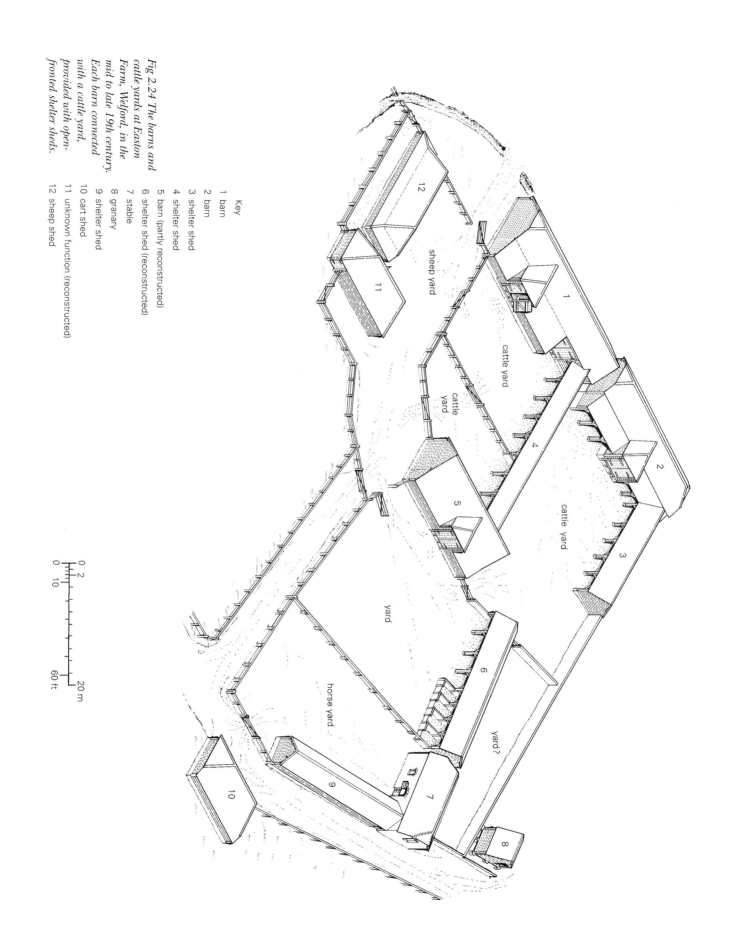

Fig 2.24 The barns and cattle yards at Easton Farm, Welford, in the mid to late 19th century. Each barn connected with a cattle yard, provided with open-fronted shelter sheds.

Key
1 barn
2 barn
3 shelter shed
4 shelter shed
5 barn (partly reconstructed)
6 shelter shed (reconstructed)
7 stable
8 granary
9 shelter shed
10 cart shed
11 unknown function (reconstructed)
12 sheep shed

sheep yard

cattle yard

cattle yard

cattle yard

yard

horse yard

yard?

0 2
10
60 ft
20 m

type of labour-saving feeding systems which were such a feature of cattle-housing in other parts of the country. This may be due to the generally small numbers of beasts kept on many farms.

The typical arrangement of the livestock accommodation on Berkshire farms was one in which the sheds lay a little distance from the barn, necessitating the carrying of fodder and litter across the yard, perhaps to a central feeding box. The compact farmstead at Kintbury Farm, Kintbury, has the barn and shelter shed on opposite sides of the yard (see Fig 2.5), and mid-century additions at Easton Farm, Welford (Fig 2.24), and Manor Farm, Chaddleworth, produced L-plan layouts of barns and shelter sheds.

Even these better-planned examples appear unsophisticated when compared both with what local model farms were offering for emulation and with what was becoming standard in regions such as Northumberland, where cattle-raising was a more intensive concern. The only comparable system recorded within the survey area was the livestock unit at Bradford's Farm, Speen, built *c*1870 as part of a model home farm (Fig 2.25). Now largely demolished, the unit had yards and shelter sheds abutting a fodder-processing range, connecting doorways allowing fodder to be distributed easily to the livestock. Nearby are two hay or straw barns – open-sided timber-framed structures providing the large amount of storage space required where so many cattle were kept – built in the early 20th century. At much the same time, a small cattle unit was added at Catmore Farm, Catmore; this had a central fodder-processing area, covered yards radiating out from this, and a small shelter shed and yard. Covered yards are not a common feature in Berkshire farmsteads; the best example within the survey area is the early 20th-century shed at Hamstead Holt Farm, Hamstead Marshall (Fig 2.26*a,b*). The reasons for the failure to adopt the covered yard at an earlier date may lie in the abundant supply of straw produced in the area, making manure conservation less of a concern than in other regions, and in the use of artificial fertilisers from the mid 19th century.

Accommodation for dairy cattle appears to have differed from that provided for fatstock. Nineteenth-century cow houses rarely survive well, the internal features having been replaced as a result of later hygiene regulations. It is possible to establish that cow houses were single-storey buildings, often completely enclosed rather than with one open side. They are often small in scale, that at Mason's Farm, Kintbury, being typical. Little Farm, Hamstead Marshall,

appears to have been built in the mid 19th century as a small dairy farm, reflecting the intensely local emphasis of this area to the south of the River Kennet. It has an L-shaped range with a small enclosed cow house and open-sided shelters, and a range with loose boxes and a fodder-preparation room was added in the early 20th century (Fig 2.27). The conversion, probably in the early 20th century, of part of the barn at Hamstead Holt Farm, Hamstead Marshall, for use as a cow house reflects the contemporary shift away from cereals towards dairy farming. Good remains of dairies were not recorded, probably indicating that liquid milk, transported immediately to the towns, rather than butter and cheese, was the principal product of this aspect of farming.

HOUSING FOR SHEEP AND PIGS

For much of the 19th century, sheep were one of the mainstays of the regional agricultural system, but their importance is not reflected in the county's farmsteads, since they required little in the way of buildings. Ewes might be taken under shelter at lambing time and in severe conditions; Caird noted 'a light thatched sheepshed with well-littered yards' on one farm, and Spearing explained that in February 'a lambing pen is made, in the corner of the field where their food is, with thatched hurdles, or the ewes are removed to a convenient lambing yard at the homestead'.[54] It is possible, but not provable, that some open-sided sheds were intended for seasonal use by sheep. At Easton Farm, Welford, there is a shed with side and end aisles, and with evidence for the use of bars across the open bays (Fig 2.28*a, b*). The form of the building, in particular the low aisles, makes it unsuited to cattle, but the structure might have been used partly for carts and implements, and for sheep when required. None of the farmsteads had elaborate fenced enclosures for sheep-handling or sheep dips. Two farmsteads retained portable huts, used to provide shelter for shepherds when flocks were being handled in remote areas (Fig 2.28*c*).

Berkshire was well situated to provide the London market with meat, and in the late 18th century the county was famous for pig-breeding and fattening. In the mid 19th century, Caird remarked that 'pigs are fed in yards in great numbers', and many farmsteads probably had pigs grubbing around in the cattle and sheep enclosures.[55] None of the farmsteads within the survey area had anything resembling buildings for pig production on a commercial scale. Instead, the typical provision might be a small range of sties, the pigs being reared probably

a

b

d

e

Fig 2.25 Bradford's Farm, Speen. This estate farm was rebuilt in the mid to late 19th century, and its centrepiece was a new livestock unit and processing range. The old barn (a; BB94/14251) was retained, but processing was carried out, probably using the power of a portable steam engine, in a two-storey L-shaped range, which also included cartsheds and granaries (b; BB94/14247). Livestock yards and shelter sheds abutted the range at the rear (c, reconstructed from documentary and site evidence), and there were further shelter sheds nearby (d; BB94/14248). The large numbers of cattle kept on the farmstead necessitated the provision of two lightly framed and weatherboarded hay barns (e; BB94/14257).

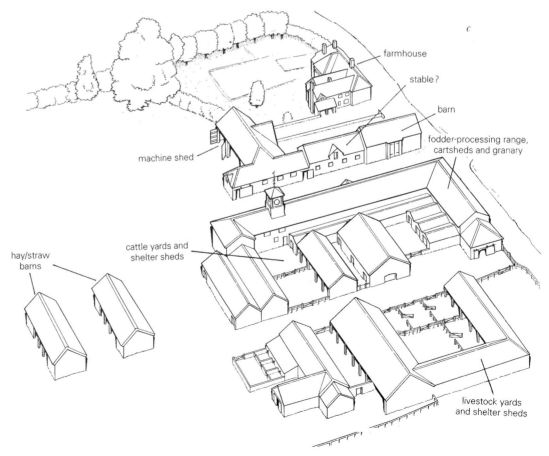

c

farmhouse

stable ?

barn

fodder-processing range, cartsheds and granary

machine shed

cattle yards and shelter sheds

hay/straw barns

livestock yards and shelter sheds

a

b

Fig 2.26 The early 20th-century cattle shed at Hamstead Holt Farm, Hamstead Marshall (a, b: BB94/14164; BB94/14168).

Fig 2.27 (below) Little Farm, Hamstead Marshall, was built in the mid 19th century as a small dairy farm with an L-shaped range of originally open-fronted cattle shelters (BB94/13931).

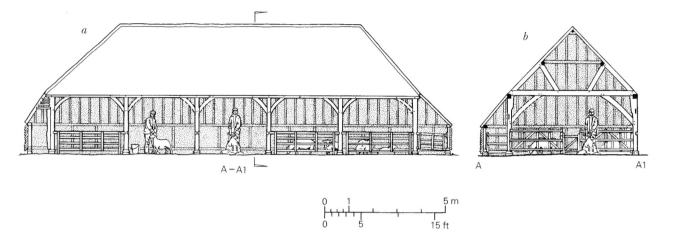

Fig 2.28 Buildings for sheep. The low eaves of the shelter at Easton Farm, Welford (a, elevation; b, section), suggest that the building was used for sheep. Portable huts, like that at Bradford's Farm, Speen (c; BB96/1716), were hauled by horse and provided shelter for the shepherd in remote locations.

exclusively for domestic consumption rather than for sale; there were two sties at Mason's Farm, Kintbury, and at South Stanmore Farm, Beedon, an aisle of the barn was converted to provide sties, with access to yards outside (Fig 2.29).

CARTSHEDS, IMPLEMENT SHEDS AND MACHINE SHEDS

Berkshire's emphasis on arable farming created a demand for carts and wagons for haulage and for implements for fieldwork. The increasing sophistication of farming in the 19th century was reflected in the growing number and larger size of the implements required; expensive ploughs, harrows, drills, reapers and many other implements were manufactured by specialist engineering companies, and became common on the farms of the region. The cost of the equipment meant that adequate shelter was essential, and the open-sided shed was the usual means of storage.

One cartshed, at Wawcott Farm, Kintbury, has a carved date of 1758 on a tie-beam, and the structure makes such a date credible. However, most of the cart and implement sheds recorded within the survey area date from the early and mid 19th century and later – from the period, that is, when improved and mass-produced machinery was becoming common. Cartsheds are usually single storey, often timber framed but sometimes of brick, with wooden posts supporting the wall-plate on the open side (Fig 2.30). Despite the regional farming emphasis, cartsheds are rarely larger than six bays long. They are frequently detached structures, set away from the livestock so as to allow generous space for manoeuvring vehicles and implements, and so as to reduce the likelihood of stock straying into them. Where incorporated into a courtyard plan, the cartsheds face outwards, for the same reasons. Shelter from sunshine and the prevailing winds influenced the direction in which the sheds faced; an alignment facing north or east was most common.

There are few variations in cartshed design. Some sheds have an aisle at the rear to give additional depth to the building. Whether these structures all date from the period when bigger, longer implements such as elevators were coming into use is not clear. One certain instance of provision for longer implements was recorded at Halfway Farm, Welford, where the early 20th-century block comprising cattle shelters and a cartshed is so contrived as to provide greater depth in two of the cartshed bays (Fig 2.30b, d). The same effect was provided at Rowles Farm, West Ilsley, by the addition of a pentice to the front of the building (Fig 2.30c). A few cartsheds, in the larger farmsteads, are incorporated within a two-storey building; the upper storey was a granary, and traps in the floor permitted the loading of grain directly into wagons (see Fig 2.19d).

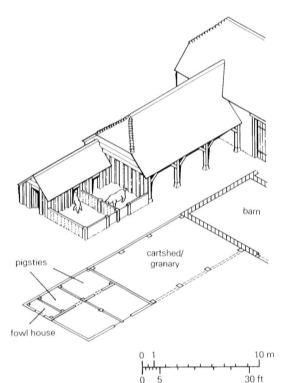

Fig 2.29 Pigsties: Mason's Farm, Kintbury (a); sties inserted into the barn visible as pair of low openings at South Stanmore Farm, Beedon (b; BB94/13905).

Fig 2.30 Cartsheds: Mason's Farm, Kintbury (a; BB94/13914); Halfway Farm, Welford (b; BB94/14202); Rowles Farm, West Ilsley (c; BB94/14149). The nearer bays in the cartshed at Halfway Farm are deeper than those at the far end, allowing larger machines to be stored (see d). The added pentice on the cartshed at Rowles Farm provided similar depth (see f). Cartsheds (dark grey) were usually built to face away from the main yard, as at Halfway Farm, Welford (d), Waterman's Farm, Kintbury (e), and Rowles Farm, West Ilsley (f).

There is some evidence for the provision of shelter for the most expensive machines used by the large arable farms. The traction engines and portable threshing machines which became common in the second half of the 19th century were larger than could be accommodated within the conventional cartshed; greater width and, especially, greater height were required. Similar accommodation was needed for the large balance ploughs, elevators and other machines used commonly from the mid 19th century.

a

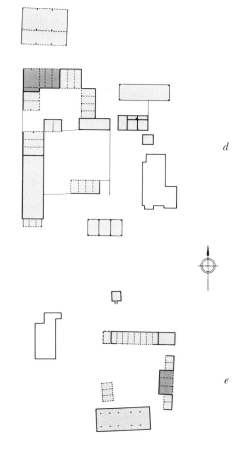

d

b

e

c

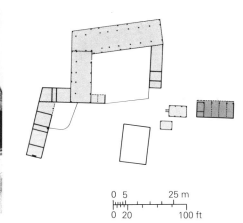

f

0 5   25 m

0 20   100 ft

a

b

c

A machine bay was added between the cartshed and the barn at Clapton Farm, Kintbury; the bay was provided with doors to give security and greater protection, and the doorway is about 60 cm (2 ft) higher than the bays of the adjacent cartshed (Fig 2.31*a*). Other farmsteads have a higher bay added to a range of cartsheds, or one cartshed bay altered to provide height for a machine (Fig 2.31*b*). At Bradford's Farm, Speen, a four-bay machine shed was built, probably *c* 1870, to house a larger number of machines; the doorways are 3.83 m (12.55 ft) high, giving ample headroom for even the tallest machines and implements (Fig 2.31*c, d*).

The existence of machine bays is perhaps a little-recognised aspect of farmstead design, but it is a phenomenon which reflects an important trend in the increasingly capital-intensive agriculture of the late 19th century. That not all farmsteads have such provision indicates that many farms depended on contractors or estates for the supply of mechanised processing, but it is not known whether the farmsteads with machine bays used their machines for contract work rather than simply servicing their own estates or farms. The unprepossessing buildings constructed to shelter the machines are an interesting demonstration of the individual progress of different farming regions. In comparison with some areas, Berkshire was slow to adopt mechanised processing, and largely omitted the phase of fixed-power operation. Partly as a result, but also for other reasons as well, the area invested heavily in the second phase of mechanisation, in which primary crop-processing had largely been removed from the farmstead. In this phase, new structures were required to house the machines which had made earlier buildings, in particular the barn, redundant.

Fig 2.31 Machine sheds. The bay added to the barn at Clapton Farm, Kintbury (a; BB94/14268), and the raised bay in the cartshed at Folly Farm, Eddington, Hungerford (b; BB96/2040), were designed to house tall machines, probably portable steam engines or traction engines. The large machine shed at Bradford's Farm, Speen (c; BB94/14255, and d), has doors with a height of nearly 4 m (13 ft).

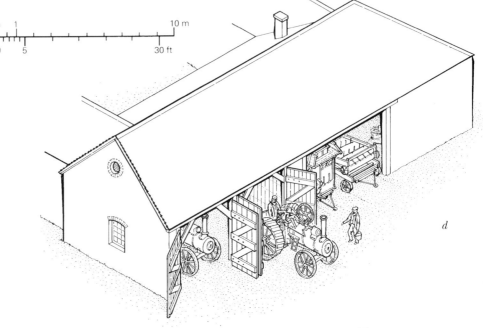

d

3 SOUTH LINCOLNSHIRE

The Survey Area

The part of Lincolnshire chosen for survey consists of two almost contiguous blocks of parishes east of Grantham and south of Sleaford (Fig 3.1). It contains two contrasting types of land: the four eastern parishes – Helpringham, Great and Little Hale, and Swaton – lie on the Black Sluice Fen (mostly about 3 m OD (10 ft) above sea level), rising to a slightly higher area (the Common) at their western ends; the western parishes (the clays) – Braceby and Sapperton, Newton and Haceby, Pickworth, Walcot, parts of Folkingham and parts of Lenton, Keisby and Osgodby – are on higher ground, though nowhere rising much above the 80 m OD (260 ft) contour. The soils of both areas are predominantly heavy clay, which is stiff, cold and wet: although rainfall is slightly lower than average, the water table is high, and the growing of satisfactory grain crops is difficult without improvement – particularly drainage – of the soil.

Even with such improvement, the area did not lend itself to large-scale arable exploitation until the mid 19th century, on account of its poor communications with the rest of the county, itself considered remote. The Car Dyke, a Roman drainage channel in the fen parishes, had once been navigable, but, although one contemporary source states that it was still capable of being used by boats in the 1850s,[1] the evidence of 19th-century maps suggests that this may be incorrect, or that only the very smallest of boats could have used it. The South Forty Foot Drain, however, was certainly navigable, and in 1851 it was reported that a steam packet was to commence operation along its entire length.[2] Even before then, the Drain provided waterborne access to the River Witham, which, in turn, rendered accessible the markets of Lincoln, Boston and the coast. For the western parishes, there was no means of water transport, and it was not until the advent of the railways that it became possible to move goods in and out of the area with ease. That occurred during the 1850s, with the opening of the Peterborough to Newark section of the London to Edinburgh line (in 1852), and of a link between Grantham and Boston, via Sleaford. The latter also had an impact on the fenland parishes, since it passed through Great Hale. In 1872 another line, also accessible to both areas, was opened, running south from Sleaford; ten years later, yet another, traversing Helpringham, linked Sleaford and Spalding. The importance of such developments for agriculture was commented upon at the time: James Caird stated in 1852 that he thought the advent of the railway would have a major effect upon the agricultural system of Lincolnshire.[3]

Enclosure was completed shortly after 1800, but problems of drainage meant that its full potential was not immediately realised. In the fenland parishes, the Car Dyke, which extends along the western edge of the fen proper, took some of the downwash from the higher land beyond, but did little to drain the fen itself. During the late 18th century, the South Forty Foot Drain, which marks the east end of the parishes, was cut; but, although it effected an improvement, there had been a major deterioration by 1800. In the following two decades, windmills were erected to lift water from the parish drains into the South Forty Foot, but not even that provided a lasting solution, and it was only in the late 1840s, when a steam pump was installed, that the land was fully secure for agriculture.[4] Although the western parishes stand higher, water was still a problem owing to the water-retentive clay soil, which required under-drainage before its potential for tillage could be realised. Such drainage had been commenced by 1850, but had not progressed very far.[5]

Settlement, Landholding and Farm Size

Settlement in both areas has long been predominantly nucleated. In some of the western parishes there is now more than one main centre, but that is the result of the amalgamation of older, smaller, parishes, each with its own village, into larger modern administrative units. Most of the farmsteads in these parishes are situated in the villages, though there are some – probably post-enclosure foundations – outside

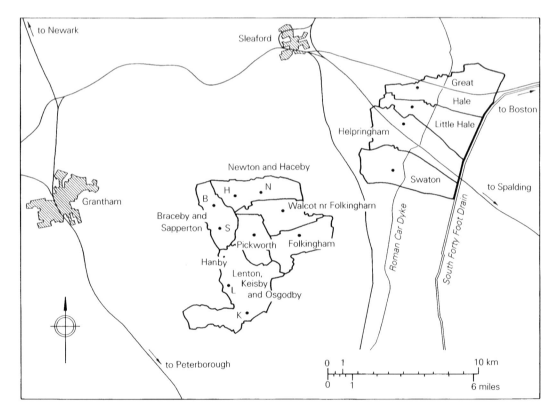

them. In one instance, Manor Farm, Walcot, the farmstead is split, the main part lying in the village centre, next to the church, and a lesser complex of buildings in the fields; it was in the latter that most of the horses and some of the wagons were kept, to save taking them back to the village each night. Settlement in the fenland parishes was also formerly largely nucleated, the centres of population lying on the edge of the higher ground, between the fen and the Common. The great length of the parishes meant that much of the newly drained land in the 19th century was so far from the villages (up to 4 km (2 miles)) that new farms were established, giving rise to a more scattered settlement pattern. In Swaton, all of which formed part of a single estate (see below), most of the land in the fen was divided between the farms in the village, some of which were provided with fenland offsteads (small semi-independent farmsteads, often with a cottage). Two farms in Swaton also had offsteads on the Common.

Landownership in both sections of the survey area was quite fragmented. In the western parishes there were parts of a number of estates. Newton and Haceby, and Braceby and Sapperton, were largely owned by the Welby estate, the centre of which was at Denton Park near Grantham. Pickworth formed part of the estate of the Duke of St Albans, and Walcot was mostly owned by the Ancaster estate, based at

Grimsthorpe, while the hamlet of Hanby (now in the parish of Lenton, Keisby and Osgodby) was the property of the Earls of Dysart (the Tollemache family), whose main residence in the region was at Buckminster: none of the major landowners was resident within the survey area itself. The Welby and Ancaster estates were amongst the largest in south Lincolnshire, and the Dysarts' lands, which were associated with those of the Manners and Heathcote families, were also extensive.[6]

The pattern of landholding in most of the fenland parishes is more complex. The exception to this is the parish of Swaton, which was almost entirely owned by the Warners of Walsingham Abbey in Norfolk; they sold their Swaton estate in 1913, but it was purchased by the Crown, and its unity is still preserved. More characteristic are Great and Little Hale, parts of which were owned by the Marquis of Bristol, who resided at Ickworth Park, near Bury St Edmunds. Most land in those parishes, and in Helpringham, was the property of lesser men, many of whom were small freeholders. Some, such as the Watling and Barnes families, owned three or four farms, but most only one. This kind of fragmented ownership is typical of much of the south Lincolnshire fenland.[7]

Most farms in Lincolnshire were held on annual tenancies, the negative effects of which on tenant improvements were overcome by the

Fig 3.1 Map of the Lincolnshire survey area.

early development of a system of tenant right. Under that scheme, outgoing tenants were compensated for investments they had made but from which they had not gained the full benefit. Such compensation covered labour and financial outlay on crops sown but not harvested, and expenditure on underdraining, manuring and other soil-improving activities, and was payable by the incoming tenant, who was the beneficiary. The system appears to have developed in about 1820, shortly after the time when tenants began to become active in improving their land. One of the reasons suggested for the early development of tenant right in Lincolnshire was that there was a large amount of land whose potential could be realised only after substantial tenant investment – of time, perhaps, more particularly than of money.

Within the survey area, farms were generally not large, but there are differences between the fenland and the western group of parishes. In the latter, the mean and median size of farm are both about 90 hectares (225 acres), the smallest farm recorded being of 31 hectares (77 acres), and the largest of 166 hectares (410 acres). In the fenland area, by contrast, the mean size is about 65 hectares (160 acres), and the median nearer 58 hectares (143 acres). Hence, although there were a few large farms – the largest being of nearly 200 hectares (500 acres), there were many more very small farms, extending right down to a smallholding of a mere 2 hectares (5 acres). This is likely to be a reflection of the large number of independent freeholders on the fen.

The 19th-Century Farming System

At the beginning of the period from which farm buildings survive in any numbers – the late 18th century – the predominant element

of the agricultural economy was grassland. According to one early 19th-century account of agriculture in Lincolnshire as a whole, this was partly a response to poor transport links, since it was thought easier to move livestock to market along poor roads than to try to transport grain.[8] The main agricultural emphasis in the survey area was twofold: the rearing of locally bred sheep, and the finishing of cattle which were imported from as far afield as Scotland and Wales. The 1801 Home Office Crop Returns show that arable acreages were generally small in the western parishes, and that wheat was the largest arable crop. In the fenland area, the arable acreage was rather larger, but, with the exception of Swaton, the main crop was oats (largely used as a fodder crop).[9]

Between 1801 and 1866, when annual statistics become available, the area under cultivation expanded, as did the proportion of arable. The most striking change occurred in the parishes on the fen, where wheat replaced oats as the dominant crop. A high proportion of the western area remained under grass in the middle of the century, perhaps largely because underdrainage had not progressed very far.[10] In general, J A Clarke, writing in 1851, thought the area to be backward and mean, particularly in relation to the feeding of cattle.[11] Despite this, the main trend in the first three-quarters of the 19th century was towards an increase in mixed farming (Fig 3.2), with the rise in the acreage of wheat suggesting that corn was being grown for market. It is difficult to date the changes accurately, but Clarke's remarks suggest that it took place at the same time as, or very shortly after, underdraining, which became widespread during the 1850s.

The timing of the changes was probably influenced by a number of factors. Although grain prices were low during much of the period between about 1820 and 1840, the local response was to increase production in an attempt to maintain farm income. Before the middle of the century, reclamation of the fen and of common land made it possible to achieve an increase by expanding the total area of land used for agricultural purposes. Once the maximum available area had been reached, the only way to increase productivity was to intensify the nature of agriculture by improving the land. Apart from underdraining, one of the main means of achieving this was to increase the amount of fertiliser and manure applied: the rise in arable production therefore partly depended upon a simultaneous improvement in the ways in which cattle were kept, leading to the adoption of a more

Fig 3.2 Simplified diagram of the mixed-farming cycle. Corn crops provide grain for market, and oats and straw for cattle fodder. As the 19th century advanced, fodder was supplemented by root crops, and by bought-in oil cake. The cattle were sold for meat, but also provided manure which was returned to the fields to improve crop yields, and was later supplemented by bought-in fertilisers. The proportion of income derived from grain and cattle varied during the course of the century. Not shown are sheep which grazed and manured the fields, but were not kept at the farmstead.

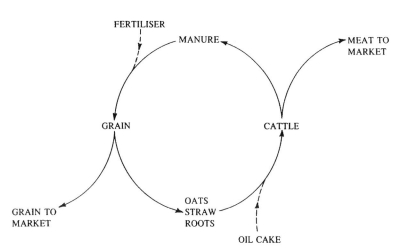

balanced mixed-farming regime than had hitherto prevailed. At the same time, the production of grain may have received an added stimulus from the construction of railways in the vicinity, by means of which the crop could be taken to distant markets.

Much of the foregoing account is derived from the western part of the survey area. The position in the fenland is more difficult to assess, largely because J A Clarke did not specifically comment upon the Black Sluice Fen in his 1851 account of Lincolnshire agriculture, but also as a consequence of the poverty of the tithe records for the area (they usually give details of cropping). It is likely, however, that, despite the better transport links afforded by the South Forty Foot Drain, the main improvements to the land did not occur significantly earlier in this area than in the western parishes, owing to the fact that drainage was not entirely satisfactory until about 1850 (see above). The effect of the change was, however, broadly similar, with a rise in mixed farming.

Within Lincolnshire, the claylands were amongst the most severely affected by the late 19th-century depression. Analysis of a sample of the annual Crop Returns, which began to be collected in 1866, suggests that between the 1870s and the 1900s, the amount of arable in both groups of parishes remained roughly stable, though there was some shift in emphasis away from wheat, particularly in the fenland area. The most significant change was a large rise in the number of cattle, implying both a continuing quest to increase arable yields by enhancing the quantity and quality of manure, and a greater emphasis on the maintenance of income by increasing the production of meat. Sheep also remained important – as they had been throughout the 19th century – providing both wool and meat, as well as producing manure which was applied directly to the fields where they were kept. These trends may be confirmed by a growth in the number of farmers described as graziers, butchers and cattle-dealers in the local Directories produced during the second half of the century.[12]

The agricultural system was influenced by the way in which cattle were fed, since, until the mid 19th century (or even later), they were fed on chaff mixed with linseed, rather than on more expensive oil cake. In this context chaff specifically relates to oats, the entire crop being chopped to make fodder for both horses and cattle.[13] This accounts not only for the relatively high acreages of oats in the survey area, but also for the presence of a specific type of building – the chaff house – to accommodate the crop (see below).

The Farmstead

The earliest extant farm buildings in the survey area date from the 18th century, and consist mainly of barns and stables, the latter often with granaries above. The same building types also predominate in the early 19th century, and on some farms may represent the first phase of post-enclosure investment. When such buildings were constructed, they appear to have comprised virtually the entire farmstead, since evidence from the tithe maps suggests that they stood in isolation, rather than in association with other structures which have subsequently been demolished or replaced by later ones (Fig 3.3). Although the early buildings are connected with arable exploitation – and the production, processing and storage of grain crops in particular – this does not mean that the picture presented earlier of a predominantly livestock economy is incorrect. The seeming contradiction between the documentary and physical evidence may reflect a situation in which cattle were kept outside (as were sheep – see below), while grain crops were probably largely grown for fodder, rather than for the market – particularly as the area was noted for the fact that it used chaff as cattle-fodder (see above).

Fig 3.3 The evolving farmstead: Old Manor Farm, Braceby (Braceby and Sapperton). The only agricultural buildings shown on the 1839 tithe map are those in a: the dovecote (dated 1707) and the barn (also 18th century) (see Figs 3.23c and 3.7b, respectively), together with the stables which form a slightly later addition to the latter. The main stable range, cattle accommodation and other buildings (b) were all built after 1839 and do not replace earlier structures of similar function.

Key
1 dovecote
2 barn
3 stables
4 trap house
5 working-horse stable
6 chaff house
7 cattle sheds
8 fowl house
9 shelter shed
10 loose box
11 cartshed
12 pigsties

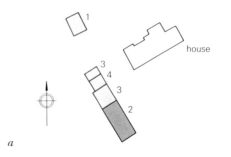
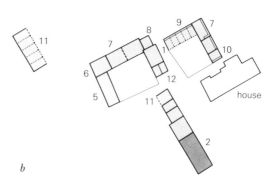

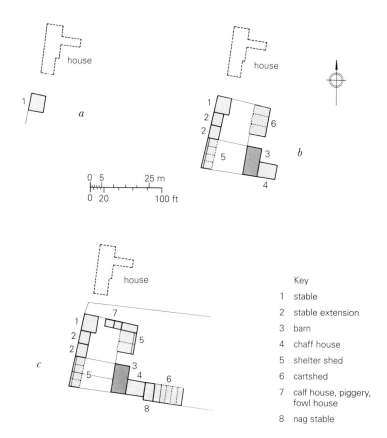

Key

1 stable
2 stable extension
3 barn
4 chaff house
5 shelter shed
6 cartshed
7 calf house, piggery, fowl house
8 nag stable

Fig 3.4 The evolving farmstead: Village Farm, Swaton. The farmstead developed piecemeal during the 19th century: a, 1790–1820; b, 1825–1850; c, 1850–1875. The resulting plan, while accommodating all the elements necessary for mixed farming, was not well integrated, the buildings being placed poorly in relation to each other.

perhaps reflecting, not just the larger numbers of cattle in the area during the post-1870 depression, but also increasing diversity in foodstuffs.

The effect of the introduction of new kinds of building on farmstead layout, and on the flows of processes around the buildings, can be clearly seen, because most farmsteads in the area reached their final form by a process of evolution during the 19th century. This can be exemplified by Village Farm, Swaton (Fig 3.4). The earliest phase of development (*c* 1800) appears to have consisted of no more than a stable with granary above; the building was next to the road, which was convenient in terms of moving horses in and out, and of taking grain to market, but nothing can be understood of the way in which the farmstead actually worked. The second quarter of the 19th century saw considerable expansion – the stable was extended, a barn and chaff house were built, and two shelter sheds constructed (one for cattle, the other probably originally for carts). With this, it becomes possible to reconstruct the pattern of processes: unthreshed corn was taken to the barn, where it was stored and threshed, before the grain was carried across the yard to the granary for storage prior to sale or use as fodder; the straw was kept either in the barn or outside until it was required in the yards as fodder and litter. The oat crop was taken from the fields to the chaff house, where it was stored and chopped; thence it was taken to the yards as fodder. Cattle and horses were moved in and out of the yards as required, and their manure was taken out to a midden or direct to the fields by carts which were also accommodated in the yard. The farmstead did not reach its mature form until the third quarter of the century, when the cartshed was converted to house extra livestock and a new cartshed was built outside the yard; at the same time, a calf house, piggery and fowl house were added at the north. The result of this was to allow greater numbers of cattle and carts/implements to be kept.

By the end of its development Village Farm provided all the accommodation required for a small mixed system, and the more recent buildings were planned with an eye to convenience. The new cartshed, for example, was better placed than its predecessor in terms of access from the fields, and the pigsties, calf house and fowl house were positioned near the house so as to be convenient for the farmer's wife, who looked after the animals housed by them and made their feed in the back kitchen. Despite that, the overall plan was not convenient – the stable, for instance, was in an awkward corner – and required the carrying of fodder and grain around the farmstead to a greater extent than can have been strictly desirable.

Confirmation of the general lack of cattle-housing before the mid 19th century comes from a description of agriculture in Lincolnshire as a whole, written by Philip Pusey, one of the leading agricultural commentators of the period. In 1843 he noted that, 'though the farm buildings of Lincolnshire are excellent, I was sorry in some of the yards to see numerous cattle standing shelterless in the midst of a snow-storm. These yards should at once be furnished with sheds, for the beast's sake and his master's.'[14] During the mid and late 19th century, the provision of large-scale and increasingly sophisticated methods of housing cattle is a recurrent theme in the national literature, particularly as agriculture was intensified. This is reflected in the farmsteads of the survey area, with open-sided shelter sheds being constructed in the second and, more particularly, third quarters of the century, after which there was a slow move to fully covered yards.

As part of the same development, new buildings were constructed for the storage and processing of fodder. The earliest kind of building connected with these functions which is found in any numbers within the survey area is the chaff house, in which chaff (the oat crop) was stored and chopped. From the middle of the 19th century, root houses and other fodder-preparation rooms became more numerous,

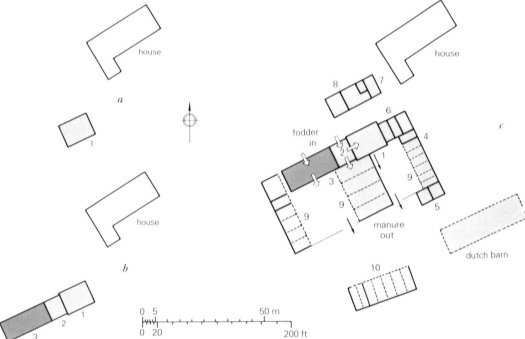

house

a

1

house

b

2 1

3

0 5   50 m

0 20   200 ft

house

8 7

6

fodder in

2

3

1

4

9

9

9

manure out

5

c

dutch barn

10

Key (above)

1 stable	6 pigsties
2 chaff house	7 fodder room
3 barn	8 nag stable, trap house
4 hen house	9 cattle shelters
5 loose boxes	10 cartshed

Key (below)

1 barn, granary	5 root house
2 stable	6 covered yards
3 chaff house	7 loose box
4 cartsheds	8 pigsties, hen house
	9 trap house, nag stable

fodder in

4

5

4

3

2

manure out

7

7

6

6

1

fodder storage

9

manure out

8

house

0 5   50 m

0 20   200 ft

Fig 3.5 The evolving farmstead: Woodside Farm, Newton (Newton and Haceby). The stages in the development of Woodside Farm (a, c 1840; b, c 1850; c, c 1860) are broadly similar to those at Village Farm (Fig 3.4), but the result is more satisfactory. Corn crops entered the barn and chaff house, where they were processed into fodder and litter which could be passed directly to the stable and cattle yards. Manure was passed out of the yards at the opposite side of the farmstead, creating a fairly simple linear flow of processes.

Fig 3.6 The planned farmstead: Hanby Lodge Farm, Hanby, (Lenton, Keisby and Osgodby). The conversion of corn crops into manure follows a similar linear pattern to that at Woodside Farm, Newton (Fig 3.5), but the fact that Hanby Lodge Farm was designed in one stage means that the layout could be more compact. Chaff was stored and processed next to the stable, where it was consumed (see also Fig 3.20c), and roots next to the feeding passage between the covered yards. The barn was a two-storey struc- ture on the first floor of which grain was stored, while the ground floor may have served as a secure and dry store for expensive oil cake and/or for artificial fertilisers.

Not all evolutionary farmsteads were so poorly integrated. At Woodside Farm, Newton (Newton and Haceby), the sequence of develop- ment is similar to that at Village Farm, but the end result must have been considerably more satisfactory (Fig 3.5): the stable is easier of access, the chaff house is well placed both in relation to the fields (from which the oat crop came) and to the yards (whence the processed crop was taken), to which it had direct access. Functional areas such as the hen house, loose boxes and pigsties which did not require access to the yards were arranged around it in such a way as to be readily accessible from both the house and a fodder- preparation room in a detached block which also accommodated the nag stable and trap house. In line with the recommendations of the 19th- century commentators, the cattle yards faced south so as to derive maximum benefit from the sun, and were sheltered on the north by the two- storey buildings; the yards were partly covered, providing shelter for the animals and protection for their fodder. In addition, the cartshed was placed outside the yard facing north so that the sun did not warp the timber of the vehicles, and there was space outside for the manœuvring of carts and implements.

It was possible for many of the same func- tions to be housed even more economically in terms of labour, though only a few single-phase planned farmsteads in the survey area aspired to this. The best example is the farmstead built in the early 1880s by the Dysart estate at Hanby Lodge Farm, Hanby, in the parish of Lenton, Keisby and Osgodby (Fig 3.6). The only

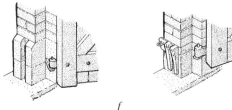

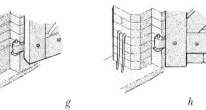

a

b

c

f　　　　*g*　　　　*h*

Fig 3.7 *The development of the barn: barns for hand threshing. The 'traditional' form of barn has a central threshing floor, identifiable from the outside by the tall double doors and storage bays. The example at Parks Farm, Great Hale (a; BB93/21412), probably dates from the late 18th century. The barn at Old Manor Farm, Braceby (Braceby and Sapperton) (b; BB96/ 9453) is much larger, and slightly earlier than that at Parks Farm, but has the same form. This kind of barn continued to be built into the 19th century, as at an unnamed farmstead on Swaton Common (NMR Buildings Index no. 91571) (c; BB93/21364), built by the Warner estate. The doors at the same farm have an elaborate mechanism for operating the top bolt (d), while on the upper stone hinge block are scratched and pencil marks made during threshing to keep a tally of the number of sheaves threshed. Below the doors in this kind of barn there is usually a timber threshold (or evidence for one), as at Johnson's Farm, Little Hale (e; BB92/31048). Such thresholds were held in place by various kinds of slot: at Rookery Farm, Great Hale (f), the slot is formed of stone; at the farm on Swaton Common it is of timber (g); while at Grange Farm, Little Hale (h), it is iron.*

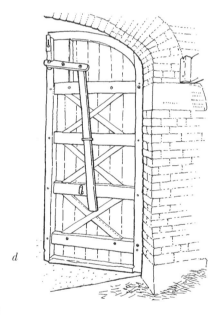

d

e

elements present at Woodside and Village Farms which are not represented at Hanby Lodge Farm are the pigsties and hen house, which may have been accommodated in a small range adjoining the house. The plan of the main block of the farmstead suggests that chaff was used on a large scale only to feed horses, as might be expected in the late 19th century when cattle were fed on oil cake, and there are only two main, parallel, flows of processes through the farmstead (one for the cattle, the other for the working horses). The trap house and nag stable are situated nearest to the house, reflecting their domestic function, and the loose boxes face the house, perhaps reflecting their use for livestock requiring extra care. The barn was readily accessible by carts, as were the root house and chaff house, while the stable and cartshed could easily be reached from the fields.

The kind of planning evident at Hanby Lodge Farm (and at the identical farmstead at The Pines, Great Ponton, on the same estate – not recorded) is an example of the application of national standards to the designing of a completely new farmstead. Few farmsteads in the survey area resulted from this kind of planning; instead, they accommodated the same processes, aimed at producing the same products, in buildings of varying dates and laid out in relation to each other with differing degrees of convenience.

GRAIN PRODUCTION

As indicated above, the earliest surviving buildings on many farmsteads are stables with granaries above, and barns (Fig 3.7). The earliest barns served a dual purpose, providing a ventilated floor on which hand, or flail, threshing could take place; at each side of the threshing floor there was space for storing the unthreshed crop and straw. Gradually, as the threshing process became mechanised, barns became smaller, and their functions changed to those of a straw store and a fodder-mixing and preparation area; reflecting this, the design of the building was radically altered. On some farms – particularly those of the mid 19th century, before the later increase in cattle numbers necessitated the provision of large areas for fodder preparation – the barn almost disappeared, becoming little more than a small room with a grain-milling or bruising machine.

The earliest barns, both in the fenland parishes and in the more westerly area, are immediately recognisable by their traditional form. The barn at Parks Farm, Great Hale, for example (one of the earliest surviving agricultural buildings in the fenland parishes (Fig 3.7a)), has the characteristic tall double

and opposed threshing doors in the long walls, though local examples all lack the projecting porches or canopies found in some parts of the country. Between lay the threshing floor, where, throughout the winter, small quantities of grain were threshed each day and winnowed in the slight draught which could be created and regulated by varying the combination of open and closed doors. By local standards, the barn at Parks Farm is quite large, but even the largest – such as that at Old Manor Farm, Braceby (Braceby and Sapperton) (Fig 3.7b) – had only one threshing floor.

Barns of this type continued to be built well into the 19th century, and remained in use (though in a different way) long after threshing had become mechanised. The parish of Swaton – which was almost entirely owned by the Warner estate – contains a particularly distinctive group of buildings of this kind, erected during the 1820s and 1830s (Fig 3.7c). The farms in the parish are generally quite small, and this is reflected in the scale of the buildings, which are also quite plain, though well finished. Particular attention was paid to the design of the doors (Fig 3.7d), beneath which were timber thresholds (consisting of planks which slotted into channels on the door jambs (Fig 3.7e–h)) which were designed to prevent the crop spilling out of the barn during threshing.

There is no evidence within the survey area for the use of fixed power for mechanised threshing – whether in the form of horse-engine houses or of fixed steam installations. Such features do exist in other parts of Lincolnshire, and their absence within the survey area may be due partly to the relatively small scale of most of the farms (even in the western parishes), and partly to the fact that arable production was relatively unimportant in the area during the first half of the 19th century. It therefore seems that hand, or flail, threshing continued until the arrival of portable machinery from the 1840s onwards.

The first farmsteads which were planned for mechanical threshing seem to have been constructed in the 1850s (Fig 3.8). It is clear, however, that the engines were mobile, rather than fixed, and it is likely that they were powered by steam, since portable horse wheels had been available a little earlier. With the advent of steam threshing of this kind, the functions of the barn underwent a transformation. As the crop could be threshed much more rapidly – in a few days, rather than gradually throughout the winter – there was no longer any need to build barns capable of storing the unthreshed crop: hence there was no need for a covered area comparable to that which lay to one side of the threshing floor in the traditional barn. In addition, the threshing floor was rendered redundant, since threshing would take place in the open air. Other processes – such as grain-milling and bruising – were probably still conducted in the barn, but did not require a great deal of space (there are later machines for this in two of the smallest barns in the region – that at Poplar Farm, Helpringham, and that at an unnamed farmstead on Helpringham Fen).[15] Hence, what had formerly been a large building dominating the farmstead became, in some cases, little more than a small room, more properly considered a processing room than a 'barn' (Fig 3.8a, b).

As cattle numbers increased later in the 19th century, barns became larger again, as they served as mixing houses for fodder – though they rarely returned to anything resembling their traditional form. One type looks quite

Fig 3.8 The development of the barn: barns in the era of mechanisation. After mechanical threshing became common, the unthreshed crop was stacked outside, as was the straw, and threshing was conducted in the open air. At Poplar Farm, Helpringham (a, b: BB92/31050; BB93/21272), grain, (and, perhaps, bought-in foodstuffs) was stored on the first floor (reached by an external stairway at the back). The only part of the building which accommodated functions traditionally associated with the barn was a small room between the open-sided bays (in the centre of (a)) in which fodder was prepared, and in which there is a later milling machine (b). Another type of barn, which appears from the outside to be of traditional form, is exemplified by Crow Lane Farm, Great Hale (c). The unthreshed corn and straw were stacked outside, where threshing took place; inside, grain was stored in the loft at the left, and the ground floor was used for storing fodder – probably including oil cake – and for preparing it prior to distribution to the livestock. The logic of this arrangement could be carried further, as at Moat Farm, Newton (Newton and Haceby) (d), where the barn was fully two-storeyed, and there was probably a separate chaff house. At an unnamed farm (now demolished) on Swaton Fen (NMR Buildings Index no. 91570) (e), the barn is similar to that at Moat Farm, but smaller, since it has no first floor for grain storage: this may reflect the fact that the farmstead was an offstead, forming part of a larger unit centred at a farmstead in the village where the grain may have been taken.

a   *b*

c

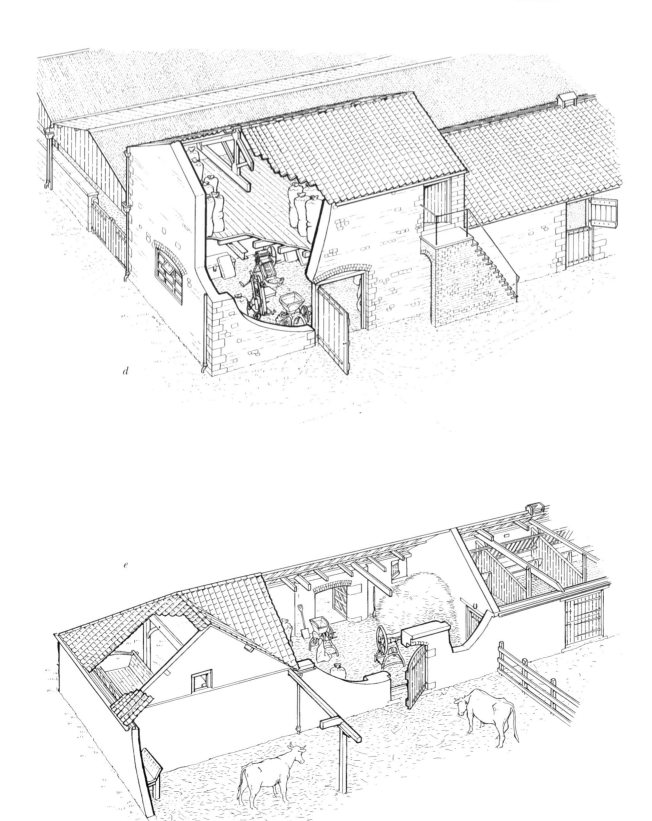

d

e

a

b

Fig 3.9 The position of granaries. Most early 19th-century (and earlier) granaries are above stables, as at Manor Farm, Helpringham (a; BB93/21276), built in the early 19th century. Some later granaries are above cartsheds and beside the barn, so reducing the distance grain had to be carried within the farmstead, as at Grange Farm, Little Hale (b; BB95/12569), built in the 1880s.

traditional from the outside, but has a loft on one side of the central processing area, which was partitioned off to form a granary (see below), as at Crow Lane Farm, Great Hale (Fig 3.8c); in other cases, a traditional barn like that at Manor Farm, Walcot, was adapted to this form.[16] An extension of this may be seen in some of the most advanced instances, where the

barn is a fully two-storeyed building: the first floor served as a granary, and the ground floor as a processing room, as at Moat Farm, Newton (Newton and Haceby), a small planned farmstead built in c 1900 (Fig 3.8d). A final type of building is a single-storey structure, like that at an unnamed farm, probably of the 1890s, on Swaton Fen,[17] which was used as a fodder-processing room with space for short-term storage of quite small quantities of crops prior to their conversion into fodder (Fig 3.8e).

What all the later varieties of barn have in common is that they were built on the assumption that threshing would be conducted by machine which, together with the power source, would be used in the open air. It was not that the mechanisation of the process required new types of building, but that there was no longer any necessity to construct barns of the large and relatively expensive traditional kind. Where barns already existed, however, there was nothing to prevent farmers continuing to use them: expenditure on their replacement would have been wasted. On many farmsteads which are predominantly of later date, therefore, there is still an early barn of traditional type.

Granaries

The process of threshing produced grain and straw which were used for different purposes and housed separately, the straw either outside or in the barn, and the grain in a granary. Grain (particularly wheat) was a valuable commodity, since some of it was a cash crop. As a result, grain was always stored in substantial buildings, which provided well-ventilated first-floor rooms where the grain could be protected from damp and vermin. The earliest granaries – which date from the late 18th and early 19th centuries – are almost always above stables (Fig 3.9a). From the middle of the century onwards, when large cartsheds became more common (see below), granaries were sometimes placed above them (Fig 3.9b). This offered a number of advantages: ventilation was better, owing to the open-sided nature of cartsheds, potential problems of the horses' breath and the steam from their bodies (particularly in winter) tainting the grain were obviated, and grain could be loaded straight into carts through trapdoors in the floor of the granary.

An alternative which was developed in the late 19th century was for the grain to be accommodated within the barn. On some of the smaller farmsteads, and some of those in which earlier, traditional, barns were adapted for use in the mechanised age, a first-floor loft was created at one end of the barn, as at Crow Lane Farm, Great Hale (see above, and Fig 3.8c). On

a　　　　　　　　　　　*b*　　　　　　　　　　　*c*

some of the later planned farms, in which the barn was fully floored, the first floor served as a granary (see above, and Fig 3.8*d*).

The distinctive architectural fittings of granaries were all connected with keeping the grain dry and free from vermin, but well ventilated. The floors were often made of close-fitting boards and were better finished than those in other parts of the farmstead; this reduced the opportunities for any grain spilt on them to be lost through seepage into the ground floor of the building, and potential points of access for pests. In some granaries – particularly those built before the middle of the 19th century – a floor of lime mixed with ash and laid on laths was used, giving a continuous and smooth surface (Fig 3.10*a*). Provision was also made for access to granaries by cats, by installing primitive cat holes in the doors, so that they could keep rodents down (Fig 3.10*b*). The other problem – that of ventilation – was solved by the installation of various types of combined window and vent (some similar to those used in stables (Fig 3.10*c*)).

STABLES

Two main types of stable are found within the survey area, one prevalent in the late 18th and early 19th century, and the other in fashion thereafter, but with an overlap between the two. The earlier kind is often on the ground floor of a two-storey building, under the granary (see above), and is well illustrated by that at Woodside Farm, Newton (Newton and Haceby), on the Welby estate (Fig 3.11*a*, *b*). The building is of stone – typical of the western group of

parishes – and has central doorways in each side wall, with a manure passage (with drains) between. The horses were stalled on each side of the passage, facing the end walls, and ventilation was provided by splayed slit vents; there were no windows, making the interior very dark when the doors were closed. Beside each of the doorways is a small recessed cupboard (approximately 30 cm (1 ft) square) in which curry combs and brushes might be kept; often there are also harness hooks near the doorways. Each of the two standings was formerly divided into two double stalls – a characteristic of stables in Lincolnshire as a whole – at the head of which was a hay rack above a manger.

The second, generally later, variety of stable had the (double) stalls arranged along the length of the building, rather than across it (Fig 3.11*c*, *d*). There was usually a central doorway in the wall opposite the stalls; between the doorway and the standing was the dung passage with its drain. As in the earlier examples, the stalls had a hay rack and manger at their heads, and, sometimes, a small grille vent above each stall. Apart from the difference in internal layout, the main change between this kind of stable and its earlier counterpart was connected with the amount of ventilation – a feature on which national commentators laid increased emphasis during the mid and late 19th century.[18] One of the main ways in which this was manifested was that the later stables were usually in single-storey buildings, which not only allowed a greater volume of air in the building by including the roof space in the stable, but also allowed vents to be incorporated within the roof to remove stale air (Fig 3.11*e–i*).

Fig 3.10 Granaries: details. Grain was a valuable commodity which had to be kept dry and secure: this led to a number of distinctive features. Floors were sometimes rendered impervious by being constructed of laths coated with lime ash: (a) shows the underside of such a floor at Manor Farm, Helpringham (BB95/12570). Granaries were often reached by external steps, and had lockable doors with cat holes, as at Johnson's Farm, Little Hale (b; BB92/31047). Ventilation was often provided by louvred windows (c: Woodside Farm, Newton (Newton and Haceby); BB93/24151).

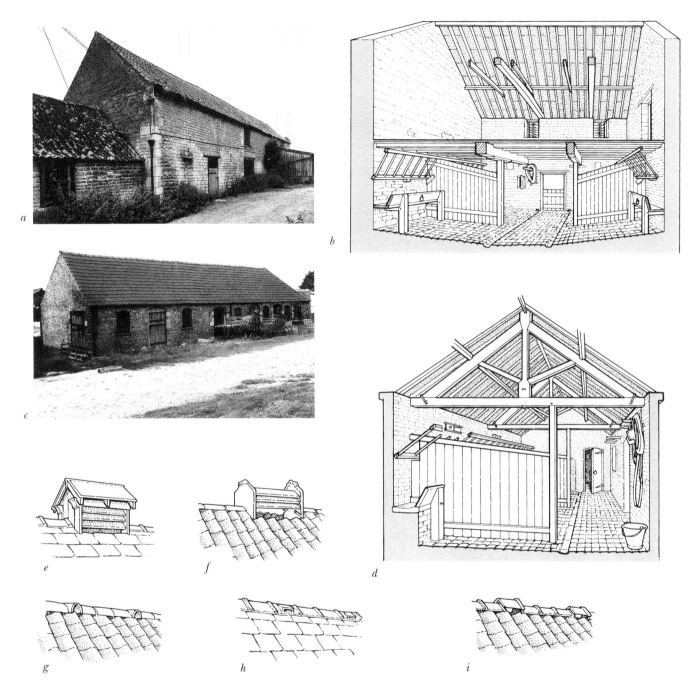

Fresh air was admitted to most stables of this kind by windows which flanked the doorway: only a relatively small area of the opening was intended to admit light, the larger area usually consisting of some kind of ventilator, sometimes with adjustable slats (Fig 3.11*j–m*).

There was no drop-feed system (whereby fodder could be placed into the hay rack from a room above the stable), in either type of Lincolnshire stable, but this did not necessarily mean that fodder had to be pushed past the horses. For much of the year, the animals were probably in the stables only for feeding and grooming, so that fodder could have been placed in the hay racks and mangers when the horses were not in the stable. When they were not working, the horses were usually loose in a yard which was separated from the cattle yards by fences. Once tractors made horses redundant, horse yards were often amalgamated with cattle yards, so physical traces of horse yards do not often survive, but the pattern can often be seen on 19th-century maps.[19]

The mangers were constructed of brick (Fig 3.11*n*), but the upstanding front of the structure was timber to prevent the horses

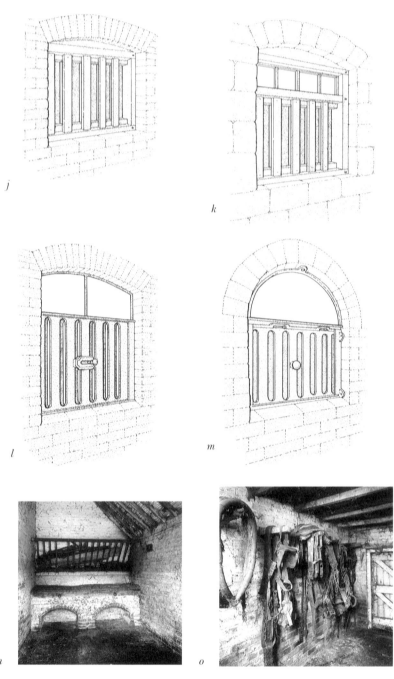

Fig 3.11 Lincolnshire Stables. The late 18th and early 19th-century stable with granary above is exemplified by Woodside Farm, Newton (Newton and Haceby) (a, BB93/24149, and b). The reconstructed interior (b) shows the main features: double stalls with hay racks and mangers, on either side of a central manure passage; a small cupboard next to the door, and, beside it, a tack hook. The later, single-storey, stable, is exemplified by Hanby Grange Farm, Hanby (Lenton, Keisby and Osgodby) (c; BB93/24134), and Rookery Farm, Great Hale (d). There is a single row of double stalls, each with a vent at its head; a manure passage runs the length of the building behind the stalls. As in the earlier example, each of the stalls has a hay rack and manger, and there are tack hooks in the side wall. The door at the end leads to a small tack room where additional gear was kept. Single-storey stables often had vents in the ridge of the roof. The forms were varied and some, like those at Hanby Lodge Farm, Hanby (Lenton, Keisby and Osgodby) (e), and Moat Farm, Newton (Newton and Haceby) (f), were decorative. The others are at Cardyke Farm, Swaton (g), a different part of Hanby Lodge Farm (h) and Grange Farm, Little Hale (i). Vented windows are found in both kinds of stable: the simplest consists of wooden slats, as at Manor Farm, Helpringham (j). Sometimes, as at Old Hall Farm, Pickworth, there is a small glazed section above (k). Late 19th-century examples were often iron, and incorporated sliding vents, as at Hanby Lodge Farm (Lenton, Keisby and Osgodby) (l), and Grange Farm, Little Hale (m). Fittings within stables do not always survive, but one of the most common kinds of manger (here (n) BB93/24140) at Hanby Grange Farm, Hanby (Lenton, Keisby and Osgodby) is of brick and is set over an arch. Sometimes rather more survives, as in the tack room at Poplar Farm, Helpringham (o; BB93/21273), where harness still hangs on the large timber pegs.

damaging their teeth; below, the brickwork was sometimes arched, leaving a recess at the horses' feet for litter. This design, which is characteristic of the survey area, found favour with the 19th-century commentators, and was illustrated by Denton.[20] As in the earlier stables, there were often heavy wooden harness pegs at the ends of the stall divisions or in the walls away from the stalls. They enabled the harness and other equipment to be stored conveniently close to the animals for which they were intended. An alternative arrangement on some of the better-appointed farmsteads was for the harness to be kept – on similar pegs – in a small separate tack room, usually next to the stable, and communicating with it by means of an internal doorway (Fig 3.11o).

CARTSHEDS

In order to move crops from the fields to the farmstead and thence to market, and to move the manure created by the animals (of all kinds) back to the fields, as well as to bring imported feedstuffs into the farm, carts and wagons were required and, in turn, had to be provided with

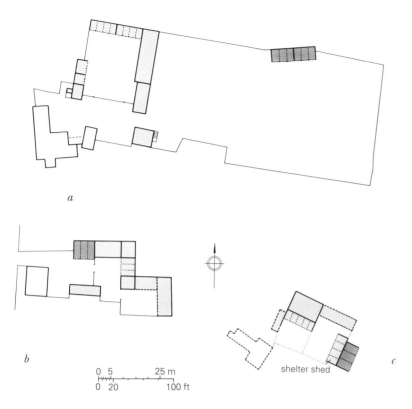

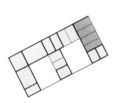

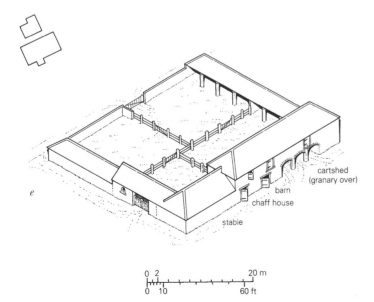

Fig 3.12 Cartsheds: position. (Cartsheds shown in dark grey.) Completely detached, as at Manor Farm, Helpringham (a). Attached, but outside the cattle yard, as at Chestnut House, Swaton (b). Backing onto a shelter shed, with access from outside the yard, as at Stennet's Farm, Little Hale (c). Fully integrated and of a single storey, as at Grange Farm, Hanby (d)(Lenton, Keisby and Osgodby). Fully integrated and below the granary, as at an unnamed farmstead (e) (NMR Buildings Index no. 91511), at Helpringham fen.

some kind of shelter. The cartshed (which, on later farmsteads, was also sometimes below the granary, see above) also accommodated the large horse-drawn implements used in cultivating the land – ploughs, seed drills and the like – sometimes in bays which were partitioned off from the others, and furnished with lockable double doors. Only a few cartsheds survive from much before the middle of the 19th century, and, where they do, they are generally only large enough for a single relatively small vehicle. During the second half of the century every farm came to be supplied with a more substantial cart and implement shed, as wagons became larger and better-built, and as implements were increasingly made of iron and became ever more sophisticated and expensive. The mechanisation of fieldwork this reflects was similar to that of crop processing. The new developments occurred at much the same time, the largest number of cartsheds being built in the third quarter of the 19th century.

Unlike many of the other buildings of the farmstead, the cartshed ideally faced approximately north (though this was by no means always achieved), since wooden wagons are damaged by direct sunlight. In addition, the cartshed needed to be placed conveniently in terms of access to and from the fields, and to have a large clear area in front of it so that large vehicles and implements could easily be manoeuvred in and out. As a result of this, cartsheds were often detached from the other farm buildings, and placed at a slight distance from them, as at Manor Farm, Helpringham (Fig 3.12a); this is particularly the case on farmsteads which evolved gradually during the 19th century. An alternative was for the cartshed to be built end-on to a range of buildings at one side of the main farmyard (Fig 3.12b). A further option was for the cartshed to be built backing onto the outer wall of one of the ranges surrounding the main yard, as at Stennet's Farm, Little Hale, where the cartshed backs onto a cattle shelter (Fig 3.12c); this is, however, less common, since most buildings apart from cattle shelters required unobstructed access from outside the yard. The majority of cartsheds of all these types are of a single storey, and consist of a number of bays open on one side, often with timber posts at the front (Fig 3.13); apart from their position outside the yards, the only feature which sometimes distinguishes them from cattle shelters (see below) is that they are often considerably deeper from front to back. Towards the end of the 19th century (and thereafter), many cartsheds were built entirely of timber – sometimes with corrugated-iron roofs from the start – and were extremely crudely constructed.

56

On some of the planned farmsteads of the second half of the 19th century, the cartshed was fully integrated with the rest of the layout, forming part of one of the main ranges. One way of achieving this was for the cartshed to occupy the angle between two ranges, as at Grange Farm, Hanby (Lenton, Keisby and Osgodby) (Fig 3.12*d*): since the cartshed faced outwards, there was no need to contrive access to the angle between the ranges from within the yards; most cartsheds in this position are single storeyed. An alternative was for the cartshed to be placed beside the barn, which, as the tallest building, usually lay at the north side of the cattle yard. Where this was done, the entire barn range was usually of two storeys, allowing for a granary to be placed above the cartshed. The advantage of this was that the grain could easily be moved into the granary direct from the barn, by means of an internal doorway and ladder, and, equally, could be loaded into carts through trapdoors in the floor of the granary (see above). This kind of arrangement, as found at an unnamed farm on Helpringham Fen (Fig 3.12*e*), built in 1858,[21] provides the most integrated plan for those elements of the farmstead connected with grain-processing and storage. By extending the length of the two-storey range beyond the barn, it also helped to provide shelter along one side (usually the north) of the cattle yard.

CATTLE ACCOMMODATION

As observed earlier, most Lincolnshire farm-steads had little or no cattle accommodation until the mid 19th century. After that, as economic imperatives demanded that agricultural activity became more intense, it was recommended that cattle were kept in sheltered conditions, since they would lose less energy in heat loss, enabling a greater proportion of the energy supplied by fodder to be turned into meat. A related concern was the quality of manure which was ultimately returned to the land: better manure was made if it was kept under cover, away from the leaching effects of rain.[22] The application of these principles led to the construction, from the mid 19th century onwards, of shelters and other buildings for the accommodation of cattle.

The simplest kind of accommodation, and the one which was most popular within the survey area, was the shelter shed. This is an open-sided shed, constructed along the sides of the main cattle yards (locally referred to as 'crew yards'), usually with a manger against the solid back wall (Fig 3.14). This protected the fodder from the detrimental effects of the weather and gave the animals some shelter,

Fig 3.13 Cartsheds: Village Farm, Swaton. Single-storey cartshed lying outside the main cattle yard at Village Farm, Swaton. The rear wall is brick, but the piers at the front are timber. The enclosed bay at the far end is a nag stable, and beyond lies the chaff house and, at right angles to it, the barn (BB93/21324).

while not depriving them of either sunlight or freedom of movement. Such structures were also relatively cheap and easy to construct, since they could be added to the sides of existing yards without a great deal of fresh preparatory construction work.

Significant numbers of shelter sheds began to be built in the second quarter of the 19th century, but their popularity increased dramatically in the succeeding twenty-five years, to the point at which few of the farmsteads which were in existence by 1880 lacked them. By then, many national commentators were advocating the fully covered yard, which was becoming popular over much of England.[23] In Lincolnshire as a whole, however, as in Norfolk, the roofing-over of yards was not popular, it being thought that the relatively low rainfall did so little damage to the manure that depriving the cattle of sunlight by keeping them fully under cover was not justified.[24] While most yards remained largely open throughout the 19th century, some were roofed over in the first quarter of the 20th, though the majority of roofs have subsequently been removed.

Fig 3.14 Cattle accommodation: shelter sheds. Open-sided cattle shelter at an unnamed farmstead (NMR Buildings Index no. 91511), at Helpringham fen. The building is broadly similar in form to a cartshed, but is less deep from front to back, and has a brick manger with hay rack above against the rear wall (BB93/21288).

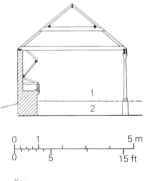

Key

1 level of manure in spring

2 ground level after removal of manure

a

b

Fig 3.15 Cattle accommodation: covered yards. Possibly the earliest covered yard found in the survey area is that at Poplar Farm, Great Hale (a; BB93/21342), built in the 1870s. The roof trusses are of unusual form in that they lack tie-beams. More typical is Poplar Farm, Helpringham (b; BB93/21275).

Fig 3.16 Cattle accommodation: covered yards. Bird's-eye view of Hanby Lodge Farm, Hanby (Lenton, Keisby and Osgodby), showing how covered yards could be fully integrated in the overall design of a planned farmstead.

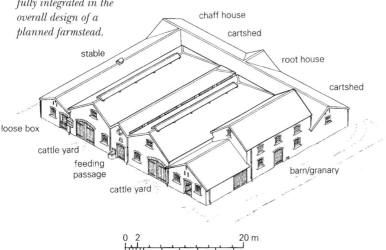

chaff house

cartshed

stable

root house

cartshed

loose box

cattle yard

feeding passage

barn/granary

cattle yard

0 2   20 m

0   10   60 ft

A few established farmsteads were, however, supplied with covered yards in the last third of the 19th century, one of the earliest being that at Poplar Farm, Great Hale, probably in the 1870s (Fig 3.15a). The roof trusses at this date were usually constructed of timber (Baltic fir), and their forms are extremely varied, ranging from the elaborate and curious structure at Poplar Farm, Great Hale, to the more conventional form at Poplar Farm, Helpringham, which was probably erected slightly later (Fig 3.15b).

Some of the completely new farmsteads built during this period were designed with covered yards. An example of this is the large planned farmstead at Hanby Lodge Farm, Hanby (in Lenton, Keisby and Osgodby parish) built by the Dysart estate in 1883 (Fig 3.16). There, the main buildings are arranged in a U-shape, with the yards in the centre, but the design of the latter is so integrated that, from the outside, the farmstead looks like a single building. Not all new

farmsteads of the period, however, were designed in this way, even on one estate: for example, Grange Farm, Hanby (Lenton, Keisby and Osgodby), another of the Dysart's planned farms, built in 1884, has open yards with shelter sheds.

On a few farmsteads there are fully enclosed cow houses, mostly built in the late 19th century rather than earlier. Only two are of any size. That at Parks Farm, Great Hale (Fig 3.17), still has its interior fittings, showing that it had a feeding passage in front of the stalls, along which fodder from an adjacent fodder room could be moved, and from which it was easy to transfer it to the manger and hay rack at the cows' heads. The building is unusual in that each double stall was separated from the adjacent stalls by a low partition with a gate, and was entered from outside by its own doorway, perhaps suggesting that each stall could be used as a loose box or fattening box (see below).

Most of the cow houses are much smaller, and their precise function is not entirely clear. Some rooms of this kind are little more than loose boxes with a manger and/or hay rack against one wall, indicating that there was a single row of three to five cattle tethered facing in one direction. In one or two instances, though, as at Grange Farm, Little Hale (Fig 3.18), the room is rather larger, and contained two rows of cattle, facing outwards, between which was a central manure passage. The general form is similar to that of byres in Northumberland (see Chapter 4), in which the relatively small number of milk cows (as opposed to fatstock) were kept. It is possible that some of the Lincolnshire examples were also for milk cows, but others may have been fattening boxes, or could have been used for young stock – or perhaps both at different times of year.

The final kind of accommodation for cattle is the loose box – an almost featureless room in which a single animal could be isolated or a small

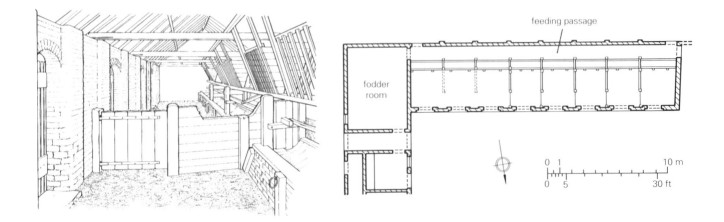

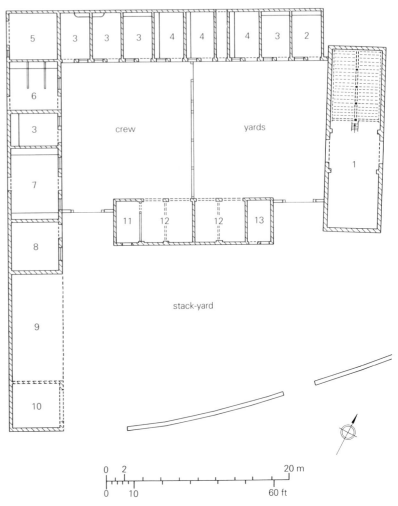

Fig 3.17 (above and above right) Cattle accommodation: cow house at Parks Farm, Great Hale. Reconstructed interior and plan of the large cow house at Parks Farm, Great Hale. The building is of unusual form, with a doorway to each double stall and gates between the stalls, suggesting that it may have been used as a series of fattening boxes. At the head of the stalls is a manger and hay rack, behind which is a feeding passage leading from a fodder-preparation room to the east.

Fig 3.18 (below) Cattle accommodation: cow house and associated areas at Grange Farm, Little Hale. In the cow house at Grange Farm, Little Hale, the cattle were stalled in two rows, one on each side of a central manure passage. At the head of each row was a manger. The precise function of this kind of cow house is not certain, but the form is broadly similar to that of byres in North-umberland (see Fig 4.32), perhaps suggesting that, like them, the room was designed to accommodate milk cattle.

Fig 3.19 (below) Cattle accommodation: loose boxes. At Manor Farm, Walcot, there is a larger number of loose boxes than usual in this part of Lincolnshire, suggesting that some cattle were fattened in them.

Key			
1 barn, granary	4 calf pens	8 cake store	12 shelter sheds
2 bull pen	5 gig house	9 demolished wagon shed	13 fowl house
3 loose boxes	6 nag stable	10 demolished implement store	
	7 cowshed	11 pigsty	

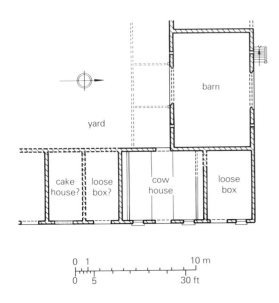

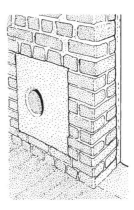

root house

cartshed

chaff house

tack room

stable

loose boxes

c

0 2   20 m
0   10   60 ft

a

b   *d*

Fig 3.20 Buildings for fodder: chaff houses. The chaff house at Village Farm, Swaton (a–b; BB93/21322 and BB93/21323) is characteristic: the room has no first floor and has a pitching door to ease loading the unprocessed crop into the building from a cart; the floor is brick so as to be easily swept and to prevent wastage of grain. By the late 19th century, chaff was used almost exclusively as fodder for horses, and the chaff house was placed next to the stables, as at Hanby Lodge Farm, Hanby (Lenton, Keisby and Osgodby) (c); cattle fodder was stored and prepared in the root house, next to the cattle yards. Chaff was chopped with the aid of machinery, and there is a socket (d) in the wall of the chaff house, through which a drive shaft from an external engine was passed.

number of cattle could be kept untethered, and usually with some kind of drain in the floor to remove the liquid manure. Such boxes had a variety of uses, and could be employed for each as occasion demanded. Hence, for example, they might house fatstock which were being finished for market, or might be used for pregnant or ill cows, for calves or young stock, or for a bull; they might also be used to house young, ill and pregnant horses. On only a very small number of farms in the survey area were there many such boxes, indicating that, unlike in some parts of the country, they did not constitute a major element of long-term cattle-housing. The only partial exceptions to that pattern are two farms (Manor Farm (Fig 3.19) and Red House Farm) in Walcot which belonged to the Ancaster estate and were constructed in the early 1880s.

Cattle fodder

Cattle required accommodation not only for themselves, but also for their fodder. During the 19th century, two main types of fodder – chaff and roots – were used, each requiring a different type of building. As noted earlier, chaff houses were designed to accommodate the oat crop (including the straw) and to provide a processing space in which it could be chopped into fodder. Since they were used for both storage and processing, they share some of the barn's characteristics in that there is seldom a first floor (Fig 3.20*a*, *b*). A typical chaff house is, however, smaller than a barn, and lacks a threshing floor: it usually has a single, smaller doorway, inside which a chopping machine (often hand-powered) might be stood. There is also usually at least one pitching door set high in one of the walls, to facilitate the unloading of carts into the building. The floor is commonly of bricks or flags, so that grain and husks could easily be swept up and so not wasted. In some of the later examples, processing was assisted by mechanical power: on the farmsteads built by the Dysart estate in Hanby in the early 1880s, evidence of this is provided by the incorporation in one of the walls of the room of a stone block with a central hole through which a drive shaft passed from an external engine to an internal machine (Fig 3.20*d*).

Only a few chaff houses in the survey area date from earlier than the 1820s; the largest number appear to have been built in the third quarter of the 19th century, with rather fewer in the last quarter. The increase in numbers between about 1850 and 1875 may reflect the beginnings of the adoption of High Farming, and roughly corresponds with an increase in buildings associated with the accommodation of cattle. The smaller number of new chaff houses built towards the end of the century is not, however, indicative of a drop in cattle numbers – or even of a hiatus in the expansion of their numbers – for, as seen earlier, the number of livestock in the area increased in response to the post-1870 agricultural depression. Instead, it is more likely that most established farmsteads had already been equipped with buildings for fodder preparation; there may also have been greater use of other kinds of fodder (roots and, more particularly, oil cake) which required a separate building of a

slightly different sort. The last suggestion may be strengthened by the fact that on later farmsteads, such as the model farms of the early 1880s at Grange Farm, Little Hale, and Hanby Lodge Farm, Hanby (Lenton, Keisby and Osgodby parish), the chaff house is associated with the stables rather than with the cattle accommodation, indicating that chaff was by then largely used as horse fodder rather than for cattle (Fig 3.20*c*).

Greater use of roots (turnips and swedes, perhaps also potatoes) and oil cake required the provision of new kinds of fodder store and preparation area: the root house and/or the cake house (the two are sometimes virtually indistinguishable, and one building may have served both purposes). The root house is a single-storey building or compartment in a larger range of functional areas, usually conveniently placed in relation to the cattle yards, and was used both for storing and chopping or pulping roots prior to their distribution to the cattle. The main distinctive feature of the building is that it often has a wide opening (sometimes with double doors) in one side, so that roots could be tipped or shovelled into it direct from carts or wagons (Fig 3.21). In some instances processing was assisted by the application of mechanical power: on at least one of the farms built in the 1880s by the Earls of Dysart in the Hanby area of Lenton, Keisby and Osgodby, one wall of the root houses incorporates a stone block with a central hole through which a drive shaft from an external, mobile, engine could enter the building (as in the chaff houses). In other

Fig 3.21 Buildings for fodder: the root house. The root house at Walcot Lodge Farm, Walcot. The building is positioned centrally between two cattle yards, and the doorway faced the entrance to the yard system, allowing carts to be backed up to the wide opening which was designed to enable roots to be tipped into the building (BB93/21410).

cases, power may have been applied, but has not left any physical traces; it is, however, likely that on most farms the chopping and pulping machines were turned by hand.

The same is likely to be true of cake-breakers, which may often have shared a building with the roots. On only two farms – both in Walcot, and built by the Ancaster estate in the 1880s – has it been possible to identify a cake house with certainty, and that only because labelled architect's plans were available.[25] There is little to distinguish the cake houses from loose boxes (see above), since they are featureless rooms with doorways of a normal size. This does not mean that it is impossible that some cake houses were similar to root houses, but it may be equally possible that in one or two instances a room identified as a loose box could have been a cake store.

PIGS

Cattle were not the only livestock kept on most farms, and the Parish Crop Returns collected annually from 1866 onwards indicate that a substantial number of pigs were kept in the survey area. Despite this, not every farm has buildings devoted to their accommodation. On those that do, such housing is usually on a very small scale and dates from the second half of the 19th century. This is likely to be because pigs could be kept in the fields for most of the time and, when that was not possible, could temporarily share the main yards with the cattle. The only requirements for purpose-built accommodation were probably for farrowing and for piglets, for the boar, and perhaps for the final stages in the fattening of the pig which supplied the farmer's family with meat.

Such pigsties as are found are of two main types (see Fig 3.22). The first is a small unlit room with a low arched opening giving access to the main cattle yards (Fig 3.22a, b), while the second is associated with small yards for pigs alone (Fig 3.22c); either kind might be combined with accommodation for fowl (Fig 3.22d; see also below). Where there was no separate yard, one of the walls of the sty usually contained a feeding trough designed so that fodder could be tipped into it from outside (Fig 3.22e–g). If there was a special yard for the pigs, the trough was usually in it, rather than in the sty itself. No matter what the plan of the sties, pigs were normally accommodated near the house, so that swill, which was often prepared in a back kitchen or outhouse, could easily be carried to them without having to be taken across the main farmyard. In a minority of instances, fodder was prepared in a meal house adjacent to the sty (Fig 3.22a).

FOWL HOUSES AND PIGEON LOFTS

Also near the house was the fowl house: poultry were kept on most farms, usually on a small scale appropriate to the farmer's domestic economy rather than to commercial agriculture, and cared for by the farmer's wife. One of the most important criteria governing the design of accommodation for fowl was that the birds should be protected from marauding foxes and other predators. Security of this kind was sometimes achieved by placing the fowl house in a loft above the pigsties, as at Moat Farm, Newton (Newton and Haceby) (Fig 3.23a), where a passage behind the pigsties contained a ladder for human access to the loft above the sties, and a hen ladder to assist the birds in climbing up to the loft. On some farmsteads, such as Woodside Farm, Newton (Newton and Haceby) (Fig 3.23b), there was a rather larger scale of accommodation, comprising a complete ground-level room and a loft over an adjacent space, and the hen house was lined with nesting boxes; the same may also have been true of Manor Farm, Walcot, where there was a small floor-level hen slot with a sliding door which could be closed at night.

There is no positive evidence for the provision of accommodation for geese or ducks, which require nesting boxes at ground level, though they may have used the lowest tier of nesting boxes in some hen houses. Many farms, however, had provision for a small number of pigeons. The only large-scale dovecote in the survey area is at Old Manor Farm, Braceby (Braceby and Sapperton) (Fig 3.23c), where the pigeon house is dated 1707, but there the building reflects the fact that the site was a long-established manorial centre. The largest 19th-century provision for pigeons is at Rookery Farm, Great Hale, where there is a pigeon loft above a meal house (Fig 3.23d). In most cases the pigeon loft is either considerably smaller, sometimes consisting of an enclosed section of the roof of a shelter shed, as at Manor Farm, Swaton; at other sites, the sole provision is a number of nesting holes in the gable of one of the major buildings.

SHEEP

Although there are no buildings specifically relating to them, sheep were kept in significant numbers, and, as discussed earlier, formed an important part of the agricultural economy of the region. Such animals provided three valuable commodities to the farmer: wool and meat, which could be sold, and manure for the arable fields. Unlike cattle, however, they did not

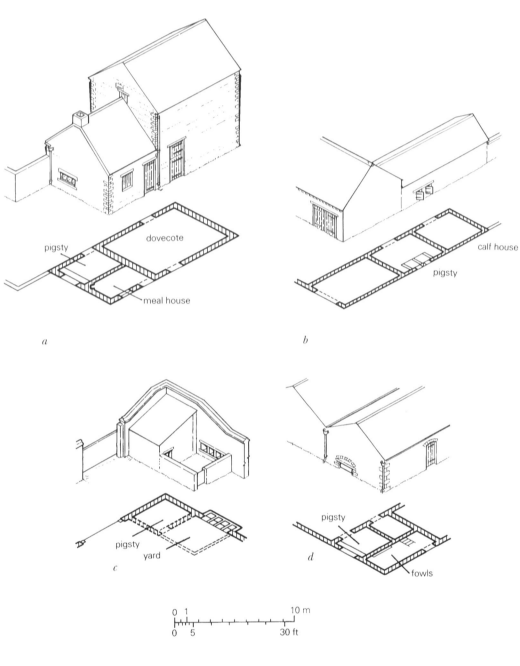

a

b

c

d

pigsty
dovecote
meal house

calf house
pigsty

pigsty
yard

pigsty
fowls

Fig 3.22 Pigsties.
The simplest kind of
pigsty consisted of a
small room with an
opening to the cattle
yard, as at Old Manor
Farm, Braceby (Braceby
and Sapperton) (a; see
also Fig 3.23c), where
the pigsty is situated
next to a meal house in
which fodder was
prepared prior to being
passed to the pigs
through the hatch in the
end wall of the sty.
Sometimes, fodder was
prepared in a back
kitchen in the house: at
Village Farm, Swaton
(b, e), hatches through
which fodder was passed
face the house. In a more
elaborate type of sty, at
Johnson's Farm, Little
Hale (c, f), the pigs were
segregated from the
cattle, having their own
small yard. More
complex still is the pigsty
at Moat Farm, Newton
(Newton and Haceby)
(d), which has a fowl
house above (see also Fig
3.23a). The pigs had
access to the main cattle
yard, and the fodder
chute consists of a
hinged hopper which
tipped the fodder into the
trough inside the sty
(g; BB93/21369).

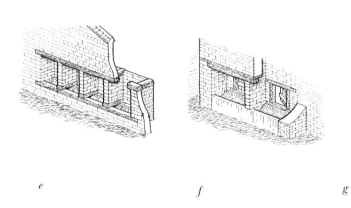

e

f

g

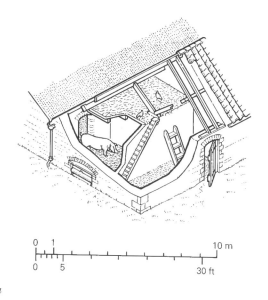

a

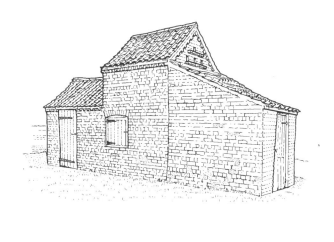

d

b

c

Fig 3.23 Fowl houses. At Moat Farm, Newton (Newton and Haceby) (a) the fowl house is above the pigsty (see also Fig 3.22 d and g): birds and humans reached the loft by separate ladders. The fowl house at Woodside Farm, Newton (Newton and Haceby) (b; BB93/24150), is larger, and contained two tiers of nesting boxes, the lower of which may have been used for geese and/or ducks. The dovecote (dated 1707) at Old Manor Farm, Braceby (Braceby and Sapperton) (c; BB95/12574), is a physical manifestation of the site's manorial status, but many farmsteads, such as Rookery Farm, Great Hale (d), had small pigeon lofts, here above the meal house attached to the pigsty (left).

require to be housed on the farmstead, but were best left in the fields, which they manured as they fed; the most that they required in the way of shelter was an ephemeral structure in the worst of the winter.[26] While some processes involving sheep – such as clipping – were better conducted under some kind of roof, they were of relatively short duration, and many took place at times of year when the cattle were in the fields, thus making it possible to use the cattle yards and shelters. At other times of year it was possible to empty cart and implement sheds for a few days.

The only hint of the presence of sheep in the surviving buildings is at an unnamed farm on Helpringham fen,[27] in which a featureless first-floor room may have been a wool store; the identification is, however, based on oral evidence, which may relate only to 20th-century use, rather than on any physical features. As will be seen in the next chapter, the general lack of accommodation for sheep cannot be taken as a measure of their importance in the agricultural economy, since even farms on which sheep formed the mainstay of the farming system often have little in the way of physical evidence for their existence.

4 NORTH NORTHUMBERLAND

For much of the 19th century, Northumberland, and particularly the far north of the county, was at the forefront of agricultural development, in terms of both farming systems and buildings: it supplied both Tyneside markets and, by coastal trade, those as distant as London. The hills in the west were suitable only for sheep-farming, but elsewhere much of the land was amenable to more than one type of agriculture. This meant that fully mixed farming could be practised over much of the area; this and the fact that many of the region's farms were of a large size meant that farmers were able to maintain their incomes even when one particular branch of agriculture suffered a seasonal setback. In addition, the versatility of the land meant that cropping regimes could be adjusted in response to long-term trends in the market for agricultural produce: as will be seen, Northumberland is one of the areas of England in which the late 19th-century depression saw a significant shift away from corn into livestock-rearing for the meat market. This is reflected in the development of farmsteads, the main buildings of the early and mid-19th century being barns (with mechanical power) for the processing and storage of grain crops, while the second half of the century saw an increase in the scale and sophistication of accommodation for cattle.

The Survey Area

The area chosen for survey falls into two slightly detached parts, both in the far north of the county (Fig 4.1). The first, the most commented-upon area, Glendale and Tweedside, is in the west of the county. This was the region in which the famous Culley family farmed from the late 18th century; it was renowned for its 'turnip soils', which permitted advanced and efficient crop rotations (see below). The land is generally undulating, and lies between about 30 and 90 m OD (100 and 300 ft) above sea level. The soils are light alluvial sands, with more gravel to the north in Tweedside: it is eminently suitable for arable farming, and light enough to grow turnips for

feeding to both cattle and sheep.[1] To the west, the land rises steeply into the Cheviot Hills, much being over 600 m OD (2,000 ft) high; the soils are mainly black peat and the ground is really suited only to sheep-farming. Farms at the foot of the Cheviots have both high and low land, enabling them to support almost the full range of agricultural exploitation.

The second part of the survey area lies further east and comprises the coastal plain between Belford and Berwick. This area is lower than Glendale and Tweedside, rarely rising above 60 m OD (200 ft), and its soils are heavier, including some boulder clay.[2] This land is less suitable for turnips, but is well adapted for wheat, pulses and grasses for grazing;[3] although different from Glendale, it is equally capable of supporting a fully mixed farming regime, with grain, cattle and sheep.

Northumberland in general has a relatively high rainfall, which, combined with a low average summer temperature – 11 to 12°C (in the late 19th century) compared to a little over 15°C at Greenwich – renders it more suitable for oats than wheat, while at the same time being beneficial for turnips.[4] The northern coastal plain is, however, slightly drier than further south, while the Cheviots shelter the Glen/Till basin from much of the rain coming from the west.[5] Strong and cold spring winds make the growing season short, but the damper, warmer climate in June produces vigorous growth. The mountains are much colder, and the winter sees deep snows, often lasting for several months.[6]

However light and dry the soil, almost all the land could be improved by underdrainage. Some of the earliest drainage schemes in Glendale were carried out by the Culleys in the late 18th century,[7] and, in the early 19th century, George Culley, together with John Bailey (estate manager for Lord Tankerville at Chillingham Park), noted that surface drains were being cut on the Cheviot hill farms with good effect.[8] Progress was made during the first half of the 19th century, and Earl Grey established a tile factory on his estate in Tweedside.[9] It was noted in 1847 that much drainage had been undertaken in the 'last few years', but much remained to be done.[10]

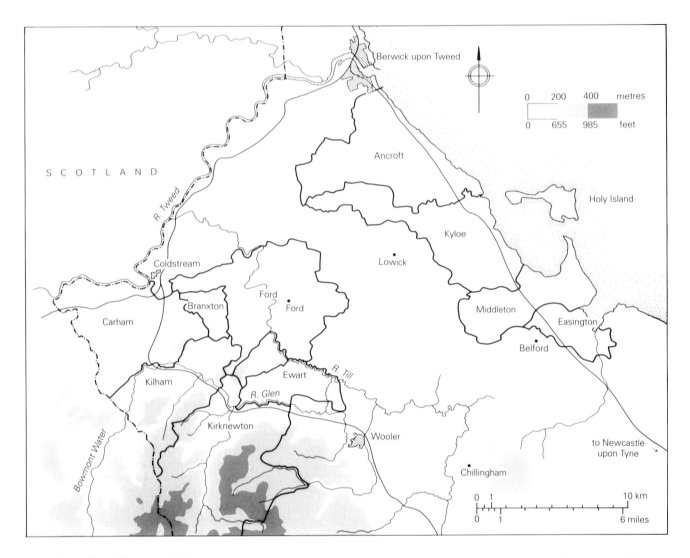

Fig 4.1 Map of the Northumberland survey area.

Landholding and Tenancy

One of the reasons sometimes adduced for the advanced state of agriculture in north Northumberland is the prevalence of large landowners, who often encouraged their tenants, either by being able to bear a greater proportion of the cost of improvements, or by such means as Earl Grey's tile factory – an investment probably not worthwhile on smaller estates. In addition, large estates were able to rationalise their lands without reference to third parties: much enclosure was completed with relative ease by the 1790s, and, although Glendale was slightly backward in this respect, it was largely enclosed by 1804.[11] Finally, large estates were able to lease large farms whose tenants had sizeable incomes and were able to afford to make improvements themselves.[12] As will be seen, there were clearly some very large

estates in the north of the county, but size did not necessarily make for enterprising landlords: for example, the Dukes of Northumberland, some of the largest landowners in the county, took no interest in improvement until the fourth Duke succeeded in 1847.[13]

In the late 19th century, a little under half the land in Northumberland as a whole lay on estates of more than 4,050 hectares (10,000 acres), compared with an average of about 16 per cent in England and Wales; 36 per cent formed part of estates of between 405 and 4,050 hectares (1,000 and 10,000 acres), leaving only 16 per cent in the hands of smaller landowners.[14] Very few of the smaller estates were situated in the north of the county,[15] the survey areas forming parts of a number of large estates. Part of the coastal area lay on the lands of Greenwich Hospital, managed (for long by John Grey) from Dilston, further to the south,

67

while another substantial area was owned by the Clarks (later Atkinson-Clarks) of Belford Hall, and a third block by the Leylands of Haggerston Castle; both the latter families were resident in the area, their seats lying immediately inland from the coastal strip. Some of the estates were of considerable size, that of the Leylands totalling 7,140 hectares (17,644 acres), but others were rather smaller: the lands of the Clarks of Belford, for example, were 1,300 hectares (3,227 acres) in extent. The western part of the survey area presents a broadly similar picture, the major landowners including Earl Grey, whose seat was at Bilton, and whose lands totalled 7,120 hectares (17,599 acres); Lord Tankerville of Chillingham Park, whose estate was 11,700 hectares (28,930 acres) in extent; the Marquis of Waterford, resident at Ford, with 2,650 hectares (6,537 acres); and the Askew-Roberts family of Pallinsburn, with 1,400 hectares (3,495 acres).[16] Most of the estate centres were either in or close to the survey area.

Corresponding with large estates there were often large units of tenure. In Glendale, farms varied from 120–160 hectares (300–400 acres) to 400–480 hectares (1,000–1,200 acres), but, where there was also mountain pasture to the west, farms might extend to 800 or 1,200 hectares (2,000 or 3,000 acres).[17] On the coastal plain there were also some large farms, with the average being about 200 hectares (500 acres). In general, it was noted that farms in the survey area were on average larger than those elsewhere in the county.[18] This kind of farm frequently occupied an entire township or even larger area, and the labour requirement was such that all the residents in the township worked on the farm, being supplied with cottages by the landlord, often immediately adjacent to the farmstead.[19]

Most farmers were tenant freeholders who, in the early 19th century, commonly enjoyed leases for twenty-one years[20] – a factor which contributed to their willingness to invest in improvement.[21] There were still some annual leases,[22] which were less conducive to advanced husbandry, especially when combined with the closed auction by which tenancies were frequently granted. Under that system rents were unsustainably high, as each would-be tenant tried to ensure that he outbid his rivals without knowing what their tenders were;[23] this was seen as one of the main factors which led to a crisis in the profitability of agriculture in the region from the 1820s right through to the 1850s.[24] Despite the advantages of the long leases, however, it seems that by the end of the 19th century annual leases were becoming more common, though without the sealed bids.[25]

The Agricultural System

Until the mid 18th century, agriculture in Northumberland was quite backward. Arthur Young, writing in 1771, was scathing about the unfulfilled potential of the area between Wooler and Rothbury – that is, immediately south of the western survey area.[26] MacKenzie, writing half a century later, stated that both parts of the survey area had been barren in the late 17th century, but that the early 19th century had seen great improvements, thanks to enclosure, drainage and the application of lime (available locally in the coastal area).[27] This is echoed by the account of Bailey and Culley, written in 1805, in which they state that the previous forty years had seen vast improvements, the value of some farms having increased threefold.[28] Colbeck, writing in 1847, made a similar point, though he thought that the improvements had occurred since 1800.[29] Part of the apparent chronological contradiction between these authors may be explained by the fact that Bailey and Culley, who were themselves in the forefront of agricultural development in the late 18th century, may have generalised from their own experience, while Colbeck may have been reflecting the more widespread pattern.

Probate inventories for the 17th and early 18th centuries show that mixed agriculture was practised on Tweedside and on the north coastal plain. While arable production was significant, livestock – both cattle and sheep – accounted for a greater proportion of overall wealth, large quantities of wool being exported through Berwick upon Tweed.[30] By about 1800, the pattern was beginning to change, the Culleys' revenue from wheat being about the same as that from cattle and sheep combined, and large amounts of grain being exported from the north of the county through Berwick.[31] As will be seen below, it is at this point that the surviving buildings begin to reflect the agricultural emphasis of the area.

According to Bailey and Culley, the most important feature of Northumberland agriculture was the maintenance of a balance between the arable and grasslands, so that there were large numbers of livestock, particularly sheep, in order to manure the land and thereby increase the yields of grain crops; similar effects were produced by the application of farmyard (ie cattle) manure and of lime.[32] A common rotation on the turnip soils of the Glendale area consisted of a number of years of grass separated by one or two years of oats, one of turnips and one of barley or wheat; on the stronger coastal lands periods of grass were succeeded by two or more rotations including fallow, wheat, peas or beans (used as fodder), followed by a further fallow.[33]

In the turnip area the system of alternate husbandry outlined above was adopted as a response to a general lack of old pasture, and supported sheep rather than cattle: cattle were kept, but only in numbers sufficient to convert straw into manure. Most of the turnips were grazed off by sheep – mobile manure factories – but a lesser amount was also fed to cattle, which were kept in yards.[34] The low price of grain which followed the repeal of the Corn Laws in 1846 caused farmers to devote more of their land to turnips, which were exported to Newcastle, probably by water, but perhaps also taking advantage of the Tweedmouth to Newcastle railway which was opened in 1847.[35] It is not clear what proportion of the crop this involved, nor how long the situation persisted, and it is unlikely that there was any fundamental shift from sheep-breeding as the backbone of the farming economy of the area.[36] Sheep-breeding was also the major – almost the only – concern of the hill farms, with ewes being sold after five or six years and younger sheep going to lowland farmers for final fattening, while farms at the foot of the hills were able to take advantage of their proximity to both high and low ground in order to breed and rear sheep.[37]

In the middle of the 19th century, more sophisticated rotations, including clover, were in use in both Glendale and the coastal plain.[38] The main improvements of the first half of the century in the hills involved drainage and the planting of belts of trees to provide shelter.[39] In Glendale and Tweedside farming changed little between 1820 and 1850, and at least one commentator thought the application of artificial manure would enable an intensification of arable farming and an increase in the number of cattle.[40]

Although the mid-century authors did not dwell to the same extent on the coastal strip, it seems clear that there was greater emphasis on wheat than in the western turnip farms, and that the first half of the 19th century saw little change of a fundamental nature. Caird exemplified the system in use by reference to Beal Farm in Kyloe Parish: the farm consisted of 410 hectares (1,050 acres), of which 113 (270) were permanent pasture supporting a large flock of sheep from which 240 ewes and 320 hoggets (yearlings) were sold each year; 60 cattle (plus calves) were kept in yards, and were fed on swedes, oil cake and bean meal.[41] While the implication of the number of sheep sold is that sheep were an important element in the farm's economy, it is clear from the acreage that the main product must have been grain – probably wheat.[42]

During the second half of the 19th century, there were marked changes in the balance of agriculture in much of Northumberland apart from the hills. The change is clear from the annual Crop Returns which were collected from 1866, and show that in the coastal area there was a dramatic decline in the proportion of wheat, accompanied by a large increase in the number of cattle and sheep. In Kyloe parish, for example, wheat fell from 235 hectares (580 acres) in 1866 to 49 hectares (101 acres) forty years later, while the number of cattle (other than milk cattle, which were always in a minority) rose from 532 to almost twice that number, and sheep more than doubled in the same period from 4,816 to 10,995. The same pattern is repeated in the western part of the survey area, though the increases in livestock are generally nearer a third than a half. The decline in wheat production was not mirrored in oats and barley, which fluctuated within a narrow range, probably largely reflecting their primary use as fodder crops. Despite that, Little, writing in 1887, noted that 'the growth of corn is on many farms a comparatively unimportant part of the business', indicating that the steepest decline in wheat had already occurred by 1886.[43] Overall, there was a marked decrease in arable: by 1890, the percentage of arable land in Tillside had fallen to 29.1 per cent, compared with 33.6 per cent in 1866, while in the coastal plain the reduction was from 33 to 23.6 per cent.[44] The result of this was that Little listed the main concerns of the Northumberland farmer as 'the breeding, rearing and fattening of sheep, the fattening of cattle, and the growth of turnips, oats and seeds'.[45] The decline in arable continued throughout the first half of the 20th century (except in the special circumstances of wartime), but an observation made by Pawson (in his 1961 survey of Northumberland for the Royal Agricultural Society) was probably already true by 1900: the farmsteads of the area had originally been designed for arable production, but the land had long been given over to the grazing of cattle and sheep.[46]

The Farmstead

The 19th-century commentators were universally scathing in their comments on the farmsteads erected before their own time. To some extent this could be a reflection of their ideals of progress, which had little time for the achievements of past generations, but the fact that no surviving buildings within the survey area date from much before 1800 suggests that the older farmsteads were genuinely found to

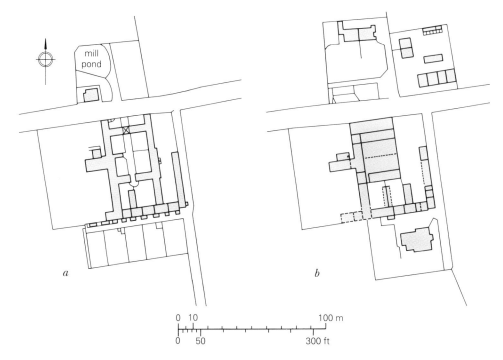

Fig 4.2 Crookham Westfield, Ford. The water-powered farmstead (a) shown on the first edition of the 25 in. Ordnance Survey map of c 1860 was completely superseded by the extant steam-powered complex (b) during the last third of the 19th century. Of the earlier buildings, only a small amount of walling in the south-east corner remains.

a   *b*

0 10   100 m

0   50   300 ft

be deficient. According to Bailey and Culley, for example, writing in 1805, 'buildings for the use and convenience of farms, were formerly very shabby and ill-contrived', though those erected in their own day were 'better adapted to the various purposes wanted for extensive farms and improved cultivation'[47] – though few enough of them in fact survive today. MacKenzie, writing in the 1820s, described the older arrangement as one in which the buildings were 'all huddled together, without any regard to cleanliness, or health',[48] though unfortunately neither he nor any of the other commentators provided more detail concerning the buildings they condemned.

By the 1840s both Grey and Colbeck were able to point to the construction of a large number of new farmsteads: Grey, in his capacity as manager of the northern estates of Greenwich Hospital, was himself involved in the design of farm buildings which, along with steadings in the far north of the county, drew praise from Colbeck.[49] According to Grey, the main advance was in the provision of buildings which were 'substantial and commodious', and were adapted to the increased production of corn and the larger numbers and better quality of livestock found in the first half of the 19th century.[50] It is clear, though, that not all older farmsteads had been replaced by 1850, for Caird, writing in 1852, deplored the state of the buildings at Beal Farm – one of the most advanced farms in agricultural terms (see above) – which were replaced only in the later 1850s.[51]

The dates of the surviving buildings reflect the pattern observed by the commentators in the first half of the 19th century, as well as the chronology of agricultural changes discussed earlier. In the Cheviot area, the buildings are difficult to date, largely on account of the lack of fundamental change in the agriculture of the region: most appear to have been constructed in the middle years of the century, and presumably replaced poorer, meaner structures. The development of farmsteads in Glendale and on the coast was more complex, as the buildings had to accommodate a number of interlocking systems – sheep-farming, the processing and storage of grain crops, and the accommodation of cattle. On the coast, development was usually piecemeal: it is typical for the buildings connected with arable farming to have been erected in the first quarter of the 19th century or shortly thereafter, together with some accommodation for cattle. Later, the cattle accommodation was expanded and improved, reflecting the late-century shift away from wheat to meat production; the rising numbers of sheep are less well represented in the buildings, though at one or two sites sophisticated sheep yards were constructed during the second half of the century. Development in the Glendale area is generally similar to that on the coast, but its timing appears to have been slightly later, the first phase tending to lie in the third and fourth decades of the century, and with four completely new farmsteads being constructed in the last third of the century (Fig 4.2). It is not entirely clear what the latter replaced, but map evidence shows that some substantial and apparently well-planned earlier complexes of buildings were entirely superseded in the last third of the century. All 19th-century farmsteads (apart from those in the hills) were designed to use mechanical power for crop-processing and, probably, fodder preparation: as will be seen, the form of power varied (horse, water and fixed steam power all being found), but it is clear that mechanised threshing had been widely adopted by the 1830s at the latest.

THE FLOW OF PROCESSES AND FARMSTEAD LAYOUT

Sheep do not need roofed accommodation, but can be left to graze in the fields all year; the only times when they require to be taken to the farmstead are when they are clipped, sorted for market or dipped, though sorting can sometimes be done in the fields, and, in the era before chemical dips, washing was often done in a stream. The result of this is that, although sheep formed an important part of the agricultural economy in all parts of the survey area, they are not often represented in the surviving buildings. In the Cheviot breeding lands, for instance, the farmsteads are small, often consisting only of one or two main agricultural buildings attached to the house – enough to provide stabling for two or three horses, stalls for a few milk cattle and accommodation for their fodder. In Glendale and the coastal strip, to which sheep were sold for rearing, such animals are usually equally unrepresented, though there are a few examples of detached handling yards; for most of the time it was more important that the animals were manuring the fields to improve arable yields.

When the corn harvest was gathered, by contrast, it required transporting to the farmstead, where it was processed and stored. On reaching the farmstead, the corn crops were stacked outside in ricks of a size which could be broken and processed in a day or half day.[52] From the rick, the crop was taken to the first floor of the threshing barn, where it was mechanically threshed. The grain was carried to granaries, which were often situated above adjacent cattle sheds, or were sometimes above cartsheds; a varying proportion was sold off the farm, while the remainder was used as fodder for cattle and horses. The straw produced by the threshing machine was passed directly into a second barn – the straw barn – where it was stored until required in the cattle yards, which were situated adjacent to the barns, and from which manure was taken out to the fields.

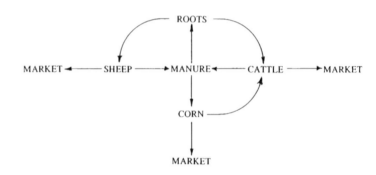

In order to accommodate these interlocking flows of processes (Fig 4.3) allowing for the most efficient use of manpower, farmsteads were generally arranged in a U-shape, or in an extended U. The threshing and straw barns, as the tallest buildings, were generally (though not always) in the centre of the north side, where they protected the cattle in the yards to the south from the cold winds (Fig 4.4). Flanking the barns there might be hemmels – open-sided cattle shelters – either in a single storey, or with granaries or storage lofts above. The east and west sides of the farmstead provided additional accommodation for cattle – such as loose boxes, and byres for the small number of milk cows kept on each farm – together with stabling and a poultry house. In one of the side ranges or at the outer end of the cattle yards there might be a root house in which turnips (and, later, oil cake) were stored and prepared prior to being distributed to the cattle. There were many variations around this basic theme. The barn ranges might form one side of the yard system, as at Crookham Eastfield, Ford (Fig 4.4c), or there might be further yards for cattle or for horses, to one side of the main U-shaped block of buildings, as at Crookham Westfield, also in Ford parish. Both the Crookhams lay on the Pallinsburn estate, and were newly constructed in the 1860s or 1870s, but the same kind of plan could result from more piecemeal development, as at Easington Demesne, Easington (see Fig 4.5), on the coastal strip, where the farmstead evolved slowly from about 1810 to 1920.

Until the 1860s, the yards – whether for horses or cattle – were almost always open. During the late 19th century shelter sheds were built along the sides of the cattle yards (Fig 4.4d), and then in some cases (though not always until after 1900) the yards were completely roofed over; new farmsteads of the period incorporated these features from the start. Where the yards were entirely roofed over, the buildings appear as one large square

Fig 4.3 Simplified diagram of the flow of processes. Corn crops produced both grain (much of which was sold) and litter and fodder for cattle, which were also fed on roots. The manure produced by the cattle (which were sold off the farm) was returned to the fields. Manure was also provided by sheep, which were kept in the fields and fed off roots prior to sale.

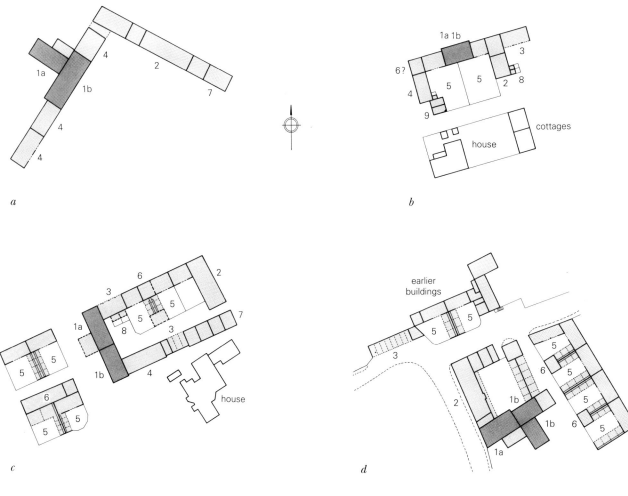

a

b

c

d

Fig 4.4 Comparative farmstead plans. The majority of farmsteads in the lowland areas were U-shaped, or of extended U-shape, in their mature form, but some, such as Goswick, Ancroft (a), began as L-shaped. At Goswick, the threshing and straw barns are set at right angles, and the cattle accommodation is conveniently disposed in relation to the straw barn from which litter was distributed. A compact U-plan is found at Cheswick Cottage, Ancroft (b), where the barn is on the north, sheltering the yards from the north wind and allowing them to receive maximum sunlight. On a larger scale is Crookham Eastfield, Ford (c), where the U-plan is extended by a low range of buildings to the south, and the barns are placed at one side so as to serve additional cattle yards to the west. The accretion of cattle yards is also shown at Westnewton, Kirknewton (d): the yards were originally largely open, with shelter sheds along their sides (see Fig 4.25). Some late 19th-century farmsteads were completely roofed, as at Thornington, Kilham (e), though the basic U-shape or L-shape of the buildings remained the same.

Key
1a threshing barn
1b straw barn
2 stable
3 cartshed
4 cow house
5 cattle yard
6 root house
7 nag stable
8 pigsties
9 fowl house

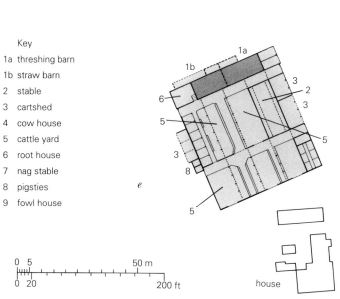

e

0   5   50 m

0   20   200 ft

or rectangle: within that, the basic U-shape or L-shape might be retained, as at Thornington, Kilham (Fig 4.4e)(built between 1880 and 1898 following a prize-winning design by J B Denton – see Chapter 7), or there might be buildings around all four sides of the yards, as at East House, Ancroft. Another characteristic of development in the late 19th century, when the number of cattle was increasing, was for detached cattle units to be built to one side of the pre-existing buildings. Such arrangements commonly consisted of a single-storey range of hemmels, each serving a separate yard. Each pair of adjacent yards was usually served by a root house, placed either between the hemmels, or at the opposite ends of the yards, as at Westnewton, Kirknewton. The accretion of extra cattle units in this period often resulted in a less regular plan than is manifested on those farmsteads which were planned in a single phase, but the new accommodation was always placed as conveniently as possible in relation to the original buildings, especially the straw barn, from which large amounts of material had to be carried to the cattle yards.

THE UPLAND FARMSTEAD

As described above, the farmsteads in the uplands are small, usually consisting only of a house with attached accommodation for a few milk cows and horses, together with their fodder. At its smallest and simplest, the farm building might consist of no more than a single room attached to the house, as at Mounthooly, Kirknewton (Fig 4.6). The sole original agricultural building has one off-centre doorway in one of the long walls, to one side of which was a single and a double stall (or open loose box) for horses, while to the other were three cattle stalls. In the back wall there is a small square pitching door (or 'hay hole'), through which hay could be loaded into the horses' side of the building. There was originally a hay rack in the horses' stalls, and there is a ground-level feeding trough for the cattle; both sets of animals were served by a single manure passage, into which the door opened. This building, together with the attached house, was probably built in the middle of the 19th century, and at that stage may have comprised the entire farmstead, unless two rough unroofed shelters (later covered with corrugated iron) against field walls nearby were built at the same date. In the early 20th century two loose boxes were built beside the stable/byre (house for milk cows), and a timber-and-iron hay barn and implement store was built behind the building.

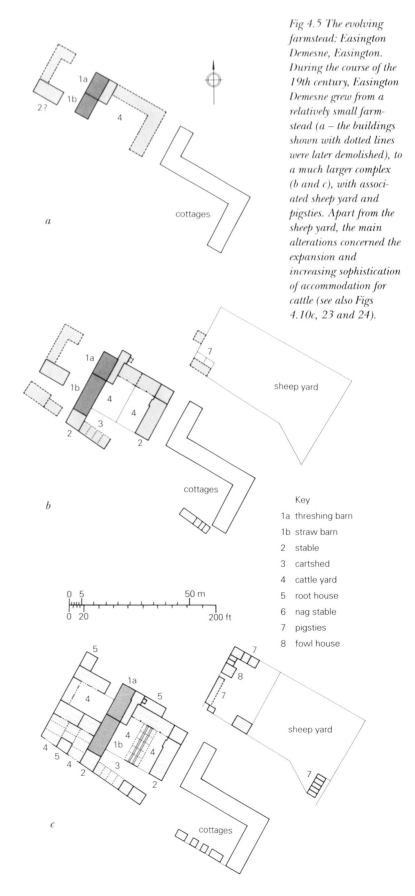

Fig 4.5 The evolving farmstead: Easington Demesne, Easington. During the course of the 19th century, Easington Demesne grew from a relatively small farmstead (a – the buildings shown with dotted lines were later demolished), to a much larger complex (b and c), with associated sheep yard and pigsties. Apart from the sheep yard, the main alterations concerned the expansion and increasing sophistication of accommodation for cattle (see also Figs 4.10c, 23 and 24).

Key
1a threshing barn
1b straw barn
2 stable
3 cartshed
4 cattle yard
5 root house
6 nag stable
7 pigsties
8 fowl house

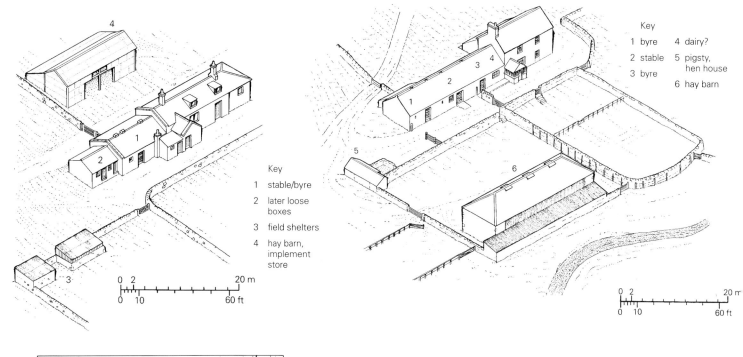

Key
1 byre   4 dairy?
2 stable   5 pigsty,
3 byre   hen house
          6 hay barn

Key
1 stable/byre
2 later loose boxes
3 field shelters
4 hay barn, implement store

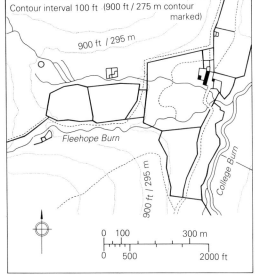

Fig 4.6 (above left) The upland farmstead: Mounthooly, Kirknewton. The original farmstead comprised the house (except for the extreme right-hand end) and the first part of the attached building to its left, which formed a combined stable and byre. The two field shelters in the foreground may have been constructed at the same time, but were probably only roofed over (with iron) later. The loose boxes at the extreme left of the main range were added in the early 20th century, as was the timber-and-iron hay barn.

Fig 4.7 (above right) The upland farmstead: Trowupburn, Kirknewton. A slightly larger upland farmstead, with separate stable and byre, and with a detached pigsty/hen house. The added hay barn is different from that at Mounthooly (Fig 4.6), having stone end walls and a narrow lean-to at the rear, which may have been used for drying wool washed in the adjacent stream.

Fig 4.8 The upland farmstead: Fleehope, Kirknewton. The farmstead at Fleehope (b) has a small 'barn' (in the centre of the range), as well as a stable and a byre. The hemmel may have been used for cattle but, as the opening is very low and the ground slopes away steeply in front of it, the sheltering, clipping and sorting of sheep are more likely uses for it, particularly since the building lies at the centre of a complex system of enclosures (a) which extend from the 275 m (900 ft) OD contour, past the buildings to the river. Those compartments were used for sheltering sheep in the worst of the winter, and for handling them during sorting, clipping and dipping.

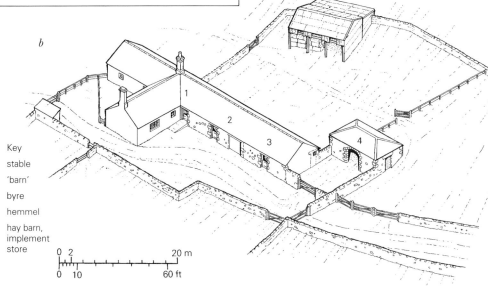

Key
1 stable
2 'barn'
3 byre
4 hemmel
5 hay barn, implement store

74

The latter type of structure was provided on almost every hill farm in the College Valley as part of a programme of estate improvement con-ducted by the then owner, Sir Arthur Sutherland, a Newcastle businessman.

Slightly larger is the farmstead at Trowup-burn, Kirknewton, on the same estate, where the house is attached to two byres, between which is a stable (Fig 4.7). In addition, there is a small detached pigsty and hen house, so that the shepherd would have his own supply of meat and eggs. In front of the house and main farm building is a large yard which may have been used for sheep-handling, and which now contains a hay barn of similar date to that described above, though with stone end walls. Against the rear of the barn is a narrow lean-to – too narrow and inconveniently placed to have been an implement shed – which may have been used for drying wool after it had been washed in the adjacent stream; apart from that, no roofed structure is associated with sheep-farming. The same is also true of Fleehope (also in Kirknewton parish (Fig 4.8)), a short distance from Mounthooly: there, a stable and byre are again attached to the house, this time separated by a room of uncertain function which may have been some kind of barn, or fodder store and processing area. In addition there is a small detached hemmel (open-sided shed) immediately to the north west of the byre, with a yard (originally open, but now roofed with iron). It is possible that cattle were allowed access to this area in the summer, but the hemmel was perhaps also used for clipping and sorting sheep (as it is today). It forms the hub of a complex system of field walls which form a series of open-air compartments into which different categories of sheep could be herded. All that sheep required for shelter were similar enclosures, or well-placed plantations of trees;[53] circular sheep folds are not a common feature in the survey area, though they do occur in some numbers in other valleys, such as Coquetdale.

An elaboration of that system is at Southernknowe (Fig 4.9), lower down the same valley, where the main part of the farmstead consists of two parallel ranges, each with two yards outside, with a droveway between the two pairs of yards. One yard was for cattle and horses, since the associated buildings probably housed a byre and stable; the other yards adjoined hemmels, and were probably used for sheep-handling. The only other agricultural buildings on the site are two small pigsties (one certainly a later addition), a later hen house and the characteristic early 20th-century hay barn.

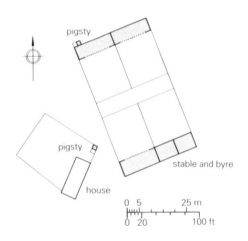

Fig 4.9 The upland farmstead: Southernknowe, Kirknewton. Apart from the stable, byre and associated yard, the main part of the farmstead was almost exclusively related to sheep-farming, consisting of three open yards, each with a hemmel.

SHEEP IN THE LOWLANDS

Each year, the older ewes and many of the yearlings were sold down from the hills, the former to market, the latter to be reared on the better lowland pasture typical of both the Glendale area and the coastal strip. The importance of sheep to the lowland areas is not reflected in the buildings. Lambing and clipping necessitated the presence of large numbers of sheep at the farmstead only on a small number of days annually, usually at a time of year when the cartshed or a cattle hemmel could be emptied for a short time. On many farms there are systems of fences and hurdles for the sorting and dipping of sheep (Fig 4.10a): none appears on the first edition of the 25 in. Ordnance Survey map, produced in the early 1860s; some are depicted on the second edition, of 1897–8, and many more on the third edition, produced in the early 1920s. The emergence of such systems may, therefore, be testimony to the increase in the number of sheep during and after the late 19th century (see above).

On three farmsteads there are more elaborate arrangements for sheep. At Beal Farm, Kyloe, built in the 1850s, there is a yard some distance from the main farmstead, surrounded on three sides by low narrow open-sided shelters (Fig 4.10b). The present structures may have been built in the 1920s or 1930s; if so, they stand on the site of an earlier yard (shown on the 1897 25 in. Ordnance Survey map) in which sheep were provided with some shelter during winter or in the course of lambing. At Easington Demesne, Easington (Fig 4.10c), a double yard lies adjacent to the main farmstead and cottages. Little can now be deduced concerning the internal arrangements: both yards contain a

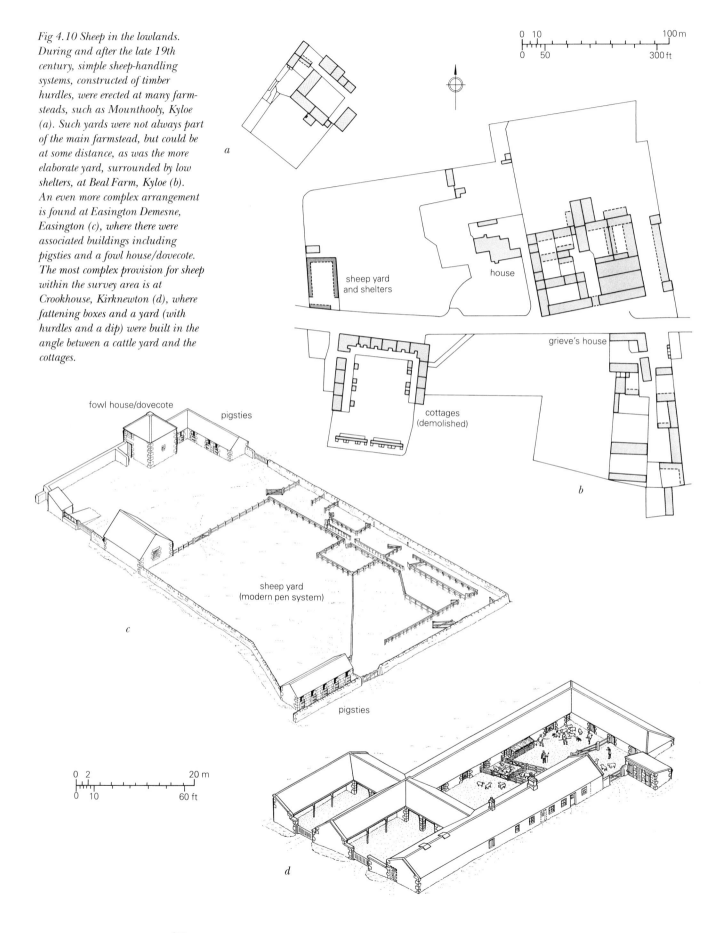

Fig 4.10 Sheep in the lowlands.
During and after the late 19th
century, simple sheep-handling
systems, constructed of timber
hurdles, were erected at many farmsteads, such as Mounthooly, Kyloe
(a). Such yards were not always part
of the main farmstead, but could be
at some distance, as was the more
elaborate yard, surrounded by low
shelters, at Beal Farm, Kyloe (b).
An even more complex arrangement
is found at Easington Demesne,
Easington (c), where there were
associated buildings including
pigsties and a fowl house/dovecote.
The most complex provision for sheep
within the survey area is at
Crookhouse, Kirknewton (d), where
fattening boxes and a yard (with
hurdles and a dip) were built in the
angle between a cattle yard and the
cottages.

0 10   100 m

0   50   300 ft

a

sheep yard
and shelters

house

grieve's house

cottages
(demolished)

b

fowl house/dovecote

pigsties

c

sheep yard
(modern pen system)

pigsties

0 2   20 m

0   10   60 ft

pigsties

d

small number of pigsties; one also has a combined fowl house and dovecote, and a low building with a central doorway in one gable, which could have been used for calves, or may have been a lambing shed. It is almost certain, however, that the main function of the yards themselves was to facilitate the handling of sheep and, perhaps, to protect young lambs.

The most elaborate arrangement found in the survey area is at Crookhouse, Kirknewton (Fig 4.10d), which stands on quite high ground near the River Glen. The sheep yard was constructed in the late 19th century, at much the same time as a cattle-and-horse unit, to the rear of which it is attached. The cattle unit forms one end of the yard, and most of one side is formed by the rear walls of two cottages. The remaining two sides consist of low ranges punctuated by openings into the yard. Details of the internal arrangement, and of the function, of the buildings are unclear, but there is an internal sheep dip surrounded by a system of fences and gates; the yard contains an external dip and further hurdles. The dip within the building could be a later addition, and it is possible that the buildings originally housed sheep during fattening: their dimensions are in the same range as those quoted by J B Denton in the 1860s as being appropriate for sheep sheds – 3–3.5 m (10–12 ft) wide and just high enough for a man to walk down.[54] Despite Denton's report that such sheep sheds won the favour of those who tried them, such systems do not appear to have become popular in the country as a whole, but it would not be surprising for such a relatively unusual or even experimental type of structure to have been built in as advanced an area as north Northumberland.

BUILDINGS FOR CORN

At harvest time the grain crops, grown on the fields manured by the sheep, were carted to the farmstead and stacked outside in ricks;[55] traditional barns for the storage of unthreshed crops were regarded at best as an unnecessary waste of money and at worst as positively detrimental to corn.[56] This attitude, combined with the almost universal use of fixed internal barn machinery for processing the grain, led to the development of a highly distinctive type of barn (Fig 4.11a). Threshing was conducted in a two-storey building (the threshing barn), which was attached to a separate building (the straw barn), in which the straw was stored after threshing.

The first floor of the threshing barn contained a fixed threshing machine, into the top of which the crop was fed (Fig 4.11b). Grain came out of the bottom of the machine (on the ground floor of the barn), while the straw was produced at the end (on the first floor), whence it was mechanically fed, along a 'straw walk', through a large opening in the end wall of the barn, and into the straw barn. The latter might be set either in line with the threshing barn, or at right angles to it (in which case the straw walk opened into its centre); it was usually the same height as, or slightly lower than, the threshing barn, and provided a single storage space, open from the ground floor to the roof.

In order to allow the crop to be loaded directly into the first floor of the threshing barn, one of the barn's side walls incorporated a large pitching doorway, usually with double doors. Sometimes, as at West Moneylaws, Carham (Fig 4.11c), the barn was built into a natural slope in the land, so that the ground was level with the first floor on one side of the building. On other occasions, particularly on the coastal plain, where the ground is much flatter, an artificial bank, or ramp, was provided to enable carts to be taken right up to the loading doorway, as at Low Middleton, Middleton (Fig 4.11d). Where this was done, the doorway often rises up through the eaves, so that a cart could be backed part way into the building.

Inside, the threshing machine was positioned at one end of the building, adjacent to the straw barn. Although the machines have long since been removed, their position can almost always be determined by the pattern of joisting in the ground-floor ceiling, since, even though the floor is now solid, the opening for the machine is defined by trimmer joists (Fig 4.12). On the first floor, the joists at the sides of the machine sometimes have mortices in their upper surfaces for posts supporting rails which extended along the side of the machine to the wall of the straw barn, and prevented the obstruction of moving parts on the machine and straw walk. The ground floor of the threshing barn (or grain-dressing floor) usually contains few distinguishing features. The threshed grain was bagged as it came out of the bottom of the machine, and was taken to the granary (see below). The two levels of the barn were linked by a stairway which was usually beside the ground-floor door, and each storey was lit and ventilated by at least one window (sometimes more).

By contrast with the threshing barn, the straw barn was a much simpler and plainer structure, sometimes slightly lower than the threshing barn. Essentially, the straw barn is no more than a covered store (Fig 4.13): it is open from ground-floor level to the roof, and its walls occasionally incorporate slit vents. The only

Fig 4.11 The Northumberland barn. The Northumberland barn consisted of two attached buildings – the threshing barn and the straw barn, shown in (a) at Fenwick Stead, Kyloe (BB95/12571), where the two-storey threshing barn lies at the right, with the lower straw barn to the left. Within the threshing barn, the machine was on the first floor, as at Lanton, Ewart (b – the machine is a reconstruction). The crop was fed into the top of one end of the machine; straw was produced at the opposite end and was fed along a straw walk to an opening in the end wall of the barn, through which it passed into the straw barn for storage. Grain was produced at the bottom of the machine, on the ground floor of the threshing barn, where it was bagged. In order to facilitate loading the unthreshed crop into the barn, the building was sometimes built into sloping land so that the first-floor doorway was near ground level at the rear of the barn, as at West Moneylaws, Carham (c). Alternatively, when the ground was level, an artificial ramp might be built up to the barn door, as was the case at Low Middleton, Middleton (d; BB94/19532).

a

b

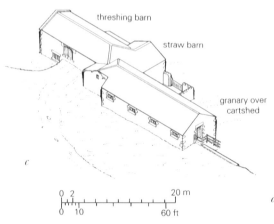

threshing barn

straw barn

granary over cartshed

c

0 2   20 m

0   10   60 ft

d

other characteristic feature is that there are usually opposing doorways adjacent to the threshing barn, through which straw could be moved into and out of the building. On many farmsteads, at least one of those doorways has been knocked out to create a larger opening suitable for 20th-century machinery.

Power

With only one exception, all the farmsteads recorded during the survey (apart from those on the Cheviot hill farms) were designed for mechanised threshing.[57] According to Bailey

and Culley, threshing machines were becoming common in north Northumberland – especially in the Glendale and Tweedside area – as early as 1797, and by 1805 were general.[58] Most of the machines appear to have been driven by water or horses, though some were powered by steam and there were experiments with wind power.[59] In the early 1840s, Grey commented that threshing machines were 'universal', and that, where water could not be used, steam was the main source of power.[60]

It is difficult to be certain exactly how far such reports accurately reflected the situation

Fig 4.12 The threshing barn: Windmill Hill Farm, Ancroft. Although the threshing machine has been removed, its position can still be determined from the pattern of the joists in the ground-floor ceiling, as trimmer joists define the sides of the aperture below the machine. The brick patch in the end wall is the lower part of the former opening to the adjacent straw barn (BB95/12573).

Fig 4.13 The straw barn: West Moneylaws, Carham. The straw barn is usually a tall building (though sometimes slightly lower than the threshing barn) with no first floor. It might be set in line with the threshing barn or, as here, at right angles to it. At the right is the end of the straw walk, by means of which straw was passed into the building from the threshing machine (here a 1930s model). The door in the end wall is a later insertion (BB95/9377).

79

on the ground, since their authors were for the most part interested in showing how advanced Northumberland agriculture was, and it has been suggested that progress was in reality rather slower, with the real expansion in numbers not occurring until the 1830s.[61] The evidence of the farmsteads recorded during the survey suggests that the new threshing barns erected during the early 19th century were almost invariably designed for mechanised processing. What is not clear, though, is the extent to which threshing machines were installed in earlier buildings still in use at that time but which were replaced later in the century.

Three types of mechanical power are found within the survey area: those produced by fixed horse wheels (gins), waterwheels, and fixed steam engines. The fixed horse wheel is characterised by a distinctive round or polygonal building adjoining one side of the threshing barn (Fig 4.14). Such installations were, from an early date, regarded as less efficient than water or steam plant; some may have existed in earlier phases of extant farmsteads and have been replaced later, though it is not certain that the north of the county was ever particularly rich in horse-powered threshing machines.[62] The dates of the few horse-engine houses which were recorded, or for which evidence (cartographic or physical) exists within the survey area, range from the early 19th century at Cheswick Cottage, Ancroft, on the coast, to the 1850s at Reedsford, Kilham, in Glendale, and possibly the 1860s at Cookstead in the parish of Ford. It has sometimes been suggested that horse power was associated with smaller farms,[63] but, within

the areas surveyed, while two of the farms were relatively small,[64] two others were over 200 hectares (500 acres) each.[65]

The most economical prime mover other than horse power was generally regarded to be that provided by water (which cost nothing),[66] despite the frequent necessity for major engineering works to create reservoirs and systems of leats (Fig 4.15). In most instances where there was an adequate supply, and a suitably sloping site, water appears to have been the preferred type of power, and in some cases it was even used on more or less level sites. West Moneylaws, Carham (Fig 4.15a), where the barns were built in the mid 19th century, is a good example of a sloping site. A mill pond was created a short distance to the east of the farmstead to collect water from streams running from surrounding higher ground. The water was then piped to the farmstead, where it entered the wheelhouse a little below ground level. It turned a breast-shot wheel which sat in a deep pit, from the base of which a leat deep underground conducted it to the west, where it emerged part way down a steep bank. On the coastal plain, even more major excavations were required for this kind of arrangement, as may be demonstrated by Low Middleton, Middleton, which was under construction in 1860. The site slopes only gently, necessitating the construction of an embanked mill pond (south west of the farmstead), from which water was led to the wheelhouse along a timber-and-slate leat (with a sluice near the threshing barn) built on a low bank, part of which formed a section of a large artificial ramp built to provide access to the first-floor doorway of the threshing barn (Fig 4.15b, c). The water entered the top of the wheelhouse, where it turned an overshot wheel prior to being taken away in a leat deep underground. The site of the outfall is not clear, but it must have been at a considerable distance from the wheelhouse, partly in order to avoid the rest of the farmstead, and partly because there is only the very slightest slope on the ground for several hundred yards.

The alternative to water power was a fixed steam engine, and this seems to have been preferred on the coast, where some of the largest farms were situated, and where there was relatively little natural relief.[67] Supplies of coal were cheaply available within both parts of the survey area, which contained thin seams of poor quality coal, largely unsuitable for commercial exploitation but adequate for local consumption.[68] Steam engines were installed from the early 19th century onwards – that is, they appear at the same date as the earliest surviving water and horse-powered systems.

Fig 4.14 Power in the barn: horse engines – Lanton, Ewart. Horse wheels were housed in circular or polygonal buildings attached to the barns. The sides of this example were originally open, having pillars at the angles. Horses turned a horizontal wheel on a vertical axle, the drive from which was transmitted to the machine in the barn by a series of gears (BB94/6084).

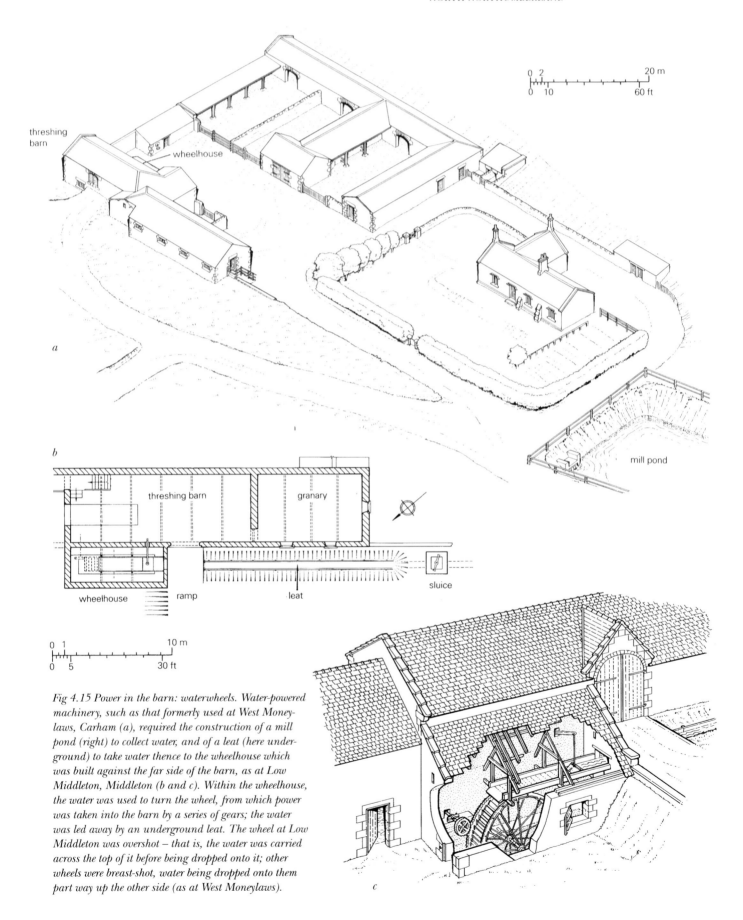

Fig 4.15 Power in the barn: waterwheels. Water-powered machinery, such as that formerly used at West Money-laws, Carham (a), required the construction of a mill pond (right) to collect water, and of a leat (here underground) to take water thence to the wheelhouse which was built against the far side of the barn, as at Low Middleton, Middleton (b and c). Within the wheelhouse, the water was used to turn the wheel, from which power was taken into the barn by a series of gears; the water was led away by an underground leat. The wheel at Low Middleton was overshot – that is, the water was carried across the top of it before being dropped onto it; other wheels were breast-shot, water being dropped onto them part way up the other side (as at West Moneylaws).

Fig 4.16 Power in the barn: steam engines. Steam engines and boilers were accommodated in lean-to buildings with tall chimneys (often demolished), such as that at Downham, Carham (BB94/19597).

Little usually remains of the steam installations. The boiler and engine were usually housed together in a lean-to (from which the tall chimney rose) against the side of the barn (Fig 4.16). The boilers and engine have long since been removed in all cases recorded, though the former are sometimes found reused for other purposes, or simply lying a short distance from the buildings; the chimneys have often been demolished.

In two instances, early 19th-century water-powered systems were later replaced by steam power. At Easington (parish of Easington), the site is on an incline, and the farmstead was originally built, between about 1810 and 1840, for threshing to be powered by a waterwheel. Later in the 19th century, however, the waterwheel was removed and the wheelhouse was extended to provide accommodation for a boiler and steam engine. Nearby, at Easington Demesne (Easington – but part of a different estate), a

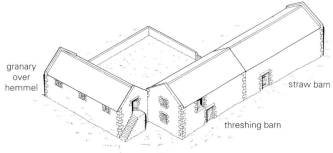

granary over hemmel

straw barn

threshing barn

0   2   20 m

0   10   60 ft

Fig 4.17 The granary: Lanton, Ewart. The granary is on the first floor of the left-hand building, above a cattle hemmel. It was reached by external steps, and grain was carried into it from the threshing barn on the right.

waterwheel constructed on an almost level site between about 1810 and 1830 was replaced in the 1840s or 1850s by a steam engine.[69] The reasons for these alterations are unclear, particularly in view of the level of investment required both to construct the water-powered system and to replace it so soon with a steam engine. While it may be that water power was found to be unsatisfactory in the parish, the possibility cannot be ruled out that some estate owners sought to keep up with the latest developments simply in order to demonstrate how advanced and prosperous they were.

According to the 19th-century commentators, the waterwheels and steam engines were not only used to power threshing machines, but were also linked to corn-crushing mills, chaff-cutters and cake-breakers – that is, to machines which assisted in the preparation of animal fodder.[70] While this may have been the case, and it is possible that such machines stood on either level of the threshing barn, there is no physical evidence to confirm it.

Granaries

After the threshing process, grain was taken from the ground floor of the threshing barn to the granary, prior to being used on the farmstead as seed or as part of the fodder for horses and cattle, or sold off the farm as a cash crop. Grain needed to be kept dry, well-ventilated and free from rodents, and in all known instances was kept in a first-floor room furnished with ventilated windows. The position favoured by the commentators was over open-sided cattle shelters (hemmels) or cartsheds, preferably adjoining the barns.[71] The advantages of such a position were that the grain was carried as short a distance as possible after threshing, and the open-sided nature of the accommodation below helped to ventilate it. If the grain was stored above a cartshed, trapdoors in the floor enabled it to be loaded directly into carts for taking to market. The commentators imply that the same could be done even if the granary was above a hemmel; while this is possible, since the cattle could be moved out and a cart backed in, only a few actual examples of this kind have trapdoors in the floor, suggesting that the grain was usually carried out.

The majority of granaries were above hemmels, probably because they often did adjoin the barns. An example of this arrangement is the earliest extant phase of Lanton, Ewart, where the hemmel/granary adjoined the threshing barn (Fig 4.17). There was, however, no direct access to the granary from either level of the barn, and the grain had to be carried from the ground floor of the barn, round the end of the building, and up an external stairway (later removed) at one end of the granary. The necessity to carry the grain outside in this way is typical even of farmsteads which were built as a single planned phase, such as Crookham Westfield, Ford, where the grain had to be carried outside from the threshing barn to the granary, which was, unusually, situated above a large root house. Carts could be backed into the root house and grain could be lowered into them through trapdoors in the floor of the granary.

On a small number of farmsteads, the granary was situated above a detached cartshed, sometimes a short distance from the barns. At Mardon, Ford (Fig 4.18*a*), the 1850s saw the construction of a large detached cartshed with a granary above. It lay on the opposite side of the farmstead from the earlier barns, but was conveniently positioned in relation to the main access to the steading, so that what was lost in terms of labour when the grain was taken to the granary may have been saved when it was removed.

In one instance – Low Middleton, Middleton (Fig 4.18*c*) – even though the threshing barn and granary were separated by the straw barn, internal access was provided. As was usual, the grain came out of the threshing machine on the ground floor, but then, instead of being taken outside to the granary, it was carried upstairs within the threshing barn, and through a doorway beside the straw walk; that gave access to a first-floor gallery along the side of the straw barn, at the far end of which another doorway led to the granary. This was a particularly efficient arrangement, since the granary was sited above the cartsheds, with which it communicated by trapdoors.

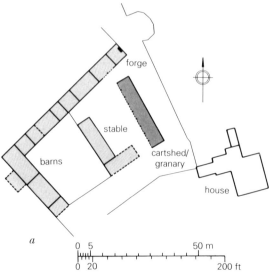

a

b

Fig 4.18 The granary and cartshed. Some granaries were placed above cartsheds so that grain could easily be loaded into the carts below for transport to market. This often meant that they were at some distance from the barn, as cartsheds were frequently situated conveniently for vehicular access, as at Mardon, Ford (a), and Windmill Hill Farm, Ancroft (b; BB95/12572). At Low Middleton, Middleton (c), there is an unusually convenient arrangement which enabled grain to be carried from the threshing barn (far right), through the straw barn on a timber gallery, to the granary, which lay above the cartshed.

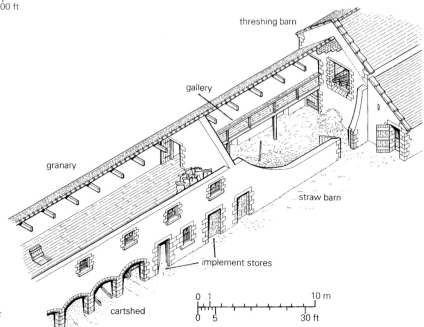

c

83

Cart and implement sheds

Few cartsheds – whether with granaries above or single storeyed – survive from before the mid 19th century. This may be a reflection of an increase in the number, size and sophistication of both carts and field implements after about 1840, as agriculture became more mechanised and more intense. Many cartsheds are, therefore, later additions to pre-existing farmsteads: some project from one side of an earlier block of farm buildings, as at Cheswick Cottage,

Ancroft (Fig 4.19*a*), while others were completely detached structures, as at Cheswick Buildings, also in Ancroft (Fig 4.19*b*). A further option, found on farmsteads which were built in a single phase as well as on those which evolved, was for the cartshed to be attached to the main building, but set a short distance in front of the cattle yards, facing inwards (Fig 4.19*c*). Finally, on planned farmsteads, such as Low Middleton, Middleton, the cartsheds might form part of the main range of buildings, but face outwards rather than into the cattle yards (Fig 4.18*c*). All these arrangements allowed carts and implements to be manoeuvred without crossing the cattle yards.

Even on some planned farmsteads, such as that at Beal Farm, where the original design of the 1850s probably included outward-facing cartsheds in the main block of buildings, further provision was sometimes required. At Beal Farm, the addition, constructed between 1860 and 1898, took the form of a detached single-storey range providing an additional thirteen bays for carts and implements, open on one side (Fig 4.20). At each end of the building there was a deeper and wider bay, with heavy sliding doors, in which mobile steam engines or large machines were housed. The only other example of specific accommodation for field engines or machines to have been identified in the survey area is at Hethpool in Kirknewton, which is situated in the Cheviots immediately below the point at which the steep ascent into the upper reaches of the College and Elsdonburn Valleys begins. There, an outward-facing cartshed had earlier been added to the rear of the stable block, and in the 1920s a machine shed was erected beside it. The reason for the provision of accommodation of this type at these two farms may be that their large arable area justified expensive mobile machinery: Beal Farm, at approximately 485 hectares (1,200 acres) in the late 19th century was one of the largest coastal farms recorded, while Hethpool was nearly 730 hectares (1,800 acres) – not as large as some hill farms, but probably (given its position on a plateau) with a relatively high proportion of arable.

STABLES

Even after mobile steam power became available, the majority of farms were still worked by horses, which also provided the only means of transport both for produce and for the farmer's family and workers. Horses were, therefore, vital to the working of the farm, and were at the same time both valuable and relatively delicate. All these factors meant that horses required to be housed in solid, dry and well-ventilated buildings.

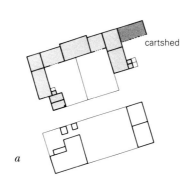

a

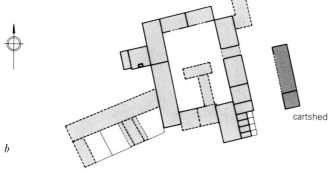

b

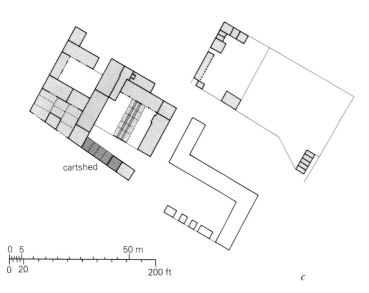

c

Working horses were generally kept separate from the riding horses used for domestic purposes (Fig 4.21). Sometimes the household animals were simply kept in an adjacent room with fittings of a higher standard, but on other occasions they were kept nearer to the house. The typical stable for working horses was a long single-storey range, along the length of which the animals were stalled singly, each with a vent, and hay rack and manger at its head, and with a drainage passage behind. Interior fittings rarely survive, since stables have long since been converted to other uses, but it is clear from surviving examples that both timber and iron were used. In the wall behind the horses there might have been one or more doorways and vented windows, and there was often a doorway at one or both ends of the manure passage. Riding-horse stables were smaller, but generally similar in layout, though some, like that at Hethpool, Kirknewton, were divided into stalls and boxes, which allowed greater freedom to each individual animal.

Stables of both kinds often included large timber hooks for saddles and harnesses, though there was sometimes also a separate tack room. In a few cases, as at Goswick, Ancroft, in the early 19th century, and Crookham Eastfield, Ford, towards the end of the century, there were adjacent rooms in which fodder was prepared. Before the middle of the century, horses were largely fed on hay, but Colbeck, writing in 1847, noted that this was regarded as old-fashioned, and that the newer and cheaper method was to use straw with boiled or crushed corn in the winter, and tares and bean straw in the summer.[72]

The 19th-century commentators were divided as to the best position for the stable relative to the other farm buildings. Ewart thought that it should be adjacent to the place – presumably the straw barn and granary – from which most of the fodder came, but J B Denton approvingly cited Scott Burn's view that, because horses required less straw than fattening cattle and calves, the stable should be placed further from the straw barn.[73] In reality, it seems that it was accessibility from the fields rather than proximity to the barn which dictated the position of the stables. Hence, for example,

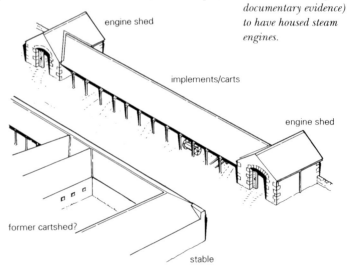

Fig 4.20 The cartshed: Beal Farm, Kyloe. A large detached cartshed was added to the planned farmstead of the 1850s. There were thirteen open-fronted bays, flanked by taller, deeper bays with doors, which are known (from documentary evidence) to have housed steam engines.

Fig 4.21 (below) The stable: fittings. Working horses were usually stalled in a single row with a manure passage behind and a manger and hay rack at the head of the stall. Fittings might be entirely timber, as at West Moneylaws, Carham (a; BB95/9379), or timber and iron, as at Hethpool, Kirknewton (b; BB94/19561). Riding horses might be kept in boxes or stalls: in either case, the interior finish of the building was generally better than that of the working-horse stable, with a boarded ceiling and plastered walls (c; Hethpool; BB94/19559).

a   *b*   *c*

Fig 4.22 The stable:
siting. Stables for
working horses (dark
grey), often associated
with yards, were usually
placed conveniently in
terms of access from the
fields. At East House,
Ancroft (a), they lay
along one side of the
farmstead, flanking the
main entrance to the
complex. Such a lateral
position was also
common in U-shaped
and E-shaped complexes,
such as that at West
Moneylaws, Carham
(b), where the yard next
to the stables may have
been used for horses
rather than for cattle.
There was certainly a
horse yard at Crookham
Eastfield, Ford (c), where
there were also separate
nag stables near the
house. Crookham
Westfield, Ford (d), had
more elaborate horse
yards with shelter sheds.

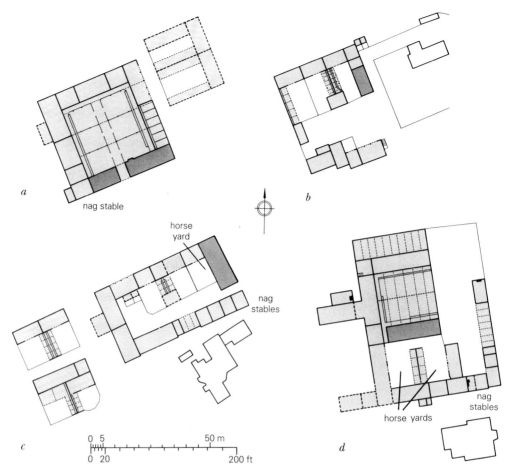

at East House, Ancroft (Fig 4.22a), where the
final form of the farmstead was a square of buildings with roofed cattle yards in the middle, the
stables were distributed on either side of the
gateway in the entrance range. In many other
cases, where the basic shape of the farmstead was
an E, the stables lay along one of the short sides
of the complex, the barns and cattle accommodation forming the other two (Fig 4.22b, c).

An elaboration of this plan is at Crookham
Westfield, Ford (Fig 4.22d; cf. 4.26a), a planned
farmstead of the late 19th century, where the
stables formed the south range of the main
U-shaped plan, but beyond them were two horse
yards with hemmels; more usually, the horse yards
lay within the main U-shape, as they did at
Crookham Eastfield (also Ford parish
(Fig 4.22c)). The presence of horse yards suggests
that horses were in the stable only for grooming
and feeding, but were otherwise kept outside, at
least during the summer, as in Lincolnshire.

FATSTOCK HOUSING

So far, the buildings associated predominantly
with arable farming have been discussed – the
barns, granaries, cartsheds and stables – and

their relationships to each other described:
interlocking with that system was accommodation for cattle and their fodder. As indicated
earlier, fatstock became an increasingly important element in the farming economy during
the second half of the 19th century. At the same
time, better methods of keeping cattle were
devised: the warmer the conditions in which an
animal was kept, the greater the weight gain per
unit of fodder, as less energy was wasted in heat
loss, while the drier the conditions, the better
the quality of the manure. The story of cattle-
housing in 19th-century Northumberland is
therefore one of increasing capacity combined
with ever greater sophistication.

Yards

The earliest form of cattle accommodation
consisted of hemmels, with open yards in front
(Fig 4.23, 4.24a); the shelters often adjoined the
barns and were either single-storeyed or had a
loft or granary above. Proximity to the straw
barn was desirable, since straw for litter and
fodder had to be taken to the cattle, which were
free to roam within both the hemmels and the
yards. Accommodation of this kind is typical of
the first sixty years of the 19th century, but

appears to have been rarely, if ever, constructed thereafter. During the last four decades of the century, most of these early systems were altered to provide a greater degree of shelter for both the cattle and their fodder. At Easington Demesne, Easington, for example, the dividing wall between the cattle yards was replaced by an open-sided shelter shed which incorporated a feeding passage (with a doorway at each end), from which fodder could be placed directly into mangers under the shelters (Fig 4.24a, b). There

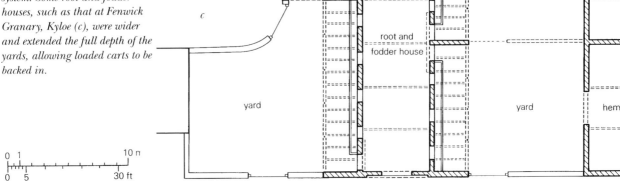

Fig 4.23 Fatstock housing: hemmels. Hemmels, with granary above, and openyards at Easington Demesne, Easington. The doorway in the centre of the range, and the feeding trough, are later additions (BB95/9360).

Fig 4.24 Fatstock housing: the evolution of the open yard. The main cattle yards at Easington Demesne, Easington, were originally open (a). During the second half of the century (b), earlier buildings (not shown on (a)) were largely demolished and replaced with further cattle accommodation, including one open and one covered yard, the latter with its own root house (left, with open doors). At the same time, the earlier yards were supplied with a covered feeding system. Some root and fodder houses, such as that at Fenwick Granary, Kyloe (c), were wider and extended the full depth of the yards, allowing loaded carts to be backed in.

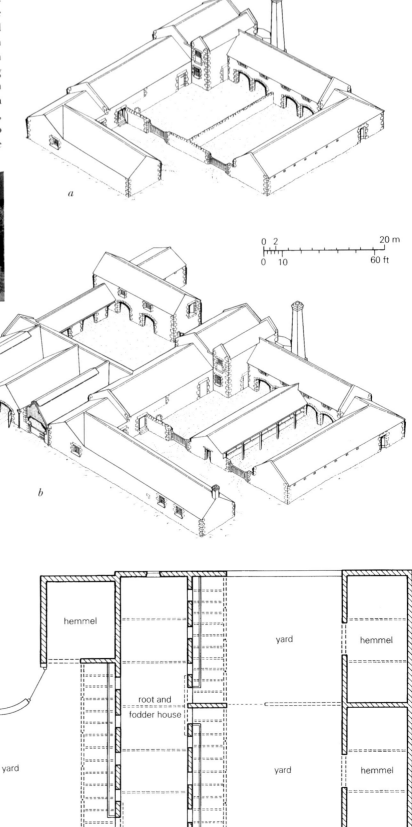

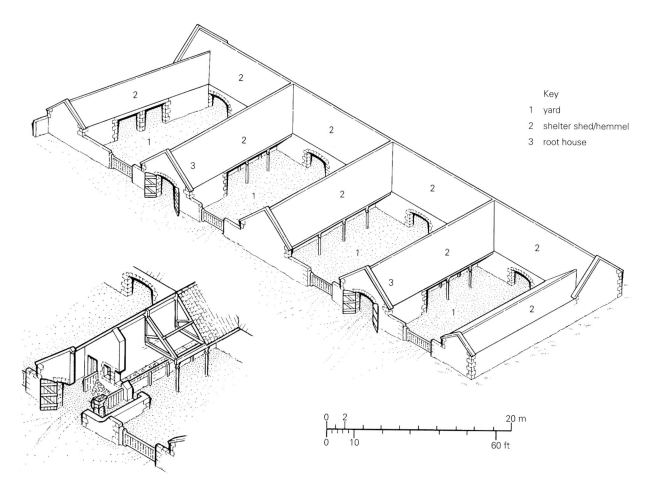

Key
1 yard
2 shelter shed/hemmel
3 root house

0 2   20 m

0   10   60 ft

Fig 4.25 Fatstock housing: shelter sheds. The late 19th-century detached cattle unit at Westnewton, Kirknewton. Open yards with hemmels at the back were flanked by shelter sheds covering mangers. Each pair of yards was served by a root house, from which fodder could be pushed into the mangers through hatches.

were many variations on this: some systems of shelter sheds lacked any kind of feeding passage; others, such as one of those at Fenwick Granary, Kyloe (Fig 4.24c), had a much wider passage into which a cart could be backed, which also served as a root or cake store and fodder-preparation area. A different arrangement, which achieved the same objectives, was for there to be a root house at the outer end of the yards, with the shelter sheds behind.

All these variations are also found on the newly planned farmsteads of the second half of the 19th century, and in farmsteads where additional cattle-housing was added to a core of earlier buildings. The latter was a very common phenomenon, separate cattle units outside the main farmyards being one of the main characteristics of farmstead development in the area at this period. One of the best examples is at Westnewton, Kirknewton, where a range of four new yards was built near the older barn and stable ranges (Fig 4.25). The new cattle unit consists of hemmels and yards with shelter sheds and root houses. The root houses have outward-facing double doors, through which fodder could be loaded into them, and the rear walls contain a doorway to each yard; between the

rear doorways are two hatches through which fodder could be pushed along the length of mangers in the shelters behind.[74]

The final refinement in the development of many yard systems was the roofing-over of the entire yard. In a few cases, this occurred before the end of the 19th century, and some planned farmsteads of that period, such as Crookham Westfield, Ford (Fig 4.26a), were designed with covered yards from the start, but often such roofs were not built until the early 20th century. Although the covering of a yard led to a reduction in the amount of sunlight and, therefore, heat which reached the cattle, that was more than offset by the ability of covered yards to retain heat better in winter. This meant that less of the energy provided by fodder was wasted in heat loss, and more could be turned into meat. In addition, covered yards protected the manure from the leaching effects of rain – something which was seen as increasingly important as the proportion of expensive oil cake fed to cattle rose during the last third of the 19th century, and which was of greater significance in Northumberland, where rainfall is relatively high, than in the drier climate of Lincolnshire.

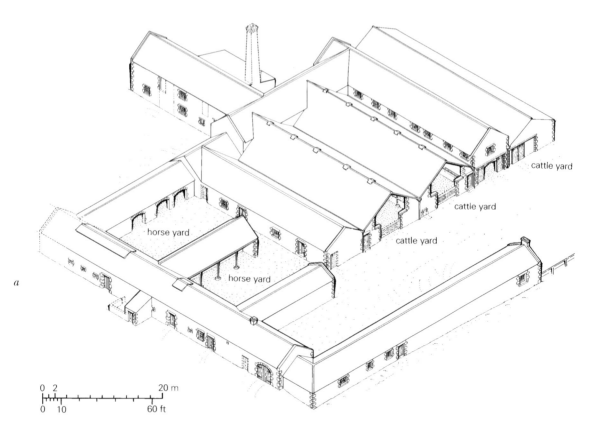

a

b

Fig 4.26 Fatstock housing: covered yards. Towards the end of the 19th century, some complete farmsteads, such as Crookham Westfield, Ford (a), were built with covered cattle yards, as were some additional cattle units, like that at Kilham, Kilham (b, BB95/9341, and c). Protecting the cattle from the cold enabled them to gain weight more efficiently, while covering the manure meant that nutrients were not washed away by rain.

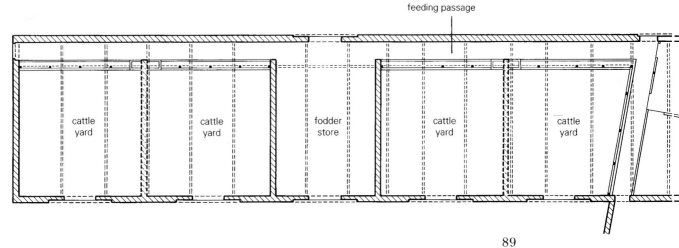

c

Fig 4.27 Fatstock housing: loose boxes. A different method of fattening cattle intensively involved keeping them in loose boxes such as those at Fenwick Granary, Kyloe (a – dark grey), and East House, Ancroft (b), where fodder was placed in the mangers through hatches in the wall between the loose boxes and the main cattle yards behind. The provision of loose boxes did not remove the need for other types of cattle accommodation, as illustrated at Fenwick Granary (a), where there were also two sets of open yards.

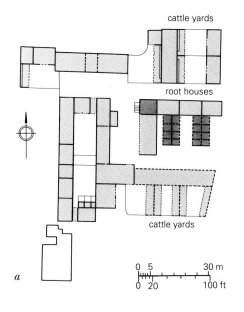

cattle yards

root houses

cattle yards

a

0 5   30 m

0 20   100 ft

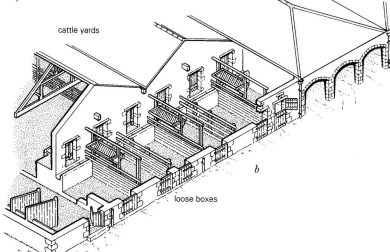

cattle yards

b

loose boxes

Loose boxes

On almost all farmsteads in the survey area, fatstock were kept in the yards for the majority of the time, but the main block of buildings usually incorporated a small number of loose boxes. Such boxes could be used for a variety of temporary purposes, such as accommodating sick or pregnant cows (or horses), calves or a bull. Most compartments of this kind have few distinctive features – they might contain a manger, and might have a drain in the floor and a window or vent, but there is no set pattern.

On two farmsteads (Fenwick Granary, Kyloe, and East House, Ancroft), there is (or at one stage was) a greater number of loose boxes (Fig 4.27), conveniently situated in relation to the source of fodder, perhaps suggesting that some cattle were fattened in them – a more intensive system of rearing which was advocated by some mid-century commentators.[75] At Fenwick Granary, the former loose boxes were attached to root houses from which fodder could readily be taken to them, while at East House the boxes were so contrived that fodder could be placed in the mangers from within the adjacent cattle yard, to which the beasts in the boxes had no direct access.

FARM MANAGEMENT AND THE DOMESTIC ECONOMY

It will be clear from the foregoing discussion that the farmsteads of the north Northumberland lowlands were often large, and housed a complex set of interlocking functions. In this, particularly when combined with the use of mechanical power, they came to resemble industrial factories, and were planned accordingly. The scale of these enterprises is underlined by the labour requirement, referred to earlier, which necessitated the construction of cottages

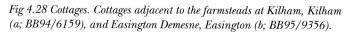

Fig 4.28 Cottages. Cottages adjacent to the farmsteads at Kilham, Kilham (a; BB94/6159), and Easington Demesne, Easington (b; BB95/9356).

a

b

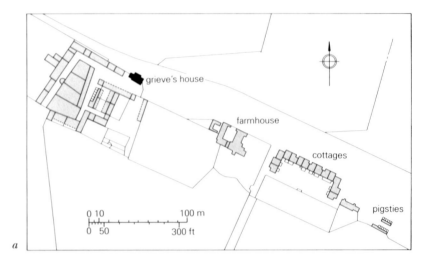

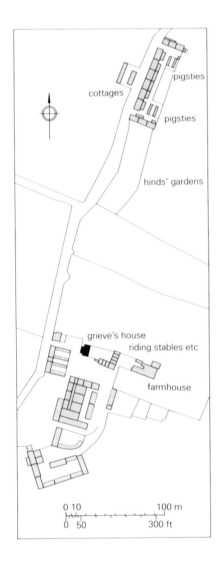

a

b

Fig 4.29 Farmsteads and townships. In many townships the sole settlement was formed by the farmstead and associated cottages, as at Goswick, Ancroft (a), and Mindrum, Carham (b). In order to supervise the labour force, there was often a grieve's house (black), placed conveniently near the entrance to the farmstead.

Fig 4.30 (left) The smithy: Mardon, Ford. Many farmsteads had their own smithies, which served the entire community (BB94/19572).

(hinds' houses) nearby (Fig 4.28). In many cases, almost the entire population of a township was employed on a single farm, and the cottages, together with the farmstead, formed the only settlement in the parish or township (Fig 4.29). This creates a very distinctive pattern of rural settlement in the region, having more in common with parts of Scotland than with much of England.

In order to supervise such a large labour force, the farmer sometimes employed a manager, or grieve, who lived on or immediately adjacent to the farmstead. Grieves' houses are usually distinguished by being larger than a mere cottage, and by their siting (Fig 4.29). At Goswick, Ancroft, for example, the grieve's house stands next to the main entrance to the farmstead. From such a position, the grieve could see everything and everybody who entered

and left the steading, and could easily supervise the labourers without having to leave his house and the office it contained. At Mindrum, Carham, the grieve's house is again placed near the main entrance, and access from it to the main part of the cattle yard was facilitated by the provision of a passage through one of the side ranges of the main U-shaped block of livestock buildings, which enabled the grieve to enter the complex without having to walk round the front. At both Goswick and Mindrum the farmer was resident close by, but that was not always the case, and at Crookhouse, Kirknewton, the only person who lived on the site was the grieve.

A further indication of the 'industrial' nature of many of these farmsteads, at least at the larger end of the scale, is that several incorporated a smithy (Fig 4.30), often placed near the stable or cartshed. This was important not

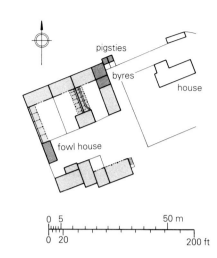

Fig 4.31 The domestic economy: West Moneylaws, Carham. Milk cows, pigs and fowl were kept on a relatively modest scale, largely to supply the needs of the farmer's and labourers' households. Such animals were often accommodated in buildings near to the house or readily accessible from it.

Fig 4.32 The domestic economy: the byre at Southernknowe, Kirknewton. Cattle were usually tethered in double stalls with a head rail. The divisions between the stalls were much lower and shorter than those in stables, and were usually of the form illustrated here. At the head of the stalls was a ground-level manger (here with later drinking bowls), and behind (not shown) was a manure passage. The floor would originally have been stone (BB94/6077).

Fig 4.33 (above) The domestic economy: the fowl house at Easington Demesne, Easington. Fowl houses contained tiers of nesting boxes, and sometimes, as here, had small entrances (with shutters) above ground level through which birds, but not predators, could gain access. In this example there is a pigeon loft above (BB95/9365).

only for keeping the horses shod, but also for running repairs to the new iron implements which were introduced during the second half of the 19th century. Not all repairs could be carried out locally, particularly to barn machinery, but many had to be and, in an area where the farmstead and cottages formed the village, the farmer had to provide the forge.

However large and well-ordered the farmstead might be, the subsistence needs of both the farmer's and labourers' households were not ignored. This concern is manifested in provision for poultry or milk cows; pigsties and pigeon lofts are also found, but are less common. On only a very small number of farms did any of these animals form a significant part of the agricultural economy as such, but that does not mean that their accommodation was of poor quality, or that it was usually badly placed in relation to the other buildings.

A good example of the general character of accommodation of this kind is at West Moneylaws, Carham, where there is a fowl house and, near the house, two pigsties (Fig 4.31); in addition, a pair of rooms in the main block of buildings may have been byres. Pigsties are

often quite near the house, since the animals' fodder was prepared in the kitchen. Byres were also conveniently placed near the house, where the milk was required, but also needed to be near the cattle yards, whence the fodder for the cows was brought. It was not always possible to meet both criteria, and the position of the byres in the overall plan is variable. Within the byre, there might be either one or two standings of cows, usually arranged across the width of the building and with a manure passage behind (Fig 4.32). The cattle were tethered (two to a stall) to posts rising from a ground-level manger to a head-height beam. There were no windows, but there were usually vents in at least one of the side walls and, sometimes, in the roof.

Fowl houses appear to have been less common, and are more varied in form. At Branxtonmoor, Branxton, two adjacent ground-floor rooms provided for hens (with tiers of nesting boxes) and ducks (with a single row of boxes at floor level). Three coastal farmsteads have quite sophisticated arrangements in which two-storey buildings contain hen houses (with hen slots and tiers of nesting boxes), above which are pigeon lofts (Fig 4.33). A few of these,

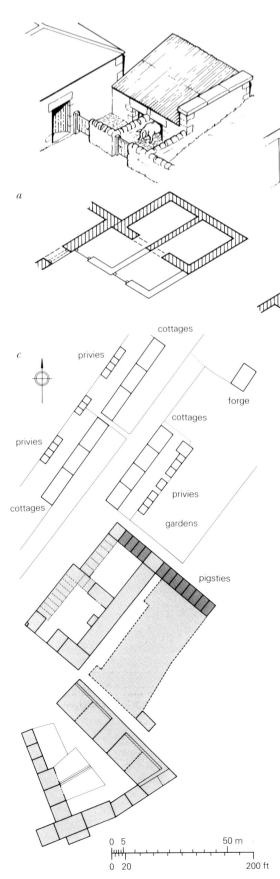

a

b

c

cottages

privies

forge

cottages

privies

cottages

privies

gardens

pigsties

0 5   50 m

0 20   200 ft

0 1   10 m

0 5   30 ft

Fig 4.34 The domestic economy: pigsties. Pigs were kept on a modest scale, often in small sties with associated yards like those at West Moneylaws, Carham (a). A slightly different arrangement is found at Kilham, Kilham (b), where there is a much larger range of sties (b and c). Even there, however, it is likely that pigs were largely kept for domestic consumption, since the sties are near to the cottages, and are sufficient in number to allow one for each cottage with two for the main house.

such as that at Scremerston Town Farm, Ancroft, are on a large scale, perhaps implying commercial egg production. In the early 19th century, Berwick had been an important centre for the export of eggs from the region, but this dropped off later,[76] and the buildings do not suggest that large-scale egg production continued to be a major feature of the region's economy.

Pigsties were usually on a modest scale, as at West Moneylaws (Fig 4.31, 4.34*a*, *b*), underlying the fact that such animals were kept only for domestic consumption. The only exception to this within the survey area is at Kilham, parish of Kilham, where there is a very long range of pigsties. Even there, however, pigs may have been kept only for subsistence purposes, since, although part of the main farmstead, the sties are next to the cottages, suggesting that the pigs belonged to the labourers (Fig 4.34). In this kind of provision even the most industrial of the large farmsteads which were geared to production for the regional and national markets shared something with the small Cheviot hill farms described earlier, in that they had to supply the daily needs of those who lived in and worked on them.

5 EAST CORNWALL

The Survey Area

The area selected for survey by the Royal Commission comprises the south-eastern part of Bodmin Moor, together with the adjacent valley of the River Lynher, flowing south to the east of the moor (Fig 5.1). The area includes parts of the parishes of Altarnun, Linkinhorne, North Hill, St Cleer and St Neot. The upland moor is a granite mass intruded through surrounding slate formations. Most of the land on the moor lies at a height of between 200 and 300 m OD (655–985 ft), but some of the higher tors rise to nearly 400 m OD; the highest point in the area is at Kilmar Tor, 396 m OD (1,296 ft). Through the centre of the survey area run the upper reaches of the River Fowey, and on the eastern side of the moor a number of brooks drain into the River Lynher, here hugging the eastern fringes of the moor. The Lynher Valley has steeply sloping sides, but away from the moor the land rises to a gently undulating plateau between 100 and 200 m OD (330–655 ft).

Cornwall's climate is mild and wet. High precipitation and humidity are pronounced on Bodmin Moor, the higher parts of which have an annual rainfall of 1,524 mm (60 in.) or more. On the granite, the soil is a gravelly loam, and much of the higher land is boulder strewn. Large tracts of the moor are still poorly drained. Away from the moor the slates support fertile loams, and there is little land which cannot be used either for grass or for cultivation. Tin and china-clay deposits gave rise to important industries in the 19th century and earlier,[1] and the landscape of the area still shows extensive remains of these extractive processes. The industries were important in the present context in so far as they provided the labouring class with alternative employment.

The area is largely one of dispersed settlement. On the moor in particular farmsteads stand alone. On the lower ground there are hamlets comprising more than one farmstead, and North Hill is a village with a medieval parish church and a sizeable number of dwellings; the other parish centres lie outside the survey area. The market towns of Launceston, Liskeard and Bodmin lie a few miles away, and are well sited to act as an exchange point for moorland and valley produce.

Landholding and Farm Size in the 19th Century

In the 19th century, when most of the surviving farm buildings were constructed, the survey area was one in which there was a large number of landowners and an even larger number of tenant farmers; a mid 19th-century writer commented on the 'immense number of small occupiers performing all the labour on the farms by themselves'. No single great estate dominated the locality. The parish tithe apportionments of the late 1830s and early 1840s show that some land was owned by the Duchy of Cornwall, the largest estate in this part of the county, but otherwise the major landowning families were of lesser significance. The most prominent resident family, the Rodds, had a mansion at Trebartha and owned much of the parish of North Hill as well as land in adjoining parishes. Some landowners owned sizeable amounts of land, divided into numerous small farms; in 1842 Thomas Stephens had about 400 hectares (1,000 acres) in St Neot, occupied by 21 tenants, and in 1840 William Marshall owned nearly 500 hectares (1,200 acres), occupying one holding of 62 hectares (155 acres) himself and letting the remainder to twelve tenants. Other landholders owned fewer properties and less land; in St Neot, William Glencross, Esquire, owned 165 hectares (410 acres), divided into two substantial farms, and Edward Geach, Esquire, had 32 hectares (80 acres), again divided between two farms. There were a number of owner occupiers. Some worked smallholdings on the moor; Thomas Mares, for example, owned 5.5 hectares (14 acres) at Berrydown in St Neot. Others, however, worked much more substantial farms, such as Carkeet, St Cleer, and Darley, Linkinhorne.[2]

In the early 19th century, tenure in Cornwall was generally leasehold for a term of lives.[3] The conditions contained in the leases were criticised in the mid 19th century as not being

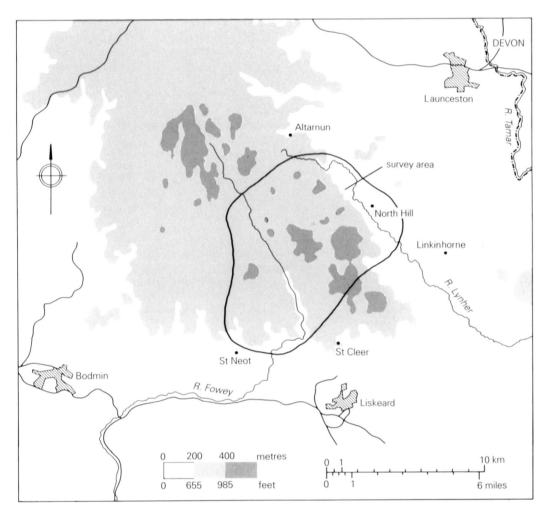

Fig 5.1 Map of the Cornwall survey area.

conducive to good farming practice,[4] and changes in these conditions were regarded as an important means of introducing better crop rotation to the county. By the end of the 19th century the leasing system had been reformed to give the landlord a greater interest in efficient management and the tenant a greater incentive to invest in good husbandry.[5]

The farms varied widely in size. The tithe apportionments demonstrate that there was a number of moorland smallholdings of less than 12 hectares (30 acres); that there was a substantial number of farms of between 12 and 60 hectares (30 and 150 acres), with farms of between 16 and 24 hectares (40 and 60 acres) being particularly common; and that holdings of above 60 hectares (150 acres) formed a little less than one-quarter of the total. Some of the largest farms lay on the moor and included extensive upland grazing; at Siblyback, St Cleer, for example, the farm, of nearly 365 hectares (900 acres), included over 20 hectares (500 acres) of land classed as 'coarse pasture'. There were, however, also large farms lying

either on the edge of the moor or on the far side of the Lynher Valley; Trebartha Barton, North Hill, was of nearly 80 hectares (200 acres), and Trebartha, also North Hill, of just over 100 hectares (250 acres).

In the mid 19th century the dominance of the small farm was regarded as one of the characteristics of Cornish agriculture which served to retard its progress towards improved management. Karkeek maintained that, while not all large farms were well cultivated, 'it is a very rare case to witness anything approaching to good husbandry on very small ones'.[6] Farm amalgamation was recommended as a way of concentrating capital so as to allow investment in improved methods of production, and this process evidently took place within the survey area in the mid and late 19th century. The farmsteads at West Tremollett, Lynher, and Botternell, all North Hill, and Darley, Linkinhorne, all result from amalgamation of two or more earlier holdings, and at most of these farms the buildings reflect the enlarged scale on which the farmer operated.

The Farming System in the 19th Century

Cornish agriculture was characterised by mixed husbandry from the late 18th century through to the late 19th century. The balance between arable and pastoral farming varied according to local conditions and over time. In the early 19th century, wheat and barley were grown on the better soils on lower lying land, and it was said that, 'the generality of farmers having an idea, that there is nothing like corn in sacks, for making money, they are very fond of the plough'.[7] The Crop Returns for 1801 demonstrate that sizeable amounts of land were used for growing wheat within the survey area: in St Cleer, over 100 hectares (251 acres) were down to wheat, and even upland Altarnun had 80 hectares (200 acres) used for this crop.

In all but the most favoured areas, however, it is likely that cereal cultivation was subservient to the needs of a livestock economy. Noting the large numbers of cattle on the heaths fringing Bodmin Moor, William Marshall remarked that 'the principal requisite is in coarse straw, to feed them with'.[8] Much of the arable land was used for the production of fodder crops; oats was the major cereal crop in 1801 within the survey area, barley may have been used partly as animal feed, and potatoes, cabbage and rape were important feedstuffs from the early 19th century.[9] Turnips were grown in increasing quantities after 1815, and effected a 'wonderful revolution in Cornish agriculture'; more cattle fodder led to an increased supply of manure, which allowed more produce to be grown.[10] Hay was grown as part of the rotation system, and it has been calculated that in many parishes, especially those around Bodmin Moor, over 60 per cent of the land was down to grass.[11]

In the first half of the 19th century, therefore, much of the county was involved primarily in livestock production. Writing in 1811, Worgan noted 'the true economy, or plan of management, of the Cornish cattle farmer. He rears cattle on mountain pasturage, to be fatted on the marshlands, and other rich grazing lands, in more genial climatures.' Cattle reared on the rather poor Cornish pastures were sold to contractors for finishing in Somerset and other grazing counties, or fattened on better land and sold for slaughter at the Royal Navy victualling yard at Plymouth.[12] Dairy farming was 'very little attended to' in Cornwall, milk cows being 'kept chiefly for the sake of rearing young stock'.[13] Farmers commonly rented their cows out to their labourers, allowing them to sell dairy produce – milk and butter – but taking the calves as profit.[14] Sheep provided a useful supplement to the farmer's income, and were used to graze the poor upland areas.

The precise relationship between cereal and livestock farming within the RCHME's survey area is difficult to determine. It is likely that the better land on the eastern side of the Lynher Valley was conducive to cereal production, and that the fringes and heart of the moor were used primarily for livestock-rearing. Mixed husbandry, however, was characteristic of both parts of the area, and any contrast was a matter of balance within a mixed economy rather than one of entirely different farming systems. The tithe surveys demonstrate the mixed nature of husbandry in the late 1830s and early 1840s. Among the farms in the eastern and southern parts of the area – that is, off the moor itself – it was common to have half or more of the land devoted to cultivation; the large farm at Trebartha Barton, North Hill, had 75 per cent of its acreage under the plough, and at the two farms at Penhole in the same region about half the land was arable. Even in this eastern area, however, there were farms with a large proportion of pasture land; only a little over 16 hectares (40 acres) of the 101 hectares (251 acres) at Trebartha, North Hill, were arable. On the moor, farms commonly had about one-third of their area under the plough, or in some cases available for growing crops; at Lamelgate, St Neot, 35 per cent of the land was arable, and at Carkeet, St Cleer, 36 per cent was described as 'arable occasionally'. Some farms on the moor had a surprisingly high proportion of arable land: 75 per cent at St Lukes Farm, St Neot, and 100 per cent at Lower Bowden, in the same parish.

In 1796 William Marshall judged that, instead of the 'wretched country, wretched roads, wretched towns, wretched accommodations, and wretched inhabitants' which he expected in Cornwall, the county was 'above mediocrity'.[15] Later commentators were, however, not so charitable about the state of Cornish agriculture. The system of management attracted particular disapproval, and in 1811 Worgan wrote that 'the general course of crops ... is extremely reprehensible; there is no circumstance evinces the truth of this assertion more, than the wretched, exhausted, foul appearance of the grounds, laid down with grass seeds; nor can it be otherwise, after having been cropped with corn, as long as they will bear any'.[16] In the middle of the 19th century the common practice of growing two successive white crops (wheat and barley) was condemned as leading to the exhaustion of the soil, and a rotation of wheat, turnips, barley or oats and two years in pasture was recommended as a means of restoring health to the land.[17]

Breeding stock and the methods of keeping animals also came in for criticism. Cornish horses were dismissed as 'a weedy, trashy race', often kept in poor conditions with inadequate fodder and shelter. The quality of horses was less critical up to the middle of the 19th century, for oxen were widely used for draught purposes. The native black cattle were falling out of favour from the early 19th century, being replaced by Devon stock; the Rodd family of Trebartha, North Hill, were among the pioneers in the use of the new breed. The treatment of cattle was defective, however. Stock were left to roam outside in winter except in the most severe weather, and many were poorly fed. Worgan observed 'that from the general deficiency of house room and comfortable farmyards throughout the county, and also of more extensive winter green crops, all cattle, particularly young stock, sustain much injury for want of more generous food, and, what is almost equal to it, warm shelter'. An example of better practice was provided by 'gentlemen, and some superior farmers', who 'house all their cattle, giving their cows cabbage, rape or the tops of turnips, and ruta baga, with straw or hay'.[18]

In the mid 19th century, Karkeek was able to report that great improvements had been made to the farming system described and partly condemned by Worgan in 1811; Karkeek used the evidence of a landed proprietor who wrote that 'we are in a transition stage, passing from a very slovenly course of husbandry, by very unequal and incomplete degrees, to a better'.[19] The process of improvement involved the development of better systems of crop rotation, the use of better fodder for livestock and investment in farm buildings. The changes did not radically alter the essentials of the farming system; much of Cornwall remained a predominantly grassland area.[20] Further efforts to eradicate poor husbandry techniques continued into the second half of the century, with further expenditure on buildings and drainage, and the more widespread use of artificial manures. The emphasis of the region's agriculture changed after 1850, with a pronounced shift away from arable production: 'instead of one half as in 1869, quite two thirds of the cultivated lands are now in grass, either as permanent pasture, or under the process of a rotation'.[21] One commentator wrote that 'our only hope and chance of agricultural progress rests on fodder crops, roots, and pasture, with such an admixture of grain crops only as may be necessary for an approved rotation, or the requirements of our animals in winter'.[22] Cattle numbers in the county increased markedly during the 1870s, from 137,000 in 1871 to 163,000 in 1880, and

this general trend is mirrored by large increases in the numbers of cattle and sheep within the survey area in the late 19th century; in North Hill, for example, there were 259 milk cows and 770 other cattle in 1866, but by 1906 the numbers were 577 and 1,320 respectively.[23] Whether the survey area participated in the county's development of early vegetable and soft-fruit production is not known, but it is likely that much of the area was not suitable for these purposes.

Pre-1800 Farmsteads

Excavation has provided evidence of the common types of farmsteads and buildings in Cornwall in the Middle Ages. The local evidence relates mainly to the moor, but it is likely also to represent a wider area. Before 1500 the farmstead was usually a small group of buildings. The principal structure was a longhouse, combining an area for human occupation with a shippon for livestock, sited at the lower end of the range beyond a passage which provided the principal or sole entrance to the two parts. The cattle accommodation provided in these buildings was commonly supplemented on medieval farms by detached cow houses and stores.[24]

The post-medieval houses of Cornwall include some dwellings which may well have originated as longhouses but which, after a long process of alternate rebuilding, became entirely domestic in function, with the lower end providing a service room. In the 18th century, longhouse derivatives were developed, with house and farm building in a linear range but with no connection between the two parts.[25] On Bodmin Moor farmsteads might have a number of outbuildings, probably similar in function to those on a medieval farmstead. A corn-drying barn, with an oven and drying kiln, formed a part of some farmsteads, and provides evidence for the cultivation of cereal crops.[26]

The Rebuilding of Cornish Farmsteads, 1800–1875

The vast majority of Cornish farmsteads date entirely or largely from the period 1800–1875. The poor condition of traditional Cornish farmhouses, and by inference of the farm buildings as well, was noted early in this period, for in 1811 the typical farmhouse was described as being 'built with mud walls, and covered with wheaten thatch'.[27] No such structures survive within the survey area, although at Middle Tremollett, North Hill, the house formerly had a cob front wall, and the rear wall of the attached bank barn is partly of cob. The replacement of houses and farm buildings of traditional type was regarded as a major contribution to the improvement of the region's agriculture, and the widespread use of stone for walling and of slate for roofing became characteristic of the 19th-century rebuilding. The typical Cornish farmstead is made up, therefore, of sturdily built granite or slate structures under stone slate roofs. The masonry is mainly uncoursed or roughly coursed rubble, but dressed surrounds are frequently used around the openings. An unusual feature is the use of slate-clad timber-framing, employed mainly on upper floors over open-fronted buildings, lightening the load on the supporting piers and lintels.

The protracted nature of the process of replacement is demonstrated by the mid 19th-century call for more investment in buildings to allow the farmer 'to carry on his business in the most economical manner – a matter of vital importance to himself, and obviously tending to give a feeling of satisfaction and confidence to his landlord'.[28] Late in the century, a report on the farming of Devon and Cornwall noted that, since Karkeek had written, 'the landlords of the two counties have spent considerable sums of money on the erection of buildings' and other improvements.[29] The ultimate success of this process is indicated by the virtually total absence of pre-1800 buildings in the farmsteads which survive today. Within the survey area, estates were probably responsible for much of the improvement, rebuilding the tenant farms and, rarely but conspicuously, constructing farmsteads such as Trebartha Barton, North Hill, for display and emulation. Although Trebartha Barton is, in its essentials, only a larger, better built and more architecturally aware version of

the type of farm common in the area, it is possible that it was intended as a model layout, albeit one which resulted from more than one phase of development.

Within the survey area, the period of most intensive rebuilding was the early and mid 19th century. Few farmsteads were built in a single phase of construction, but the tithe maps of the late 1830s and early 1840s show that many buildings which survive today were present at that time. The great majority of the bank barns which form the heart of most farmsteads were in existence by 1850, and on most sites later additions to farmsteads took the form of relatively minor structures except where new farmsteads were created or old ones thoroughly remodelled by an estate. The early and mid 19th-century farmsteads provide substantial evidence for the type of husbandry dominant in the survey area during this process of improvement.

Farmstead Layout and the Flow of Processes

The efficient layout of buildings was perhaps a less important consideration on the majority of Cornish farmsteads than on farmsteads in some other areas, for most complexes were relatively small. As a result, the movement of materials – crops to the processing area, fodder and litter to the livestock, dung to the midden – and of animals – between the fields and the farmyard – was less critical than, for example, on a large Northumberland mixed farm. Nevertheless, the distinctive form of the Cornish farmstead shows that a particular solution was devised to meet local needs.

The essentials of the Cornish farming system involved a number of linked processes in which livestock were central. Cereal and root crops were grown in the fields and brought to the farmstead for storage and processing. Cereals were threshed to provide grain and straw, both used for fodder and the latter also for litter. Roots, straw and grains were chopped, cut and milled or bruised to provide feedstuffs for cattle. Most cattle were kept in the open air for much of the year, but were often housed during the winter months. The manure from the cattle and other animals was stored and then taken to the fields to enrich the arable lands. Fieldwork and haulage were undertaken by draught animals – mainly oxen at the beginning of the period, then increasingly horses – which required housing, as did other animals such as pigs and poultry. The vehicles and implements used on the farm also required shelter.

Apart from the cultivation of the crops, the grazing of the cattle, and the spreading of the

Fig 5.2 The flow of processes in a Cornish farmstead. This example is based on Great Hammett, St Neot, and shows the buildings grouped around a large yard. The proximity between the farmhouse and the pigsties and calf house is evident in this farmstead.

Key
1 mowhay
2 chall barn
2a first floor, crop-processing
2b ground floor, livestock
2c ground floor, draught animals
3 granary
4 shippons
5 midden
6 calf house
7 pigsties
8 house and dairy

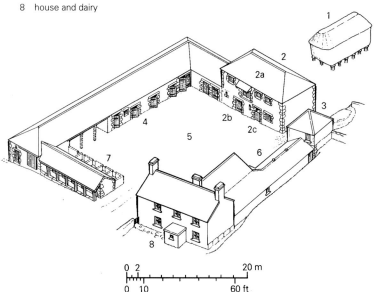

manure, all these processes were undertaken within the farmstead, although not necessarily within a building (Fig 5.2). Cornish farmsteads commonly have a stackyard or 'mowhay', an area of usually flat land (1 on drawing). Here cereal crops were stacked in ricks, which were broken up as and when the crops were processed. The buildings of the fully developed farmstead were dominated by the 'chall barn', a dual-purpose structure with a horizontal division of functions. The first floor was a barn (2a), and the ground floor provided accommodation for cattle (2b) and other animals (2c). The barn lay in close proximity to the mowhay and was used for cereal-processing (threshing and winnowing) and for the storage of the resulting straw; grain might be stored either in the barn or, in some of the larger farmsteads, in a granary, sometimes a separate first-floor room, sometimes a free-standing building (3). Straw was dropped down to the farmyard and taken into a fodder-preparation area on the ground floor of the chall barn. Here it and other raw materials were converted into fodder for the livestock, housed in adjacent areas within the chall barn and in other buildings within the farmstead (4). Some of these other buildings might be of two storeys, with the upper floor used for the storage of hay and straw. Manure from these buildings was stored in a midden in the centre of the farmyard (5). Draught animals were housed either in the chall barn (2c) or in a free-standing building, and there was usually separate accommodation for a few calves (6) and for pigs (7). The sties were often sited near to the farmhouse with its dairy (8), the source of food for the pigs.

The chall barn dominated the Cornish farmstead both architecturally and functionally (Fig 5.3). It was usually the largest building, frequently being the only storeyed structure within the complex, and it housed the central processes connected with the running of the farm economy. At Tressellern, North Hill, the stable was incorporated within the chall barn (Fig 5.3a), and the only other structures, all built later, were some small animal shelters, one of them some distance from the farmstead. Where buildings were added to farmsteads over a period, informal plans resulted, with the components of the farmstead dispersed, apparently haphazardly, over a wide area, as at St Lukes Farm, St Neot (Fig 5.3b).

Where farmsteads were laid out to an overall plan, a very compact grouping might result, with ancillary buildings arranged closely around the principal structure. On some farms, little apart from the chall barn was required. Linear arrangements of dwelling and chall barn served some small farms such as Toddy Park, St Neot (Fig 5.3c, g) and Trefuge, North Hill (Fig 5.3h), and

continue the type of plan common in the 18th century. At Nodmans Bowda, North Hill (Fig 5.3d, i), a stable and trap house were attached to the dwelling, and the livestock accommodation provided by the chall barn was supplemented by some small shelters.

In larger farmsteads, the chall barn still had a pivotal position, often within the type of U-plan or quadrangular grouping advocated by Hanoverian improvers (Fig 5.3e). Two estate-built farmsteads represent conventional ideas on planning most perfectly. Trebartha Barton, North Hill (Fig 5.3f), was built in a number of stages in the early 19th century, and was substantially complete by 1840. An eye-catcher house lies on the south side, facing away from the farm buildings; a large chall barn is sited on the north side, its height and length providing protection from the cold winds; closing ranges provided accommodation for cattle and other animals; and all the buildings together sheltered a sunny open yard where livestock could be kept in favourable conditions. Many decades later, Botternell, North Hill (Fig 5.3j), was rebuilt by the Duchy of Cornwall, and again the principal buildings were grouped around a large open yard. The chall barn, of a slightly different type by this date, dominates the higher northern block, and lower livestock ranges completed a U-plan, later made into a quadrangular plan by the addition of a fourth building for cattle. That the Hanoverian model might result from piecemeal development is evident at Great Hammett, St Neot (Fig 5.3k); here the courtyard plan developed in a number of phases from the early 19th century, with single-storey shippons, pigsties and calf houses grouped around the chall barn.

Some of the most dispersed farmstead plans result from the amalgamation of two or more earlier holdings. Darley, Linkinhorne, is a rare example of a site which in its mature phase of development is not dominated by the chall barn. This building, of modest size, survives from an early phase of development; once perhaps central to the farmstead which it served, it became peripheral when two farms were amalgamated and the whole site remodelled in the mid 19th century (Fig 5.3l). The rationalisation of the two earlier holdings shifted the balance of the farmstead by creating a largely new U-plan arrangement of shippons and stables. The true emphasis within the regional agricultural system is perhaps best reflected in this farmstead, where the buildings around the livestock yard overshadow the chall barn and demonstrate that stock-rearing was clearly the primary aspect of the farm's economy.

On many farms, the accommodation provided within the farmstead itself was supplemented by field shelters. These may have been built in response to the criticism that cattle were poorly

a

b

c

d

Fig 5.3 The layout of the Cornish farmstead. At Tressellern, North Hill, the chall barn is the only substantial farm building, and contained accommodation for cattle and horses (a; BB95/ 390). St Lukes Farm, St Neot, offers a contrast, having small buildings scattered over a wide area (b; BB95/430). Some small farmsteads have a linear plan of house and barn, as at Toddy Park, St Neot (c; BB95/433, and g), and Trefuge, North Hill (h). On others, the house and chall barn are detached (Nodmans Bowda, North Hill, d, BB95/10763, and i). More formal court-yard plans are common in larger farmsteads, as at Lynher, North Hill (e; NMR 15017/46), Trebartha Barton, North Hill (f), Botternell, North Hill (j) and Great Hammett, St Neot (k). The layout at Darley, Linkinhorne (l), results from the remodelling of the farmstead following the amalgamation of two separate hold-ings. (Chall barns shaded dark grey on plans.)

e

Key

1 chall barn

2 stable

3 shippon, cow house

4 cartshed

5 granary

6 fodder stores

7 pigsties

8 calf house?

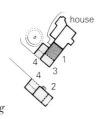

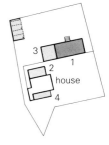

g

h

i

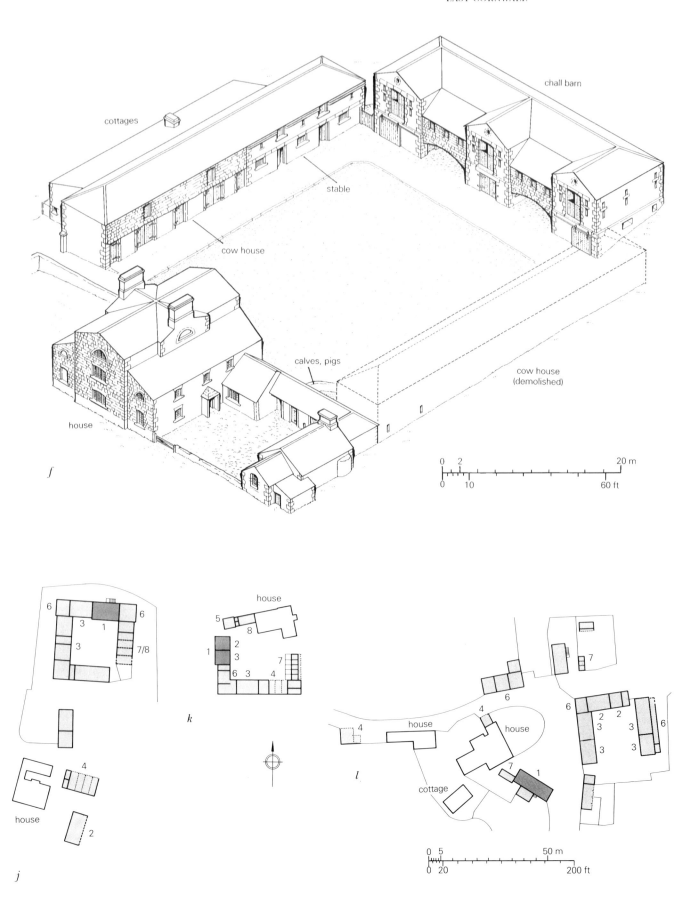

cottages

chall barn

stable

cow house

calves, pigs

cow house
(demolished)

house

f

0 2   20 m

0   10   60 ft

6   6

3   1

3   7/8

4

house

2

j

house

5

8

1   2
3

6   3   4   7

k

house

4

house

6

4

house

4   7

7

6

2   2

3   3   6

3

7   1

cottage

l

0 5   50 m

0   20   200 ft

housed, often having little more shelter than that provided by a lee hedge.[30] Some of the shelters are positioned on the line of field boundaries, allowing them to be used by stock in a number of different fields. Those which survive are well built, answering the criticism aimed by Worgan at their predecessors. They have few internal features, and appear to have been intended to give shelter only from the fiercest weather.

The Buildings of the Cornish Farmstead, 1800–1875

THE MOWHAY

The mowhay or stackyard was an enclosed piece of land next to the barn used to stack cereal crops awaiting processing. In the pre-mechanised era threshing was spread over a long period, and provided valuable employment in

Fig 5.4 The Cornish chall barn. Chall barns vary widely in size, but conform in their chief characteristics, having a first-floor barn over ground-floor shippons (a). Many were built into a hillside to permit easy access to the barn, as at North Bowda, North Hill (b, c; BB95/9900, BB95/10701). Small barns could be built against the farmhouse, as at St Lukes Farm, St Neot (d; BB95/431), but most are free-standing or attached to other farm buildings. At Great Hammett, St Neot (e; BB95/412), East Tremollett, North Hill (f; BB95/356), Lynher, North Hill (g; BB95/383) and Carkeet, St Cleer (h; BB95/10760), the ground floor included an ox house or stable as well as a shippon, but the largest, at Trebartha Barton, North Hill (i; BB95/361), was used entirely for cattle and fodder-processing. The small barn at East Castick Farm, North Hill, has a small root house in an outshut against the rear (j; BB95/9896).

a

c

d

b

the quiet winter months. An undated plan of a farm at Dreynes, St Neot, shows two large rectangular 'mowstands' or rick stands,[31] and a number of farms within the survey area retain remains of either platforms or stands for ricks. The most complete survival is at Carkeet, St Cleer (Fig 5.5), where the rectangular stand (*c*11 x 3 m (36 ft x 9ft)) was made up a grid of flat iron bars supported by short granite posts and bearer beams.

THE CHALL BARN

The workings of most Cornish farmsteads revolve around the chall barn, a Cornish term for the building type known more widely as a bank barn. It is associated very strongly with the rebuilding of the region's farmsteads in the 19th century, and Worgan, writing in 1811, describes the improved 'modern farmhouse ... built upon a more liberal plan'; it had 'every

convenience possible under one roof. The building is called a chall-barn; the ox and cow challs being under the chamber for thrashing the corn.' Worgan's published account includes a number of model farm plans, and each incorporates a chall barn.[32] The building answered the need identified by Worgan for better cattle accommodation on Cornish farmsteads, and at the same time provided an upper floor for the processing and storage of cereals.

Bank barns are common in the northernmost counties of England, in particular in the Lake District. Here there is tenuous evidence for the development of the building type in the Middle Ages, and dated examples from the late 17th century still exist.[33] The ancestry of the building type in the south west of England is not fully understood. Excavation has provided nothing to indicate that medieval or early post-medieval farmsteads incorporated a building corresponding to the chall barn, and the earliest known example of the type in the south west dates from 1755.[34] The building type appears, therefore, not to have been developed in this region, but was very widely adopted in Cornwall in the period when most of its farmsteads were being rebuilt on improved lines. Some of the chall barns within the survey area may date from the late 18th century, but most were constructed in the early and mid 19th century.

The chall barn is prominent within Cornish farmsteads because it was often the largest building (Fig 5.4). It commonly has a hipped

or, less frequently, a half-hipped roof. The building is often built into sloping land to allow easy access at two levels; cattle entered the ground floor from the front of the building, and access to the barn was gained from the higher level at the rear. Lack of a suitable slope did not, however, preclude the construction of a chall barn, for there are many examples in which either a ramp or steps were required to reach the barn.

Cereal processing and storage in the chall barn

The upper floor of most chall barns provided a single room, used as a barn for the processing of cereal crops and the storage of grain and straw (Fig 5.6). Some of the larger buildings, such as those at Carkeet, St Cleer, and Lynher, North Hill, have a separate granary or hay loft, this arrangement reflecting a similar division on the ground floor between the main cattle area and an ox house or stable. Most barns have a pair of opposed doorways positioned roughly centrally in the long side walls; the larger barns have two pairs. The rear door gives access out to the stack-yard, but the front door was used only for light and ventilation and for throwing materials down to the yard. The doorways are commonly sheltered by a canopy, often hipped, and at Carkeet a pentice extends the whole length of the front elevation to protect the first-floor openings. Ventilation was often provided by slit openings

Fig 5.5 The mowhay at Carkeet, St Cleer (BB95/10748). In the foreground are the remains of the rick stand, and the chall barn lies in the background, the door to the barn reached by a ramp next to the wheel pit.

Fig 5.6 Barn processing in the era of flail threshing. The first-floor barns usually provided a single undivided space open to the roof. The barn at Great Treverbyn, St Neot (a; BB95/8128), originally had opposed doorways, but the opening in the left-hand wall was later blocked and replaced by a new doorway. At Trebartha Barton, North Hill, the barn (b; BB95/375) has four-leaf doors and ventilation slits to allow some control over light and ventilation (c; BB95/376). The barn at North Bowda, North Hill, provides evidence for the persistence of flail threshing into the early 19th century, for the roof trusses in the central threshing area have high collars, giving ample headroom for the operation of the flail (d; BB95/10704, and e).

or by windows, but in some barns the entry of light and air could be controlled only by the opening or closing of parts of the four-leaf double doors.

The processing of grain crops, involving threshing and winnowing, was undertaken at first using traditional flail techniques. These persisted in Cornwall well into the 19th century. The barns of the period frequently have sufficient headroom to allow the free operation of the hand flail, and opposed doorways in the long side walls created a through draught used to blow away the chaff during winnowing. It is likely that the barn was also used to store straw, to be employed both as litter and as fodder for the livestock. Whether fodder preparation was undertaken in the barn or in the feedwalks is not clear, but the lack of internal connection, in the form either of ladder access or trapdoors, between the barn and the shippons perhaps suggests that most hand-powered fodder-processing was undertaken on the ground floor rather than in the barn. Straw must have been dropped down from the doorway in the front wall of the barn to the yard, and taken directly into the feedwalk.

In 1811 it was said that 'threshing machines are become very general, few farms of any consequence being now without them'.[35] The introduction of mechanised working, however, had very little impact on barn design. Barns built for mechanised working have many features – for example, the opposed doorways sheltered by canopies, characteristic of those constructed for traditional methods of working. There was certainly nothing like the gravity-feed system from threshing machine to a grain-bagging level characteristic of Northumberland barns of the same period (see Chapter 4); in Cornwall, the more limited scale of operation meant that the benefits to be gained from efficient grain-processing were outweighed by the advantages of the dual-purpose chall barn, with its livestock-housing on the ground floor.

Some of the new machines may have been worked by hand, for Worgan reports that 'a thrashing machine, to be wrought by hand, has been invented by a gentleman of this neighbourhood ... The cost of one of these is about 12l. It thrashes wheat remarkably well, and does very well for barley and oats, if carefully fed ... A man and woman, or man and boy, are the force required.'[36] The use of such machines would leave no structural trace in the barn, and it is impossible to assess on the evidence of buildings how widely they were used. Heavier sources of power were also adopted. Worgan states that the new threshing machines 'are mostly wrought by horses, a few by water, and I have heard one of them by steam; but I believe it has not answered'.[37] Richard Trevithick provided two steam engines for threshing in 1811 and 1812, but, despite the familiarity given by the county's mining industry, this form of power was not widely adopted on Cornish farms, perhaps mainly because supplies of south Wales coal were difficult to obtain.[38]

Horse power enjoyed many advantages over water power as a means of driving threshing machines. The capital expenditure required was affordable by many landlords and farmers, especially when small portable engines came into use; the farms might already have horses, and in its most basic form the horse engine, or 'horse whim', was a simple piece of equipment requiring little or no shelter.

The date at which horse engines were adopted on a wide scale is unclear. It is difficult to reconcile Worgan's statement about the widespread use of the horse engine in the early 19th century with what is known of the development of different types of engine and of their housing on Cornish farms. Heavy horse engines required structural support and shelter, and in some parts of the country horse-engine houses, with their distinctive plan and shape, were being constructed from the early 19th century.[39] Tithe maps for the parishes in the Cornwall survey area, however, indicate that in the late 1830s and early 1840s there were no horse-engine houses in the region. In Cornwall these begin to appear only in the mid 19th century. Over sixty examples have been recorded, distributed over all parts of the county.[40] Within the survey area, one horse-engine house was recorded, and this was added to the 1838 chall barn at Lynher, North Hill (Fig 5.7a, b, c).

If Worgan was correct about the common use of horses for driving threshing machines, the horse engines employed must have been of lighter construction, requiring neither support nor shelter. Little is known about the introduction of this type of light installation. Portable and fixed wheels erected in the open air outside the barn were certainly known in the mid 19th century, but it is possible that earlier versions were in use on Cornish farms some decades earlier. The type of open-air installation set up in the late 19th century at Toddy Park, St Neot, may well represent the habitual method of working on small farms from at least as early as the mid 19th century (Fig 5.7d). The light horse wheel could be erected behind the barn to drive a threshing machine inside the barn. This form of mechanised working leaves little evidence in the building; the drive shaft could pass into the barn through the open doorway, or a small opening could be inserted into the barn wall to allow the shaft to connect with the threshing machine.

a

b

Fig 5.7 Horse-powered barn processing. The horse-engine house at Lynher, North Hill, was added to the barn in the mid 19th century (a; BB95/6550). The heavy gearing has been removed from the interior (b; BB95/379), but its general form can be reconstructed (c). Smaller open-air horse engines were probably common in Cornwall. At Toddy Park, St Neot, the circular paved walkway for the horse survives in part, and holes in the walls of the buildings show the position of the drive shaft which took power into the barn (d).

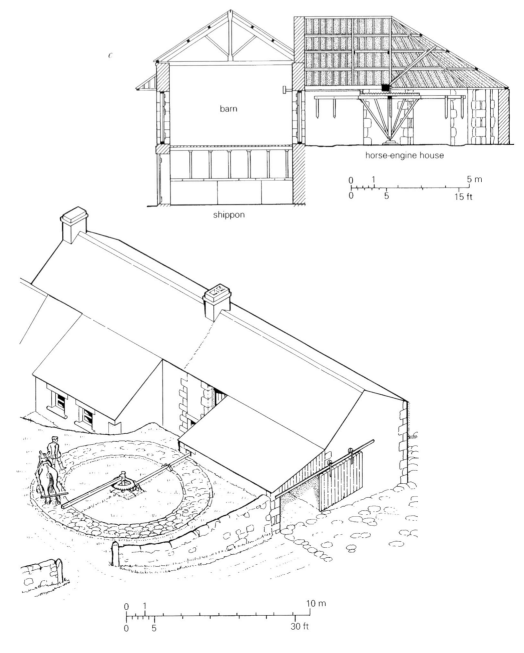

c

barn

horse-engine house

shippon

0 1 5 m
0 5 15 ft

d

0 1 10 m
0 5 30 ft

From the middle of the century, portable horse engines combined with threshers were available, and such machines meant that processing could be conducted entirely outside the barn, leaving the building as a space mainly for storage.

A water-power system was more expensive to install than a horse engine, although it was cheap to run once all the initial costs had been incurred. Necessary work might include the diversion of a water course; the creation of a reservoir; the construction of a leat or launder; the creation of an adequate fall of water, sometimes involving major earthworks; and the installation of a wheel and gearing. The expenditure and complex legal arrangements required for this work were beyond the means of many small farmers and landowners, and water-power installations are found mainly, although not invariably, on the larger farmsteads, such as Darley, Linkinhorne, and Siblyback, St Cleer. There is interesting documentary evidence for co-operation between landlords of adjacent farms at Penhole, North Hill, for in 1864 an agreement was reached to share the costs involved in creating a water-power system; the agreement states that 'it would be a great improvement ... (to the estates) ... if sufficient water power for working agricultural machinery ... were provided'.[41] The shared use of the resource persisted until the early 20th century, each farm having the use of the water power for three days each week.

On farms with a water-power system, the waterwheel was sited against the rear wall of the barn, its level being determined by the need for a good fall of water (Fig 5.8). At some sites, the wheel was sheltered within a wheelhouse, but on others it was open to the elements. Drive was usually taken from a toothed spur wheel and transmitted into the barn by a system of gears. Water-power systems were installed to drive threshing and winnowing machines, but, when portable steam engines took over this work in the more accessible areas in the late 19th century, the water power continued to be used on some sites to turn millstones, probably for the preparation of fodder rather than of grain. The best survival is at Trefuge, North Hill, where the stones are set over the wheel pit.

Livestock accommodation in the chall barn
There are a number of basic types of chall barn, which may be classified according to the way in which cattle were accommodated on the ground floor. Each type might have a number of variant forms, determined by the overall size of the building. There is a typological evolution towards a widely accepted standard layout, but there is only tenuous evidence within the survey area for a chronological development in line with the typology. The most that can be claimed is that some of the buildings which are thought to be of early date lack the sophistication in terms of plan demonstrated by later examples. The buildings at Lower Penhole, North Hill, and Great Treverbyn, St Neot, may date from the late 18th or early 19th century, and both have a single doorway on the front wall into the ground floor. The details of the internal arrangements are not clear, but it is possible that cattle were tied in a single row running the length of the building, perhaps with a feeding passage against the rear wall. A later, mid 19th-century example of the type is the chall barn at Lower Bowden, St Neot (Fig 5.9a). The rebuilding of Botternell, North Hill, by the Duchy of Cornwall in the late 19th century also incorporated a chall barn with a single long row of tyings, extending into other buildings in the courtyard layout (Fig 5.9b). The adoption of this plan by the Duchy probably reflects contemporary opinion that infection was less easily transmitted where cattle were stalled in a single row than in buildings where the beasts faced each other across a feeding passage.[42]

Most chall barns were planned to provide standings and tyings for cattle arranged in rows across the building. Some layouts were more convenient than others. At Great Hammett, St Neot (Fig 5.10a), the ground floor was divided into two rooms, the smaller an ox house or stable, the larger a shippon for cattle. The shippon has a single doorway in the centre of the front wall, and cattle were tied in rows facing the end walls. Feeding the cattle would have been awkward, for the plan fails to provide a passage giving easy access to mangers. The chall barn at Littleworth, St Neot (Fig 5.10b), also fails in this respect; here the ground floor is divided into two small shippons, and the cattle were tied to face the central dividing wall.

The more convenient plans provide separate access for beasts and for feeding. The majority of chall barns are based upon a system of rows of cattle facing into feedwalks running from front to back across the building (Fig 5.11). The feedwalk might be a simple passage providing easy access to the mangers, but in the better buildings it was wide enough to give space for the storage of feed-stuffs and for mixing fodder; these wider feedwalks have a double doorway in the front wall. Small hand-powered machines for fodder-processing – chaff-cutters, root-choppers, and cake-breakers – were probably set up in the larger feedwalks. The feedwalk was divided from the cattle by low slate or granite partitions, against which were set mangers or troughs. The cattle were tied to wooden stiddle (or studdle) posts, and stood on raised standings draining to a gutter.

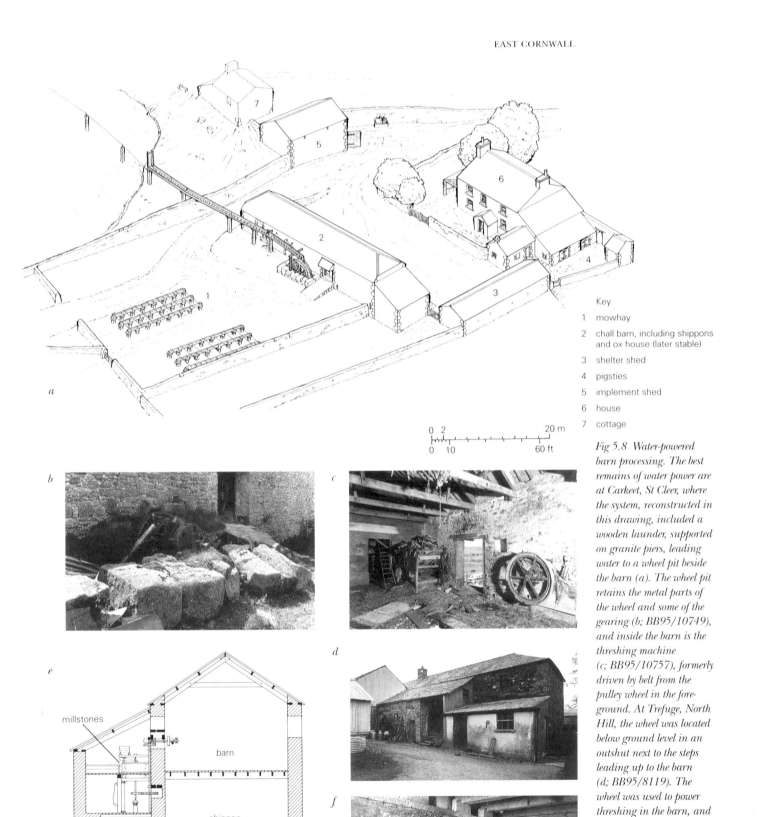

Key

1 mowhay
2 chall barn, including shippons and ox house (later stable)
3 shelter shed
4 pigsties
5 implement shed
6 house
7 cottage

Fig 5.8 Water-powered barn processing. The best remains of water power are at Carkeet, St Cleer, where the system, reconstructed in this drawing, included a wooden launder, supported on granite piers, leading water to a wheel pit beside the barn (a). The wheel pit retains the metal parts of the wheel and some of the gearing (b; BB95/10749), and inside the barn is the threshing machine (c; BB95/10757), formerly driven by belt from the pulley wheel in the fore-ground. At Trefuge, North Hill, the wheel was located below ground level in an outshut next to the steps leading up to the barn (d; BB95/8119). The wheel was used to power threshing in the barn, and was later applied to turn millstones grinding corn for fodder (e; reconstruction of the water-power system). The millstones were later driven from a shaft turned by belt drive from a tractor (f; BB95/8125).

109

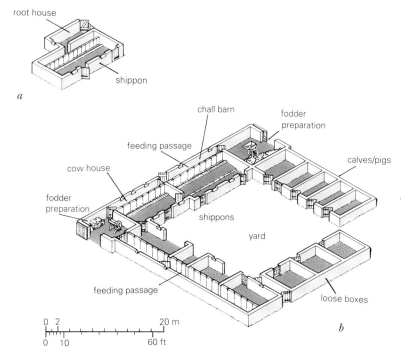

a

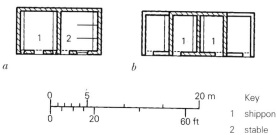

Fig 5.9 (left) Livestock accommodation in the chall barn (1). In some chall barns, cattle were tied in a single row running the length of the building, as at Lower Bowden, St Neot (a). At Botternell, North Hill, the rows extended beyond the chall barn into other buildings around two sides of the yard, connecting with a fodder-preparation room at either end of the main range (b).

a

b

0   5   20 m
0   20   60 ft

Key
1   shippon
2   stable

Fig 5.10 (above) Livestock accommodation in the chall barn (2). The plans of Great Hammett, St Neot (a), and Littleworth, St Neot (b), illustrate the type of shippon in which cattle were tied in rows across the building but which lacked a feeding passage.

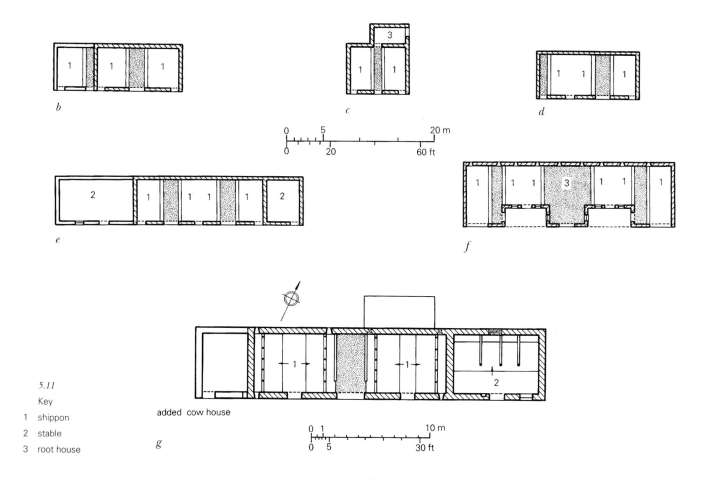

b

c

d

0   5   20 m
0   20   60 ft

e

f

5.11
Key
1   shippon
2   stable
3   root house

g

added cow house

0   1   10 m
0   5   30 ft

a

h

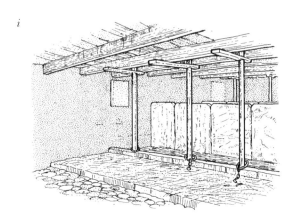

i

Fig 5.11 *Livestock accommodation in the chall barn (3). The view of Trefuge, North Hill (a; BB95/8121), shows the typical form of the cross-shippon chall barn, with multiple doorways into the ground floor; the wide double doorway (later blocked and converted to windows) opened into the feedwalk, the narrow doorway to either side into the shippons, and the doorway at the extreme left into a second feedwalk (see plan, d). The plans (feedwalks shaded) show how this type of chall barn could be adapted to meet the requirements of different farms: Nodmans Bowda, North Hill (b); East Castick Farm, North Hill (c); Trefuge, North Hill (d); Lynher, North Hill (e); Trebartha Barton, North Hill (f). The plan of Carkeet, St Cleer (g), shows the internal arrangements in more detail, with troughs and stiddle posts, and internal views of the shippon at this farm (h; BB95/10758, and i) show the low, dark accommodation. At Trewithey, North Hill (j), short wooden partitions divided the rows into double stalls, with cattle tied to stout posts. At East Castick Farm, North Hill (k; BB95/9897), a root house was contained in a lean-to against the rear wall of the barn.*

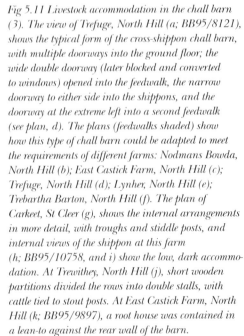

k

j

Fig 5.12 Cattle shelters. At Carkeet, St Cleer, a shelter shed, formerly open fronted but later enclosed, was built at right angles to the chall barn (a; BB95/10751). At Dozmaryhill Cottage, St Neot, a moorland smallholding, the farmstead lacks a two-storey chall barn, and cattle were accommodated in two shippons divided by a central feedwalk, with, at the low end, a small loose box or fodder room (b; BB95/ 6556). Small linhay-type buildings were also built on some farms, providing a loft over accommodation for cattle; the linhay at Darley, Linkinhorne (c; BB95/10715), had the floor removed when it was converted to shelter machinery.

Ventilation was sometimes provided by slit openings, more rarely by windows, but often the only light and air entering the shippons came from the doorway openings.[43] Manure was removed from the stalls through the doorway used by the cattle, and probably piled in the centre of the yard to decompose before being taken to the arable fields.

OTHER CATTLE ACCOMMODATION IN THE CORNISH FARMSTEAD

The chall barn was the principal building for livestock on many Cornish farms, and could combine shippons with a separate room for oxen or horses. Where more accommodation was required, a lean-to could be built against the end wall of the chall barn, and at some farms a full two-storeyed extension was added; at Nodmans Bowda, North Hill, the ground floor of the extension has both a shippon and a feedwalk, with a straw or hay loft over (Fig 5.11b).

On a number of farms, there was a need for more cattle accommodation than could easily be provided by the chall barn and some limited extensions. Other buildings, sometimes attached to the chall barn, sometimes detached, were grouped around the farmyard, in some cases producing a developed courtyard plan (Fig 5.12). At Lynher, North Hill, a detached L-shaped range was largely made up of shippons, and at Carkeet, St Cleer, an open-fronted shelter shed was built on the lower side of the farmyard. Some farmsteads have a type of small linhay building with an open shelter on the ground floor and a hay loft over. The front wall appears to have been entirely open, with a superstructure of short 'loft posts' jointed to principal rafter trusses.[44]

A number of farmsteads have quite sizeable detached cow houses of two storeys, the upper floor being used as a hay or straw loft (Fig 5.13). Some of these cow houses bear a resemblance to the Devon linhay, having an open ground floor but, unlike the Devon linhay, an upper floor with a slate-hung, timber-framed front wall, lightening the loading on the granite lintels and on the piers defining the ground-floor bays.[45] Those buildings with an open ground floor provided a simple shelter connecting with the farmyard, but those with a stone ground-floor wall by definition provided enclosed accommodation. Their doorway openings demonstrate that the pattern of shippons and feedwalks common in chall barns was also a feature of these buildings. The hay loft usually has pitching eyes on the front wall, allowing fodder to be loaded into the upper floor.

At two of the larger farmsteads the additional accommodation for cattle was integrated within a

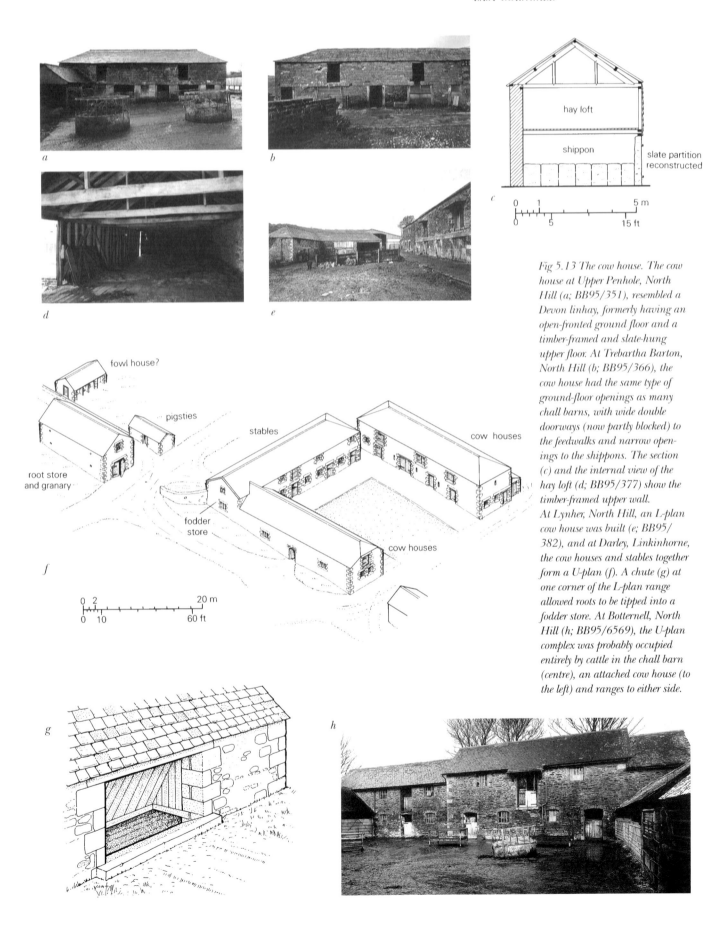

a

b

c

hay loft

shippon

slate partition
reconstructed

0   1   5 m
0   5   15 ft

d

e

fowl house?

pigsties

stables

cow houses

root store
and granary

fodder
store

cow houses

f

0   2   20 m
0   10   60 ft

*Fig 5.13 The cow house. The cow
house at Upper Penhole, North
Hill (a; BB95/351), resembled a
Devon linhay, formerly having an
open-fronted ground floor and a
timber-framed and slate-hung
upper floor. At Trebartha Barton,
North Hill (b; BB95/366), the
cow house had the same type of
ground-floor openings as many
chall barns, with wide double
doorways (now partly blocked) to
the feedwalks and narrow openings to the shippons. The section
(c) and the internal view of the
hay loft (d; BB95/377) show the
timber-framed upper wall.
At Lynher, North Hill, an L-plan
cow house was built (e; BB95/
382), and at Darley, Linkinhorne,
the cow houses and stables together
form a U-plan (f). A chute (g) at
one corner of the L-plan range
allowed roots to be tipped into a
fodder store. At Botternell, North
Hill (h; BB95/6569), the U-plan
complex was probably occupied
entirely by cattle in the chall barn
(centre), an attached cow house (to
the left) and ranges to either side.*

g

h

Fig 5.14 Stables. On most Cornish farmsteads, stables were small buildings. At East Castick Farm, North Hill (a; BB95/9893), the stable, in the right foreground, lies a little distance from the barn, and at Lower Bowden, St Neot (b; BB95/427), it is set beyond the end of the range of pigsties, with easy access to the fields. The large farmstead at Trebartha Barton, North Hill, has an extensive stable (c; BB95/364), divided into two rooms, with space for perhaps eight horses. A large hay loft over the stable stored fodder, and the upper walls were used to provide nesting boxes for pigeons.

layout which included both the housing of live-stock and a system for feeding them. At Darley, Linkinhorne, the mid 19th-century remodelling produced a U-plan, with two-storeyed ranges on three sides of a large yard (Fig 5.13f). To east and west were cow houses with hay lofts, and to the north were stables, again with a fodder loft. In the angle between the stable and one of the cow houses was a root house, supplied through a chute in the rear wall; the root house connected directly with a feeding passage running the length of the cow house. The other, detached, cow house has a root house at the rear, connecting with feeding passages within the building. The second large farmstead, Botternell, North Hill, was laid out on a U-plan by the Duchy estate in the 1890s. The linking range was made up of the chall barn, a cow house with loft over, and, at either end, a fodder-preparation room. One of the flanking ranges was a single-storey block of cow houses, with a feeding passage along the rear wall connecting with a root house. The other flanking range was made up of calf houses.

The covered yard for cattle did not form a part of the Cornish farmstead. Recommended from the mid 19th century as a way of accelerating the fattening of livestock and of maintaining the quality of the manure, it was deemed inappropriate to the needs of the area. The mild climate may have had a bearing on the issue, but perhaps more influential were the fact that manure quality was a less vital concern in Cornwall than in more dominantly arable regions, and the practice of selling livestock on for fattening in other counties. The absence of the covered yard in Cornwall may be a reminder that the county was one where stock were raised, but not finished.

STABLES AND OX HOUSES

Until the mid 19th century, the ox was in common use on Cornish farmsteads as a draught animal. It is, therefore, likely that the separate room provided on the ground floor of some chall barns was originally used to house oxen. At Carkeet, St Cleer, the present stable fittings are clearly insertions, and it is probable that they date from a refitting when the ox house was converted for use by horses. No possible ox house retains original features which allow a positive identification.

Whether as part of the chall barn or as detached structures, stables are not prominent components of the Cornish farmstead. On the small farms of the region, few horses were required for fieldwork and haulage, there is little evidence for the provision of a system of horse yards common in more predominantly arable areas, and there is a general absence of riding-horse stables. Stables for two or three horses were sometimes provided within the chall barn, as at Lynher, North Hill, and a number of farmsteads have detached stables (Fig 5.14). These are usually small, two-storeyed buildings, with a hay loft reached by ladder from the room for the horses. At two of the larger farms, probably with a sizeable amount of arable land, more extensive stabling was incorporated into a formal courtyard plan. At Darley, Linkinhorne, the larger part of one range in a U-plan layout was used for stabling, with a tack room and a fodder room at one end. At Trebartha Barton, North Hill, two adjacent rooms provided accommodation for perhaps eight horses; a wooden stall division survives, and there is evidence of a drop-feed system from the hay loft. In contrast to shippons, stables have windows providing light and ventilation, and the better rooms have sloping cobble floors.

CALF HOUSES, PIGSTIES, POULTRY HOUSES AND SHEEP SHEDS

Calves were the most important product of many Cornish farms, but it is likely that they were kept outside for much of the raising period before sale for further fattening. Many farmsteads do, however, have outbuildings which could have been used for shelter during severe weather and in the early weeks of life. Small buildings, sometimes sited near to the farm-house, as at Trebartha Barton, North Hill, and perhaps attached to a range of pigsties, as at Lower Bowden, St Neot, were used for calves, which might have been hand fed using waste from the dairy (Fig 5.15).

Pigs were kept on most farms, and ranges of pigsties are a common feature of Cornish farmsteads. It is, however, frequently difficult to determine their date; in many farmsteads they are likely to be late additions to the complex. The common presence of pigsties within the farmstead rather than attached to cottages probably indicates that the system of cow rent described by Worgan in 1811 had decayed by the middle of the 19th century; it would appear that the farming family rather than labourers were taking advantage of dairy waste to fatten swine.

a

b

Fig 5.15 Calf houses. Calves were often kept in a small range adjacent to the farmhouse. At Trebartha Barton, North Hill (a; BB95/6560), the courtyard beside the house has (to the right) a wash house with an external boiler for preparing feed, and (to the left) a range providing calf houses. At Lower Bowden, St Neot (b; BB95/426), the calf house is at the near end of the range of pigsties, and lies closest to the house.

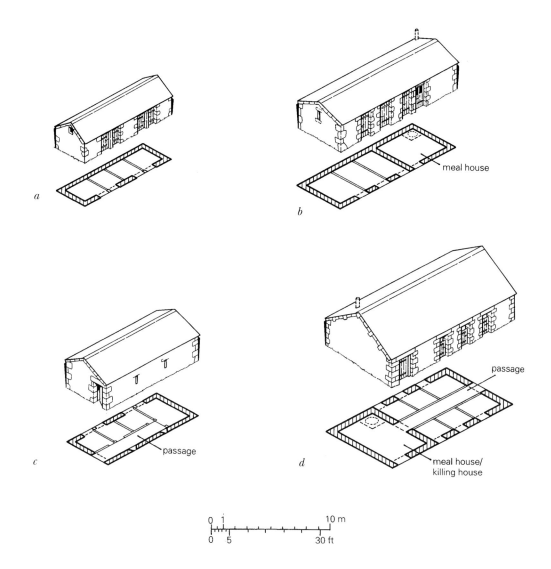

a

b   meal house

c   passage

d   passage

meal house/
killing house

0   1   10 m
0   5   30 ft

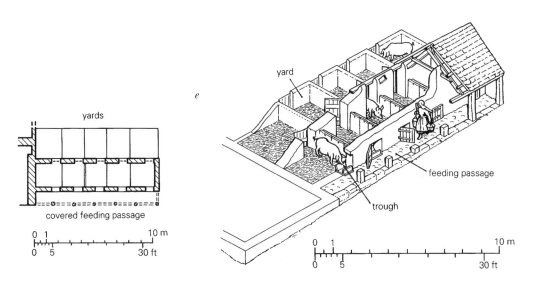

e

yards   yard

covered feeding passage   feeding passage

0   1   10 m   trough
0   5   30 ft

0   1   10 m
0   5   30 ft

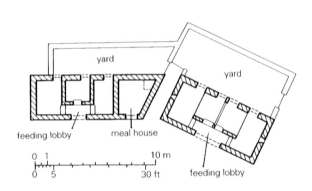

Fig 5.16 Pigsties. Trefuge, North Hill: sties with no yards (a); North Bowda, North Hill: sties with meal house (b); Lynher, North Hill: sties with feeding passage along rear wall (c); West Tremollett, North Hill: sties with central feeding passage and meal house at one end (d); Great Hammett, St Neot: sties with yards and covered external feeding passage (e); Great Treverbyn, St Neot: sties with shared yards and feeding lobby, one range with meal house (f); Carkeet, St Cleer: interior view showing troughs and low granite partitions (g; BB95/10754).

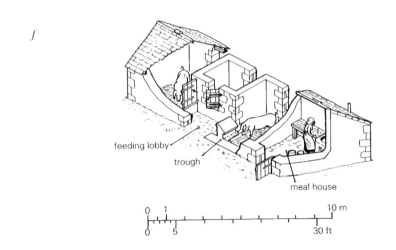

Pigsties have a variety of plan forms (Fig 5.16). A meal house was sometimes incorporated within the piggery, but the usual proximity of the sties to the farmhouse, the source of kitchen and dairy waste for swill, suggests that fodder preparation was usually undertaken here, by the farmer's wife, who was commonly responsible for this aspect of dairying. Where the farmstead included farm labourers' cottages, as at Trebartha Barton, North Hill, further pigsties might be provided. Some pigsties connected with individual yards, as at Great Hammett, St Neot, and others with a small shared yard, as at Great Treverbyn, St Neot. Others, like those at Lower Bowden, St Neot, appear to have lacked any form of connecting enclosure, and may have been used specifically for fattening.

Some farmsteads also had a killing house, at best a room with a boiler for heating water, and beams and hooks for hanging carcases. The meal house in the piggery at West Tremollett, North Hill, appears to have been used also as a killing house, despite its proximity to the sties; it had a boiler in one corner, and there are two beams with hooks.

Hen houses are not a common feature of Cornish farmsteads. Hen lofts, with a small entrance hole high in a wall, are found in a few cases, but are not often set over pigsties, as they are in other parts of the country. Pigeon nesting boxes were, however, often provided in the upper walls of chall barns and stables.

The poorer upland areas on and around Bodmin Moor were grazed by large numbers of sheep, but, as in other parts of the country, this important aspect of the regional economy is poorly represented by permanent buildings. Sheep needed shelter in only the most severe conditions and during the lambing season.

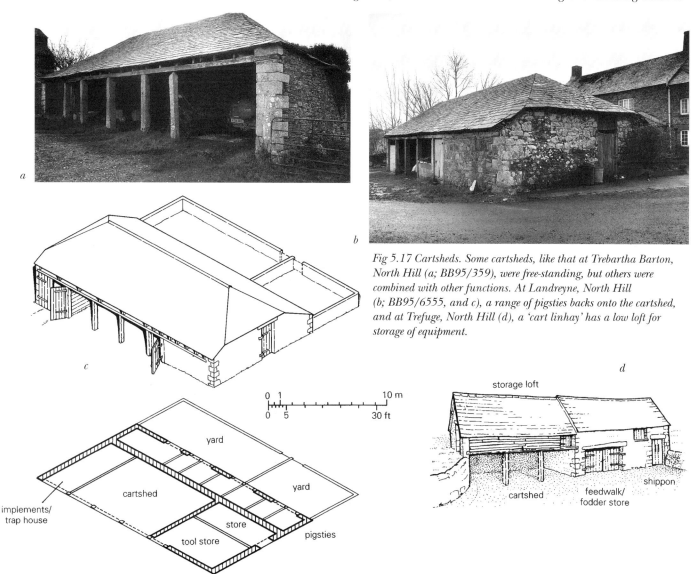

Fig 5.17 Cartsheds. Some cartsheds, like that at Trebartha Barton, North Hill (a; BB95/359), were free-standing, but others were combined with other functions. At Landreyne, North Hill (b; BB95/6555, and c), a range of pigsties backs onto the cartshed, and at Trefuge, North Hill (d), a 'cart linhay' has a low loft for storage of equipment.

Some of the shelter sheds which form a part of a number of farmsteads may have been used for sheep, but none of these structures has structural evidence which demonstrates this conclusively. The farmyards were doubtless used for sheep-handling, but nothing survives of the hurdles used during marshalling and segregating the animals.

CARTSHEDS

Large cartsheds are not a feature of Cornish farmsteads. Carts and wagons were certainly used, but even the largest farms required only a few vehicles. These were easily accommodated in an open-fronted shed of at most five or six bays, defined by roughly squared granite piers supporting the wall plate (Fig 5.17a). At Landreyne, North Hill, the four-bay cartshed was combined with a range of pigsties and a tool store (Fig 5.17b, c). At Landreyne and at Trebartha Barton, North Hill, the cartshed faces north in the recommended manner to protect the vehicles from the sun and the driving rain.

GRANARIES AND CIDER HOUSES

On the larger farmsteads, perhaps those growing cereals for sale rather than mainly for fodder, a granary was commonly provided on the first floor of the chall barn. Such rooms had their own separate entrance at the rear and sometimes, as at Lynher, North Hill, a loading door in the front elevation (Fig 5.18a). The granary at Lynher has wooden partitions dividing the room into grain bins. Where chall barns lack a separate granary, grain was probably most commonly stored in the barn to await processing into animal fodder. At Lower Bowden, St Neot, there are grain bins at one end of the barn (Fig 5.18b). Granaries

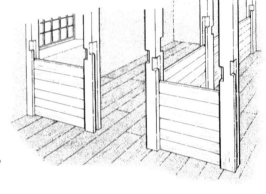

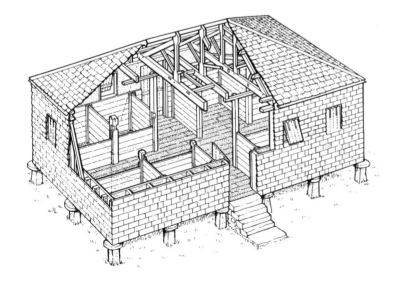

Fig 5.18 Granaries. At Lynher, North Hill (a; BB95/ 380), the granary, which retains its corn bins, was located over the stable in the chall-barn range. Grain bins at Lower Bowden, St Neot (b), allowed storage within the barn itself. The largest granary recorded was at Trebartha Barton, North Hill (c); this detached building was raised on staddle stones, and formerly had wooden bin divisions (reconstructed in drawing). A smaller granary of the same type survives at Trefuge, North Hill (d; BB95/8120).

Fig 5.19 Cider-making. Apple mills were once common in Cornwall, but now survive mainly as garden ornaments, as at Siblyback, St Cleer (a; BB95/6568). At Lower Penhole, North Hill, a substantial outbuilding (b; BB95/ 354) was used for cider-making, and retains its apple press (c; BB95/355).

detached from the barn formed a part of a few farmsteads. At Great Hammett, St Neot, a small first-floor room in a range near to the chall barn was used as a granary, and two farmsteads have free-standing granaries, timber-framed and raised on granite staddle stones. The early 19th-century granary at Trebartha Barton, North Hill (Fig 5.18c), is a substantial building and indicates that the farm produced cereal crops for storage on a considerable scale, but most other granaries are smaller.

Apple-growing and cider production were never as common in Cornwall as in Devon, but nevertheless were an important aspect of the farming economy. The first edition Ordnance Survey maps show that many farms had small orchards adjacent to the farmstead, although 19th-century commentators were very critical of their condition; Karkeek calls them 'very much neglected', and in 1890 many orchards were described as 'pitiable'.[46] Cider-making required a room for an apple

120

a

b

mill and a press, and many farmsteads had a cider house or 'pound house' close to the farmhouse and orchard. Over 120 mills or presses have been identified in the county as a whole, with a marked concentration in the east.[47] Within the survey area, however, cider production has left few traces in the buildings of the farmstead, and there are no certain examples of purpose-built apple-storage buildings or of cider-making rooms. A small addition to the chall barn at Trewithey, North Hill, is known to have housed an apple mill, a number of which survive in the area, in use as garden ornaments, as at Siblyback, St Cleer (Fig 5.19*a*). A cider press is known to have been inserted into the chall barn at Trebartha, North Hill; and a cider press remains in an outbuilding at Lower Penhole, North Hill (Fig 5.19*b*, *c*).

MISCELLANEOUS BUILDINGS

The rebuilding of the farmstead at Darley, Linkinhorne, in the mid 19th century produced two buildings of unusual and noteworthy form (Fig 5.20). One provided three ground-floor rooms with very specific functions, identified in the early 20th century as a potato house, a manure house and a carpenter's shop. The manure house has two wide doorways, and the flanking rooms each have a single doorway. The first floor of the building provided storage space. The second building is again of two storeys. The ground floor was a root store, with a wide entrance in both gable walls, and the first floor was a granary. The two buildings may have made more permanent and specific provision for functions carried out on other farms in buildings of nondescript form, and comprise part of a remodelled farmstead with a clear emphasis on livestock-raising.

Fig 5.20 Two buildings at Darley, Linkinhorne. The potato house, manure house and carpenter's shop (a; BB95/10722), and the root store and granary (b; BB95/10720).

6 CENTRAL CHESHIRE

The dominant emphasis in Cheshire agriculture has for many centuries been dairy farming for cheese production.[1] This continued to be important in the area even after the late 19th-century contraction in farmhouse cheese-making elsewhere in England. The main reason for this agricultural bias is that Cheshire is one of the wettest parts of England, while yet being relatively mild – a combination which leads to rich vegetation and high-quality grassland.[2] As a pastoral area, Cheshire's experience of the post-Napoleonic and late 19th-century depressions was less intense than that of grain-producing areas, and the story of its agriculture from the late 18th to the early 20th century is of the slow evolution of a traditional system, rather than of fundamental changes in emphasis.

The Survey Area

Two areas of the county were selected for survey (Fig 6.1). The first consists of seven parishes at the western side of the Cheshire plain, lying to the west of Nantwich, one of the main cheese markets in the county. The second area is at the east of the plain, on the north side of the Dane Valley, immediately north of Congleton. The plain is not completely flat, but consists of low hills and shallow valleys: most of the land in the survey areas lies between the 50 and 120 m OD contours (160–400 ft).

The soils of central Cheshire consist of varying proportions of clay and sand. The detailed picture is both complex and confused, but, in general terms, the eastern area has slightly lighter, drier and more sandy soils than the west, much of which is too wet in winter for arable agriculture to be successful. Although the clays were suitable for pasture, they could be improved by draining. Writing in 1813, Holland commented that some underdrainage had been undertaken in the recent past, but that much remained to be done. In 1845, however, Palin, in his prize essay on Cheshire farming for the Royal Agricultural Society of England, noted a similar situation, perhaps suggesting that little progress had been made during the intervening thirty years. More telling may be a remark made

some years later by Caird, who noted that many tiles had been laid, but the full benefit had not been felt because the drains were not properly constructed. Whatever the reason, it is clear that by the middle of the 19th century there was still considerable scope for improvement.[3]

Landholding and Tenancy

Cheshire is a county of great estates, over half the land lying on estates of over 1,200 hectares (3,000 acres) in 1873.[4] This seems to have been a long-standing phenomenon, though Holland noted in 1813 that there was also a considerable number of smaller landlords.[5] Perhaps partly as a result of this, the pattern of ownership in each parish was fragmented: few landlords – even the large ones – owned entire villages or parishes. Hence, for example, within the western part of the survey area, the Tithe Awards reveal that, while the Tollemache family was the largest single owner, its lands were interspersed with those of considerably lesser owners – often possessing only a single farm – as well as with larger blocks of land belonging to the Crewe estate and the Marquis of Cholmondeley. A broadly similar pattern existed in the eastern block of parishes, though much of the parish of North Rode was owned by the Daintry family, which was resident in the parish. In general, this remained the position throughout the second half of the 19th century, as is revealed by the records of the National Property Valuation of 1910.[6]

There was an active land market in the early 19th century, and possibly later as well. In 1813 Holland noted that a large number of new landowners, who had made their money in 'trade', had recently appeared in the county. This, he commented, was not necessarily disadvantageous, since new owners were often possessed of greater resources than their predecessors and sometimes more amenable to new ideas, so that they were prepared both to invest and to experiment.[7] An example of this may be seen within the eastern survey area, in the parish of North Rode, where, in about 1810, the main estate was bought by the Daintry family, who had made their fortune in textiles and banking in Macclesfield. Within a

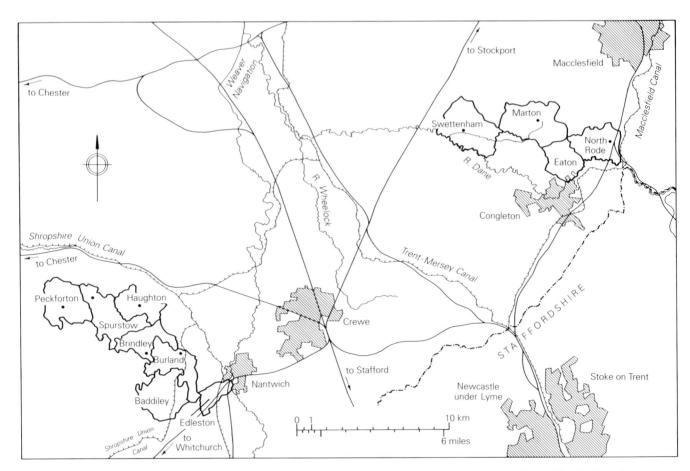

*Fig 6.1 Map of the
Cheshire survey area.*

very short time, a new main residence – The Grange – was built, together with an adjoining home farm (now Bell Farm – see below), and the tenants' farms were also almost completely rebuilt in the ensuing decade.

Whether the Daintrys also reorganised their lands into new farms is not known, but, slightly later, the Tollemache estate was subject to radical reorganisation. In 1824–5 the Tollemache estate purchased 160 hectares (400 acres) from Lord Alvanley in mid Cheshire; later, in *c* 1840, the Tollemaches purchased a larger area from the Mostyn estate in the Peckforton area. In both cases, the land was largely interspersed with farms already owned by the Tollemaches, and, as the leases expired, the opportunity was seized to rationalise the tenanted farms into units of about 80 hectares (200 acres). This involved the restructuring of some existing farms, and the creation of a number of completely new ones – about fifty in the case of the Peckforton area.[8] Hence, despite the fact that much of the arable land in Cheshire was enclosed before the age of parliamentary enclosures,[9] the first two-thirds of the 19th century saw the continued creation of new units of exploitation and, as a result, the construction of new farmsteads.

The sizes of units of tenure were extremely varied. In the 1840s, farms in the western area ranged from 185 hectares (458 acres) down to 6.5 hectares (16 acres), though with few below 17.5 hectares (43 acres) and not many above 80 hectares (200 acres); the average size was 46 hectares (113 acres), though this appears to have increased slightly by the early 20th century. Farms in the eastern survey area were generally rather smaller, having an average of about 38 hectares (93 acres) in the 1840s, again rising a little by the First World War. It is possible that the trend towards larger farms had already begun before the 1840s, since during the Napoleonic Wars most tenancies in Cheshire as a whole were stated to be between 20 and 40 hectares (50–100 acres).[10]

Tenant farmers generally enjoyed freehold tenure, but the terms on which they held the farms were subject to change during the 19th century. Before then, leases for lives were normal, but, by the early years of the 19th century, leases for a fixed number of years – usually fourteen or twenty-one – were becoming more common. The trend towards shorter leases continued thereafter, and by the middle of the century annual tenancies were widespread;[11] this was certainly the practice on both the Tollemache and the Crewe estates.[12] Rents were generally amongst the highest in England, averaging about 30s an acre (and more near the industrial towns) during the Napoleonic Wars, and slightly more in the middle years of the century.[13] According to Holland, the reason for this was the high prices which the main products of the farms – cheese and butter (see below) – were able to command, as well as the necessity for the landlord to provide high-quality buildings if dairy herds were to be maintained.[14]

The 19th-Century Farming System

Writing in the early 18th century, Defoe remarked upon the national significance of dairy farming in Cheshire, and stated that 'the soil is extraordinary good, and the grass, they say, has a peculiar richness in it, which disposes the creatures [sc. cattle] to give a great quantity of milk, and that very sweet and good'. Even at that remote period, 14,220 tonnes (14,000 tons) of cheese were annually supplied to London, with other markets as far distant as Bristol and York, as well as in Ireland and Scotland, also being supplied in quantity.[15] In general terms, this remained the case throughout the 18th century, and in the early 19th century most Cheshire cheese was still of a slow-ripening variety which was sent to London. In the middle of the century, though, there was a change to faster-ripening cheese, which was more to northern taste and could be sold in the rapidly expanding industrial towns.[16] Thereafter, some parts of the county saw a change in emphasis towards liquid milk for the same northern and midland urban markets, but this did not necessitate a fundamental change in agriculture. The main impact concerned the way in which cattle were fed, rather than housed, since it became necessary to maintain an even supply of milk (a 'level dairy') throughout the year, rather than the natural seasonal supply which was acceptable for cheese-making.[17]

The stimulus to change to liquid milk production came from a number of directions. First, there were the newly created northern urban markets, which, particularly after the cattle plagues of the mid 1860s (especially harmful to urban dairy herds), increasingly required milk to be brought in from the countryside.[18] The advent of cheap and rapid transport – in the form of railways – enabled Cheshire to provide such markets with milk, despite its perishability. During the 1840s, railways were opened from Crewe to Manchester and Birmingham, and from Macclesfield to Manchester, but it was not until the 1860s and 1870s that the network of local lines required for the milk trade came into being,[19] and some parts of the county, particularly the west and centre (including the western survey area), were never well served and perhaps partly for that reason did not abandon cheese production to the same extent as areas further north.[20] A further impetus to switch from cheese to milk in the last third of the 19th century came from the increasing competition from foreign cheeses – from the Netherlands, New Zealand and the North American continent – and from the introduction of the American system of making cheese in factories.[21] Cheshire was, however, less affected by the latter than some cheese-producing parts of England, with slightly under a quarter of farmhouse producers in the whole country being located there in 1933.[22]

The dominance of dairy farming meant that there was very little arable land. In the early 19th century, Holland reported that leases often stipulated that no more than a quarter of a farm could be ploughed,[23] and one analysis of the tithe returns for the county as a whole indicates that about 70 per cent of the land was down to grass, though it has been suggested that this figure is rather high.[24] The latter contention may be supported by the fact that the 1870 Parish Crop Returns show that 61 per cent of the county was under permanent grass, though the figure rose again later in the century.[25]

Within this overall pattern of land use, the detailed picture of crop rotations is so complex as to defy classification, with extreme local variation.[26] The basic principle, though, was always the same – to maintain the quality of the grassland. The most common feature of the rotations was that between them the land was laid down to pasture for a number of years.[27] Within the rotations, the grain crops were primarily grown to furnish straw for the cattle,[28] and the most frequently encountered grain crops were oats and barley, used primarily for fodder.[29] Potatoes were also a common crop in the county as a whole, from as early as the beginning of the 19th century, but, after about 1830, turnips and swedes became increasingly important as winter fodder for the cattle.[30]

As a result of this pattern of land use, agriculture in Cheshire was less subject to the post-Napoleonic and late 19th-century depressions which were so much a feature of corn-growing districts. There was a post-Napoleonic collapse in the price of cheese, but it was neither deep nor long-lasting,[31] and, even at the end of the century, there was little fundamental change of agricultural emphasis of the kind seen in a more arable area such as Lincolnshire.[32] This does not mean, however, that there was no improvement in farming techniques or intensification of production; indeed, the developing urban markets demanded a considerable increase in production.[33]

Writing in the 18th century, Arthur Young noted that 'cold clays are beneficial soils for cheese; in general, the worst land makes the best cheese', and commented that liming and other means of improving the land lowered the quality of cheese.[34] It is not clear how widespread this opinion was, but Marshall, writing half a century later, noted that the management of grassland was 'reprehensible throughout the county', and it is clear that some farmers much later in the century were still not convinced that manuring improved pasture and the cheese produced from it.[35] By the 1820s it appears that at least the Tollemache estate was adopting more advanced techniques, since a model lease stipulated that all the manure produced in the farmstead was to be spread on the pasture.[36] Twenty years later, Palin and Caird were able to report major improvements in the quality of grassland, which they largely attributed to the application of bones, as well as manure.[37] Earlier, marling and liming had been carried out on a large scale, and it is likely that the cumulative effects of such treatment, combined with the advance of drainage (see above), was also partly responsible for the improvement noted in the middle years of the century.[38]

The Farmstead

The buildings of the Cheshire farmstead reflect the same gradual improvement of a fundamentally stable farming system, as has been discussed above in relation to the fields. Identical processes, carried out in the same order, required to be accommodated in the late 19th century as earlier. The dominant impression conveyed by the buildings is, therefore, one of slow refinement aimed at greater economy and efficiency within the farmstead. The degree to which these aims were achieved can be seen in the layout of the buildings and the way in which it allows for the integration (or otherwise) of the processes which they were designed to accommodate. Although many Cheshire farmsteads were built in more than one phase, and overall plans can be considered only when they had reached their mature form, owing to the general stability of the farming system there are enough near-complete examples from the early 19th century for it to be possible to discuss farmsteads

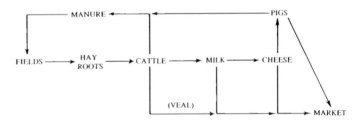

at that date as well as later. Since the processes housed in the buildings remained broadly similar throughout the period from which buildings survive, they will be described first.

THE FLOW OF PROCESSES

The concerns of a dairy farmer were (and largely still are) to provide high-quality fodder and good accommodation for his cattle (Fig 6.2). During the summer, neither impinged greatly on the farmstead except at milking time, since cattle are kept in the fields; after November, however, both animals and fodder have to be protected from damp and, in the case of the beasts, from cold. The basic 19th-century processes which had to be accommodated in the farmstead (Fig 6.3) therefore began with the storage of hay or straw (brought in from the fields in summer) for fodder and litter: they were taken to the farmstead and stored in a place convenient for any necessary processing (such as the chopping of straw) and for distribution to the cattle. Space also had to be found in the vicinity of the cow house (locally known as a shippon) for other fodder, such as roots (or, later, bought-in oil cake). Cattle were accommodated indoors in such a manner that they could be fed and mucked out with a minimum of effort. Once removed from the shippon, manure had to be stored in a midden before being taken out to the fields to assist in improving the quality of the pasture. The shippons also had to accommodate the twice-daily milking process, and were best placed with ready access to the house, in the back of which was the dairy, where the farmer's wife turned the milk into cheese. Whey and other by-products from that process were too valuable a commodity to be thrown away, and were fed to pigs, which were also best kept near to the dairy, so reducing the distance their feed had to be carried. The pigs themselves both provided another product – pork – for the household and for market, and produced more manure, which eventually found its way onto the fields. In addition to this basic flow of processes, the farmstead

Fig 6.2 Simplified diagram of the dairy-farming cycle. Hay and roots were produced in the fields and fed to the cattle, which produced milk. The milk might be sold at market or turned into cheese, which was sold; cattle also produced calves, which were sold for veal. The waste products from cheese-making were valuable fodder for pigs, which provided yet another saleable commodity – pork. Manure – produced by both cattle and pigs – was spread on the fields to enhance crop yields.

Fig 6.3 The flow of processes: Haycroft Farm, Spurstow. Hay and straw were stored on the first floor of the main range, whence they were passed, within the building, to the cattle on the ground floor. Root crops and other fodder were stored and processed in the ground floor of the angle of the L-shaped range, before being passed (again internally) to the cattle. Other fodder was taken to the stable, where it supplemented hay, which was stored in the loft before being lowered into the hay rack. Milk produced by the cattle was taken to the dairy in the back of the house (not fully recorded), whence it was sold as either milk or cheese. The waste products from cheese-making were used as pig fodder, supplementing other feedstuffs, which were prepared in the meal house (with the chimney). Manure from the cattle, pigs and horses was stored in the midden in the centre of the farmyard, prior to being taken out to the fields.

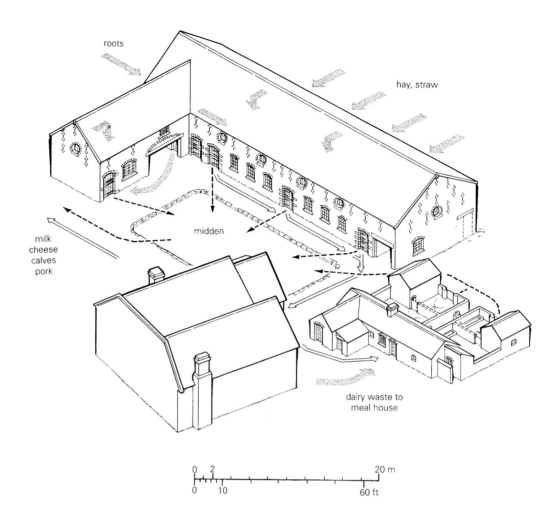

roots

hay, straw

milk
cheese
calves
pork

midden

dairy waste to
meal house

| 0 | 2 | | 20 m |
| 0 | 10 | | 60 ft |

had to accommodate the carts, implements and horses required for work in the fields, as well as fodder for the horses, which, like the pigs and cows, also produced valuable manure.

The close relationship between most sections of the cycle of processes meant that from an early date the main functions of fodder storage (and, sometimes, processing) and cattle housing were frequently accommodated in the same building. Horses and their fodder were similarly housed in a single building, which, together with the cartshed, was often attached to the shippon range. The overall plan was commonly an L-shape, though there are examples of more elaborate U-shaped or extended U-shaped plans on some of the larger farms, and some of the smaller early farmsteads were arranged in a single range or in two ranges placed parallel to each other.

Although there are a few earlier buildings in the survey area, most surviving complexes date largely or wholly from one of two main periods

in the 19th century. The earlier period is characterised by a particular form of shippon and fodder-storage/processing arrangement, and dates from the first quarter of the 19th century. Thereafter, in the second and third quarters of the century, the older layout was superseded by a new one, in which shippon plans were subject to a degree of variation, though the number of types is restricted. As will be demonstrated, so universal was the basic late 19th-century type, that examples continued to be built well into the 20th century. All the changes in arrangement witnessed by the extant buildings represent attempts to find the best and most economical way of accommodating the largely unchanging functions.

PRE 19TH-CENTURY FARMSTEADS

Writing in 1794, Wedge was unimpressed by the siting of farmsteads, apart from those of recent construction, though he thought they were generally in good repair.[39] Two decades later, Holland was able to say that, while the state of farm buildings in the county was very varied, there had been a great improvement in the buildings, though there was more to be done.[40] The only significant information he supplies concerning the older buildings is that they were generally thatched, rather than slated like the newer ones, while a 1773 survey of the Tollemache estate indicates that the buildings then in existence were generally timber framed (one was constructed of mud) (see Fig 6.4).[41]

Survivals from before the very end of the 18th century are rare in the survey area and, probably, more widely within Cheshire. The oldest building to have been located by the survey is the barn at Peckforton Hall Farm, Peckforton, perhaps dating from the 17th century (Fig 6.5). The building, which has stone ground-floor walls and timber framing above, is four bays in length, and originally had an off-centre threshing floor with tall opposed door-ways on either side. It would appear that the building was designed to be open to the roof throughout, in the manner of a traditional threshing barn, and it is possible that such was its function. Given the long-standing dairy tradition of Cheshire agriculture, though, it may be that, while there certainly was a threshing floor, the building was used in a less specialised way than threshing barns in arable areas, also serving as a general store and processing area for hay, straw and any other fodder crops required for cattle, which were housed in detached structures.

A second building on the same farmstead, constructed more crudely, but in similar fashion, probably dates from the early 18th century, and

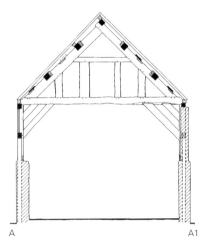

A   A1

Fig 6.4 (above) Early buildings on the Tollemache estate. Vignette showing timber-framed buildings on the Tollemache estate in Bunbury at the end of the 18th century (Cheshire Record Office, DTW2477/8/27, p 27) (AA96/363).

Fig 6.5 An early barn: Peckforton Hall Farm, Peckforton. The 17th-century stone and timber-framed barn at Peckforton Hall Farm, Peckforton, is a rare survival in the survey area. Although considerably altered in the last two centuries, the original form of the building, with an off-centre threshing floor marked by tall double doors in each side wall, can still be detected.

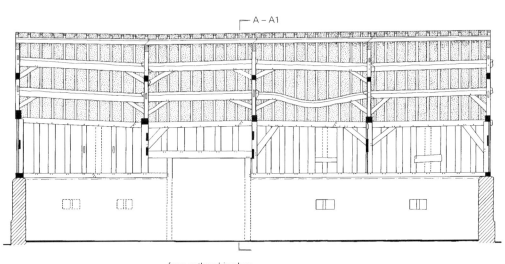

former threshing bay

may have been two-storeyed, with accommodation for cattle or horses on the ground floor and a loft for crop or fodder storage above. Detailed interpretation is, however, impossible, owing to the presence of later fittings for a shippon on the ground floor.

At Green Butts Farm, Spurstow, there is a large T-shaped range of fully two-storeyed buildings, constructed of brick on the ground floor, with timber above (Fig 6.6). The building, though much altered, appears to be of 18th-century date, but more precise dating is impossible. Its last use was as a series of shippons below haylofts, but all the present fittings date from the 19th and 20th centuries, and the original function(s) of the building are uncertain. Apart from a few fragments, such as a timber-framed wall embedded in later buildings at Folly Farm, Swettenham, nothing further can be said of buildings erected earlier than the middle of the 18th century.

No surviving buildings within either survey area appear to have been erected between then and the very last years of the century. However, the opportunity was taken to record Demesne Farm, Doddington (outside the survey area), a model farm of the 1780s (Fig 6.7), designed by Samuel Wyatt, who had been involved in the construction of a number of farmsteads elsewhere in the country, including the Home Farm on the Holkham estate in Norfolk, one of the leading improving estates of its day. The central building is a barn with two threshing floors,

each with deep porches and tall threshing doorways. Between the porches are shelter sheds for cattle, while beyond the ends of the barn are radiating ranges providing accommodation for both fodder (near, but not directly communicating with, the barn) and, at their outer ends, cattle and horses. The whole plan was designed with an eye to both show and convenience, with attention being paid to the reduction of labour required for transferring materials from one part of the farmstead to another. The form of the barn suggests that there was a larger arable element on the farm than appears to have been usual in Cheshire, but, as at the earlier Peckforton Hall Farm, it is possible that at least some of the storage space within it was used for straw and hay, with the fodder preparation areas beyond the ends of the building being used for roots and other types of fodder. However it functioned in detail, Demesne Farm was probably the most advanced farmstead in Cheshire in its day, and represents an important experiment in the integration of functions which was to be the major achievement of the 19th century.

THE 19TH CENTURY

The main building of the farmstead throughout the 19th century was the shippon, frequently, though not always, with a hayloft above. This provided for the accommodation of the most important element of the farming economy – the cattle – together with much of its fodder.

Fig 6.6 Eighteenth-century farm buildings: Green Butts Farm, Spurstow. The surviving 18th-century buildings consist of the T-shaped range in the centre of the present farmstead. Only the shell – brick with timber framing above – remains, and few details of the original internal arrangements can now be understood (NMR 4834/36).

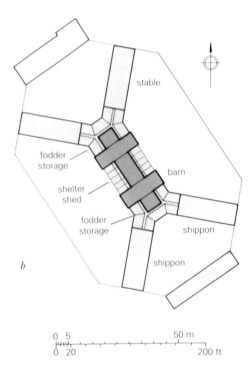

a

b

Functionally linked areas included stores and processing rooms for other kinds of fodder, stables and cartsheds. It was common for all these to be housed in ranges which were either attached or linked by a roofed passage (a drift house, through which carts and animals could pass and under which carts could be unloaded in shelter (Fig 6.8)), or in buildings placed in very close proximity to each other (Fig 6.9). Also related were other functional areas, such as the midden, farmhouse and piggery: the last tended to be set slightly apart from the main block(s) of buildings, since its relationship with the dairy (in the house) was more important (see above).

Shippons, hay stores and barns
The earliest kind of 19th-century combined shippon and fodder store may be exemplified by that at Moss Bank Farm, Marton (Fig 6.10*a*). There, the building consists of four bays, one end bay being a cartshed, and the rest containing two small shippons flanking a barn. Accordingly, the barn is a single bay in length: at one side there is a winnowing door, while at the other there are traditional large double doors, set within a shallow projection or vestigial porch. Unlike the shippons, the barn was originally unfloored, and, in its side walls, there are wide and tall openings giving access both to the shippons themselves and to the lofts above them. This arrangement enabled hay or other crops, which were loaded into the lofts through pitching eyes, to be passed down into the barn

Fig 6.7 Eighteenth-century farm buildings: Demesne Farm, Doddington. Demesne Farm, Doddington, was built as a model home farmstead in the 1780s, and was designed by Samuel Wyatt. The buildings are both attractive (a) and conveniently laid out (b). The barn (dark grey) was used for the storage and processing of cereal crops, while roots and other fodder were stored in the compartments beyond the ends of the barn which communicated with the shippons and stables in the radiating arms. At some times of the year, cattle were kept in an open yard with shelter sheds against the barn (BB91/21843).

Fig 6.8 The drift house: Brindley Hall Farm, Brindley. The drift house is a covered wagon way between the two ranges of an L-shaped block of buildings, through which carts could gain access from the fields to the main farmyard. It also provided a covered area from which hay and straw could be unloaded from carts into the first-floor storage areas (BB94/6097).

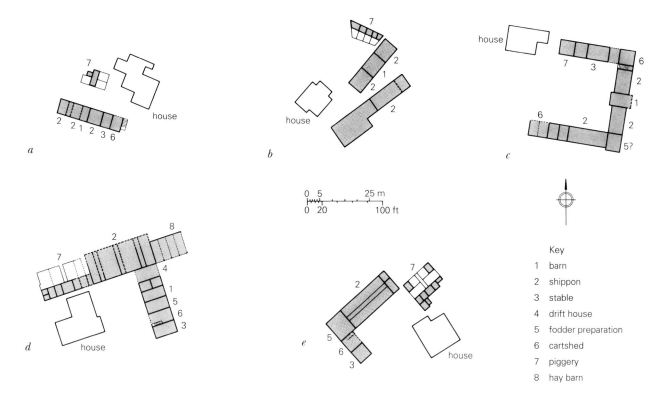

0 5 25 m

0 20 100 ft

Key

1 barn
2 shippon
3 stable
4 drift house
5 fodder preparation
6 cartshed
7 piggery
8 hay barn

Fig 6.9 Comparative farmstead plans. The simplest form of plan is a single range of buildings and, near the house, detached pigsties, as at Green Farm, Burland (a). At Gorseymoor, Eaton (b), the farmstead is rather larger, having two parallel ranges and detached pigsty. Full courtyard plans are relatively uncommon except on some model farmsteads of c 1800, such as Rode Hall Farm, North Rode (c). More common are L-shaped plans, such as that at Haycroft Farm, Spurstow (e), where there is a large piggery behind the house, or the extended plan at Manor Farm, Peckforton (d), where there is an attached hay barn. The common feature of all the layouts is that the fodder storage and preparation areas are placed near to the shippons in order to reduce the amount of labour required for the distribution of fodder.

for processing (including threshing), and then to be transferred to the cattle in the flanking shippons with a minimum of effort (Fig 6.10b – Hill Side Farm, Peckforton).[42]

This kind of layout is also found on some much larger and more elaborate farms, such as those built in North Rode by the Daintry family in the first quarter of the 19th century. At Dobford (Fig 6.10c–d), for example, the barn is very similar to that at Moss Bank Farm, but the shippons are much longer, and the vestigial porch is a later addition. Perhaps of greater interest is the estate's home farm (Bell Farm, formerly The Grange) (Fig 6.11). This is a very grand farmstead, originally attached to the house and forming part of the same architectural scheme. In the middle of the north range is a three-bay unit containing a central barn (Fig 6.11b), with flanking cattle accommodation of similar form to that at Moss Bank Farm (though the precise form is not certain, owing to later alterations). Because the farm had a

6.10c

a

Fig 6.10 The barn, c 1800. Barns of the late 18th and early 19th century were not detached structures, but consisted of a compartment within a multi-purpose building, usually closely related to the shippon ranges to which prepared fodder from the barn was taken. At Moss Bank Farm, Marton (a; BB94/6087), the barn is a single bay, marked by the large doorway set within a vestigial porch. To each side of the barn was a shippon with hayloft above, of similar type to that at Hill Side Farm, Peckforton (b). Hay and straw were loaded into the lofts through the round pitching eyes; they could then be passed internally into the barn, whence they could easily be transferred to the cattle in the flanking shippons; roots and other fodder were stored and prepared in the barn prior to distribution to the cattle. Similar plans could be adapted for larger farmsteads such as that at Dobford, North Rode (c, d; BB94/13559), where there are more shippons. Details of the original plan are not entirely clear, but it is probable that some fodder was prepared in the rooms (which also communicated with further shippons in the side ranges) at the ends of the shippons.

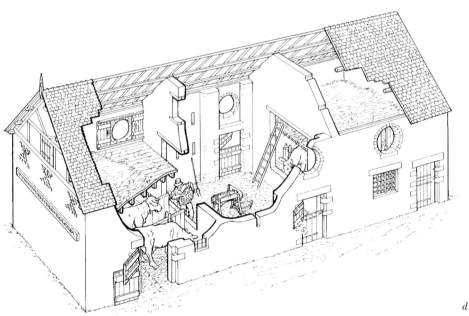

d

b

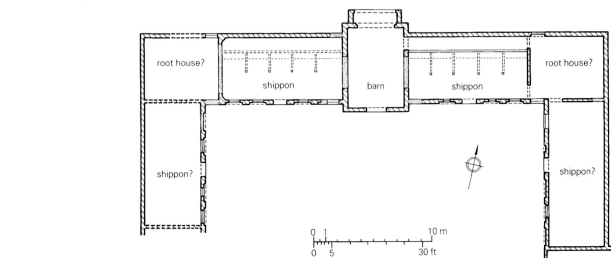

root house?

shippon

barn

shippon

root house?

shippon?

shippon?

0 1   10 m
0 5   30 ft

131

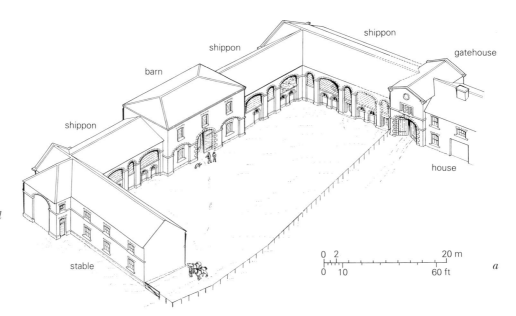

Fig 6.11 Planned farm-stead of c 1800: Bell Farm, North Rode. The plan of the north range (a) is similar to that at Dobford (Fig 6.10c–d), with a central barn (b; BB94/13562) and flanking shippons. The east range to the left of the gatehouse contains further shippons (c; BB94/13577), and the west range contained stables. Beyond the gateway in the east range is the attached house. Although the barn block (b) is three bays long, only the central bay with the large doorway formed the barn, which was similar to that at Dobford (Fig 6.10d). The shippon (c) contained a central feeding passage (byng) into which hay was dropped through the trapdoor in the ceiling (left foreground), before being passed through the openings in the side walls to the cattle which were stalled facing towards the passage.

large number of cattle, the accommodation extends east and west of the barn block, and there is yet another shippon in a return range at the east. All the cattle accommodation was lofted: the first floors are amply provided with pitching eyes and vents, so that hay could easily be loaded into the building and would then be kept both dry and well ventilated.

The shippon in the east range (Fig 6.11c) is of particular interest, since it contains many features which were later (in varying combinations) to become widespread in the county. The building is divided internally into three areas of unequal width, all entered from the north: a narrow central feeding passage, locally referred to as a 'byng' (derived from fodder 'bin'), into which the cattle, which were tethered in the wider outer sections, faced. Only the west standing and the byng were lofted, the east standing being in a lean-to, or 'shoring'. Hay was loaded into the loft through pitching eyes; when it was required in the shippon, it was lowered into the byng through trapdoors in the floor, whence it was passed to the cattle through large openings in the side walls. Other types of fodder – such as roots – would have been prepared in the barn in the central block and taken by hand or barrow across the front of the farmstead and into the north end of the byng, whence they could be fed to the cattle through the same openings. (The apertures on the east side, where there is a load-bearing wall above, have arched heads; those to the west, above which there is no wall, have straight heads: this pattern was repeated throughout the 19th century.) Behind the cattle there were passages which were used to provide access for milking and the clearing-out of manure.

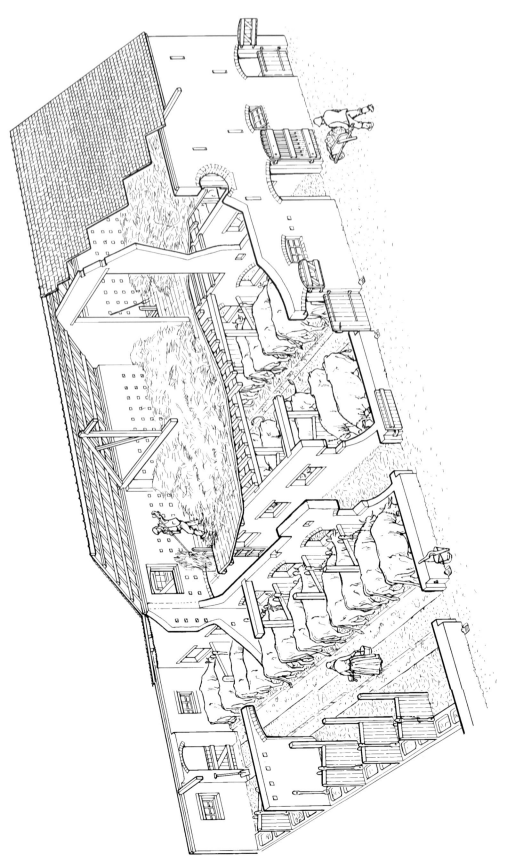

Fig 6.12 Cross shippons: Brindley Hall Farm, Brindley. The shippons were arranged across the building, and extended into a lean-to at the rear. Hay was pitched down from the well-ventilated loft (reached by Jacob's ladders) into the byngs which lay between the shippons. From the byngs (which had slatted doors), the hay was passed through apertures in the side walls to the cattle in the adjacent shippons; roots and other prepared fodder were also distributed to the cattle in this way. Behind each row of cattle was a drainage and manure passage, also used for milking. The two shippons shown here are double – two rows of cattle share a manure passage; at the right-hand end of the building (not cut away) is a shippon in which there was only a single row of cattle. (For a plan of the entire farmstead, see Fig 6.13c.)

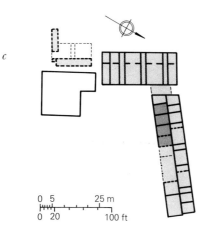

Fig 6.13 Barns on farm-steads with cross ship-pons. The south range of the main block of build-ings at Burland Farm, Burland (a), contained cross shippons; the barn (dark grey), here two bays in length, lay in the east range, which was attached to the shippon range by a drift house (see Fig 6.8). A slightly different kind of barn is that at Fox Hall Farm, Swettenham (b). The main part of the barn (in the foreground) is one bay long with wide doorways to each side, and is open to the roof. The first floor of each of the adjacent bays was open to the barn, providing extra storage space. (The structure within the main bay is a later engine house.) At Brindley Hall Farm, Brindley (c), is a larger and more complex arrangement incorpo-rating four rooms (dark grey) for fodder storage and processing.

a

0 5   50 m
0 20   200 ft

b

c

0 5   25 m
0 20   100 ft

After about 1820 new forms of shippon and hay storage were gradually introduced, some dissociated from the barn, which was also of a different kind. The commonest type of cow house within the survey area is the so-called 'cross shippon', in which the shippons lie across the width of the building, sometimes, as at Brindley Hall Farm, Brindley, extending out into a lean-to behind the main range (Fig 6.12). There is often a series of double shippons, each with a passage for access and mucking-out down the centre, and served by a byng to either side; at the outer ends of the building the last byngs usually each had a single shippon beyond. Haylofts extended the full length of the building, above both shippons and byngs, and fodder was dropped down into the latter through trapdoors, exactly as at Bell Farm, North Rode (above). Farm hands gained access to the lofts internally, by means of Jacob's ladders which rose through the traps. The system was extremely compact, but the ship-pons were usually low, making for poor ventila-tion and lighting, and the cows were so close together that the spread of disease was difficult to control.[43]

Where this plan was adopted, the 'barn', or fodder-processing area, did not communicate directly with the byngs, and usually lay in a range at right angles to the shippons (Fig 6.13a), often separated from them by a drift house (see above); processed fodder was carried across the yard to the byngs. On most farmsteads of any size, there appear to have been two single-bay rooms for fodder storage and processing, one probably for corn crops and one for roots. A relatively early example of this kind of arrangement, which may show a stage in the evolution from the early 19th-century type of barn bay, is at Fox Hall Farm, Swettenham (Fig 6.13b), certainly in existence by 1839 (when it is shown on the tithe map), and probably built after about 1810. There, the barn is one bay in length, and is open to the roof, with wide doorways to either side, those to the west being contained in a vestigial porch. The lofts over the bays at each end are open to the barn, suggesting that unthreshed corn and straw were stored in them and that threshing and other processing was carried out on the ground floor of the barn. The ground floor of the bay to the south of the barn has an external doorway to the west and no access to the first floor: the function of the room is unclear, but comparison with other sites suggests that it could have been a root store.

There was less uniformity in the design of barns, even on the same estate, than of ship-pons, but most are variations on a theme. At

134

Burland Farm, Burland, for example, the barn (built in the mid 19th century) is a single room two bays in length (Fig 6.13*a*). One bay has doorways to either side, that opening into the main farmyard being wide, but the other bay probably originally had no separate external doorway. One of the largest late 19th-century farmsteads in the western survey area, Brindley Hall Farm, Brindley, had no fewer than four rooms which were used for fodder storage and preparation (Fig 6.13*c*): two have side doorways into the main yard, the other a doorway and a window. Details of the way in which this arrangement functioned are not entirely clear, but the principle is the same.

A more convenient overall plan, which seems to emerge in the last third of the 19th century, was for the cattle to be tethered along the length of the shippon range, with a single central byng and with manure passages running the length of the outer walls (Fig 6.14). As with cross shippons, there were often haylofts above the shippons, so that hay could be passed down into the byng and thence to the cattle in the familiar fashion. This kind of arrangement not only allowed slightly greater space for each animal, but also overcame many of the problems of ventilation, since no beast could be far from one of the vented windows which punctuated each of the side walls.[44] The other advantage was that the fodder-processing area could be placed at one end of the building – usually in the angle between the two ranges. This meant that root crops and other feedstuffs could be taken directly from the processing room, through an internal doorway, into the byng, thus allowing the easiest possible movement of processed fodder.

Details of the arrangement in the processing area have almost always been removed in more recent adaptations of the buildings, but it appears that there may sometimes have been two rooms – perhaps a root store and a processing area – though this is by no means certain. In at least one instance – Haycroft Farm, Spurstow – there is clear evidence for the former existence of double doorways to one of the rooms, probably indicating that roots were loaded into it directly from carts. At Newhall Farm, in the same parish (though part of the Crewe rather than of the Tollemache estate), a single-bay barn with double doors to the yard was situated adjacent to the processing area. As in farmsteads with cross shippons, therefore, there was a degree of variation in the precise form and plan of the accommodation for fodder storage and processing, but most types are drawn from the same canon.

Despite the continued popularity of shippons with haylofts above, and the undoubted convenience of the arrangement, there were thought to be serious drawbacks, in relation to both the cattle and the crop above. The loft insulated the cows from the cold[45] – where shippons extended into lean-tos, the underside of the roof had to be lined – but impeded ventilation, with a consequent increase in the risk of pneumonia and other diseases. Despite numerous vents in the side walls, the hay above was not as well ventilated as was desirable, particularly in such a damp region, where it might be brought in from the fields imperfectly dried. There was therefore a risk of damp and mould, compounded by the damp heat generated by the cattle below.[46]

In view of these criticisms of the traditional plan, some farmsteads – though a minority until the 20th century – were designed with single-storey shippons: in almost all, the shippon was arranged lengthwise and the fodder-processing area was placed at one end of the shippon range for ease of communication. At Newhall Farm, Spurstow, the internal arrangement of the shippon has been removed, but the building is so wide that it must have contained a double row of cattle with a central byng and two mucking-out passages. In other examples, such as Moss Bank Farm, Marton (Fig 6.14*c–e*), there was only a single line of cattle, with a byng extending along one side of the building and a manure passage along the other. This kind of plan was adopted on farms both large and small: Moss Bank Farm has a medium-sized set of buildings, but at Sunnyside Farm, Spurstow, much the same arrangement is found in miniature (Fig 6.14*f*). The same basic principle was adopted right up to the late 1920s, when some of the last traditional farmsteads – those built by the County Council as part of the national smallholdings movement – were constructed (see below).

Where the shippons were of a single storey, some other type of accommodation had to be found for the hay. This usually took the form of hay barns – tall brick (later, iron) buildings with one side fully open and the other three at least partially so, to allow for the greatest possible flow of air around the crop (Fig 6.15). Buildings of this kind were already known rather earlier, one of the earliest being at Bank Farm, North Rode, where a three-bay open-sided hay barn supplemented the accommodation provided by the lofts on one of the early 19th-century farmsteads built by the Daintry family. Such an early date is relatively unusual, but during and after the last third of the century a number were constructed to provide additional hay storage on farmsteads where hay was already stored above the shippons. This may be a symptom of an intensification of farming, perhaps resulting from the requirement for greater amounts of winter fodder if cows were to be kept in milk all year in order to supply the fresh milk market (see above).

On a few of the larger farmsteads, intensification and/or expansion meant that additional accommodation was required for cattle, and extra shippons were built, either in detached buildings or attached to one of the pre-existing buildings. A particularly compact arrangement survives at Brindley Hall Farm, Brindley, where

extra shippons were accommodated in a lean-to against the back wall of the range which housed the stables, cartsheds and fodder-processing areas.

Original layouts and fittings survive only very rarely in shippons dating from 19th and early 20th centuries, almost no matter what their form (Fig 6.16). The reason for this is that, from the 1880s onwards, there was an increasing amount of regulation of shippon design in the interests of hygiene and in order to reduce the risk of disease spreading amongst the cattle. New drains were often required, and floors had to be replaced

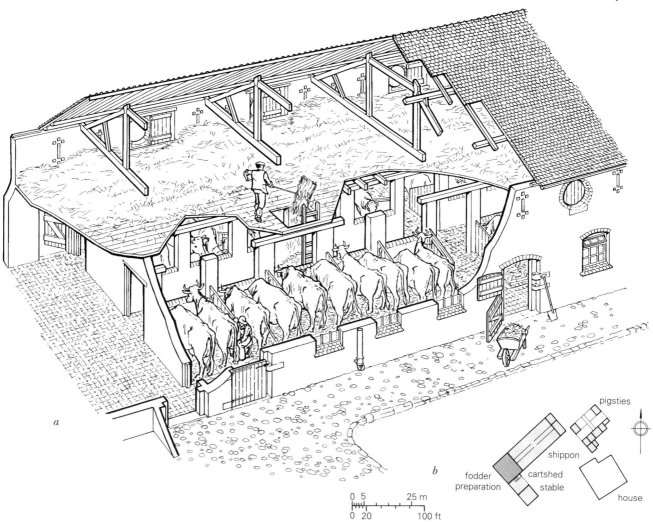

Fig 6.14 Lengthwise shippons. In the late 19th century, shippons were arranged along the length of the building rather than across its width, as at Haycroft Farm, Spurstow (a and b). One consequence of this was that there was a single feeding passage, and it was possible for the fodder-preparation area (grey on b) to be placed so as to communicate with it directly. There was a manure passage behind each row of cows, and a central cross passage facilitated movement within and through the building. As in buildings with cross shippons, hay was stored in the loft and pitched into the byng through traps.

Some later 19th-century farmsteads had single-storey shippons, as at Moss Bank Farm, Marton (c–d, BB94/6086, BB94/6091, and e). The processing room lies in the taller building at the back, and communicated directly with the shippon. Most of the fittings in the shippon (d) are 20th century, but the brick wall with openings which divides the shippon from the feeding passage (right) is original, and is similar to the side walls of the byngs in (a). This kind of plan was very flexible, and could be applied to a much smaller farmstead, such as the miniature one at Sunnyside Farm, Spurstow (f).

with concrete for ease of cleaning, while cross shippons became unusable without major alterations following an insistence that cows should stand back to back, rather than facing each other, to lower the risk of cross infection.[47]

Although it was generally believed to be desirable for calves to be kept entirely separate from their mothers,[48] it is rarely possible to identify calf cotes with certainty. This may be partly because they need have been little different from large loose boxes, of which most farms had at least one. Rooms of this kind were generally almost featureless, save that they might sometimes have a drain in the floor for the removal of liquid manure, or a manger for fodder: they could be used for a variety of purposes at different times – in addition to housing calves, they might be used as bull pens or places for sick or pregnant cows.

Power for processing

The small quantity of arable crops grown on most Cheshire farms meant that large investment in mechanical power for processing was not worthwhile. The most common aid to threshing and to fodder preparation was the

c

d

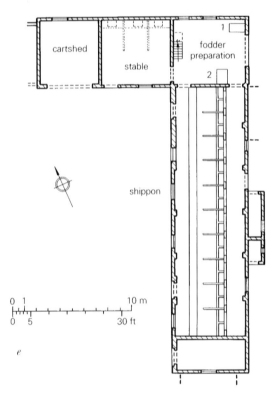

e

Key
1 later engine bed
2 later grain mill

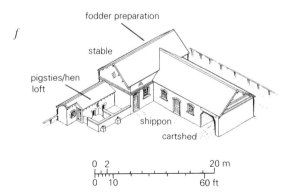

f

Fig 6.15 Hay barns. Most hay barns were detached structures and, in the 19th century, were brick, as at Burland Hall Farm, Burland (a; BB94/19562); the boarding in the gable wall blocks a formerly open arch. By the end of the 19th century, and in the 20th century, similar barns were constructed in iron, as at Cloud View Farm, North Rode (b; BB94/3723), built in 1929. Slightly less common are farmsteads, such as Swanley Hall Farm, Burland (c), with attached hay barns (dark grey).

a

b

external and, probably, portable horse wheel. Such machines are transient, and physical evidence for them is consequently very rare, save that there is sometimes a socket in the rear wall of one of the processing areas, through which the drive shaft was passed. The absence of such evidence is no indication that horse wheels were not used, however, since the shaft could equally well have been passed through a doorway; alternatively, some processing may have taken place entirely outside. It is possible to be certain that horse wheels were once widespread in the county, as they are depicted on the first edition of the 25 in. Ordnance Survey plans (surveyed during the 1870s), where they appear as small circles of broken lines (Fig 6.17).

The dates at which portable horse wheels were used are difficult to assess. Such implements became available in the 1840s, but they probably did not become popular until the mid 1850s. By that time, mobile steam engines were also in existence, though they do not seem to have been greatly favoured at least until after the 1870s maps were produced – perhaps the investment was too great for the limited amount of work they could be expected to perform. That some mobile steam engines were used, however, at least on a few of the larger farmsteads, is indicated by the presence of the remnants of line shafting in the processing rooms (Fig 6.18a). Usually, the engine would

c

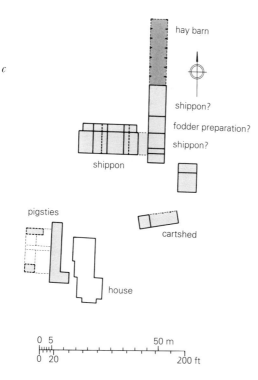

hay barn

shippon?

fodder preparation?

shippon?

shippon

pigsties

house

cartshed

0 5   50 m

0 20   200 ft

Fig 6.16 (below) Shippons: Peckforton Hall Farm, Peckforton. A rare example of a shippon with some original features. The floor has been coated in concrete to meet 20th-century hygiene regulations, but the feeding trough and stall divisions are unaltered (BB94/13610).

have been stood outside, and would have worked the line shaft via a belt drive, but in one instance – Brindley Hall Farm, Brindley – the engine may have been stood inside. The evidence for this is that next to one of the three fodder storage and preparation areas there was a room of similar proportions (now much altered) which was described in the 1910 national property valuation as an engine house.[49] While this does not necessarily reflect the area's original function, there is no other obvious use for the room, and the presence of line shafting confirms that it was associated with a powered system at some stage. There is nothing to suggest that the engine was fixed, since there is no evidence for a boiler or chimney, and it may be that the room was used as a fuel store and standing for a mobile engine, or by 1910 it may have housed a small oil engine. No example of fixed steam power was found within the survey areas, but a small number of Cheshire farms – perhaps the larger ones – did have such engines, as exemplified by Bridge Farm, Tetton, Moston (Fig 6.18b).

Cartsheds, granaries and stables

What grain was produced by the farm had to be stored, as in arable areas, in dry and secure conditions. The usual place was above the cartshed, which normally – in the mid and late 19th-century farmsteads – adjoined the barn or processing area. This was convenient for loading the granary with grain produced in the barn, as well as offering the advantage of being elevated

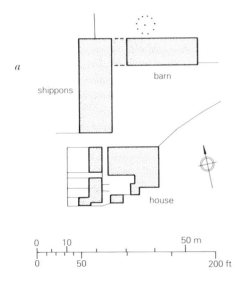

a

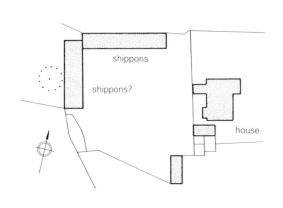

b

a

b

Fig 6.17 (far left) Power for processing: portable horse wheels. Brindley Lea Hall Farm, Brindley (a) and Cappers Lane Farm, Spurstow (b). Portable horse wheels placed outside the buildings were often used to assist processing inside. They have been removed, and there is usually little physical evidence for their former existence, but the early editions of the 25 in. Ordnance Survey maps (here reproduced in simplified form) show them as circles of dotted lines.

Fig 6.18 Power for processing: steam power. Line shafting and a corn mill in the processing room at Moss Bank Farm, Marton (a; BB94/6088), indicate the probable former use of a portable steam engine (later replaced by an oil engine). More unusual is evidence for fixed steam power, such as that indicated by the chimney at Bridge Farm, Tetton, Moston (b; BB94/13581).

Fig 6.19 Cartsheds and granaries. At Baddiley Farm, Baddiley (a), the cartshed (dark grey) is in the same range as the barn; the granary above it is reached by steps in the west bay of the cartshed. There is a more complex plan at Edleston Farm, Edleston (b), but the form of the cartshed (dark grey) is similar to that at Baddiley Farm, and at Brindley Hall Farm, Brindley (d), where the cartshed lies between the processing rooms (left) and stables (right). When cartsheds were added to pre-existing farmsteads, as at Field's Farm, Eaton (c), they might be detached and of a single storey. The appearance of cartsheds is exemplified by Tattenhall Farm, Tattenhall (e; BB93/34748).

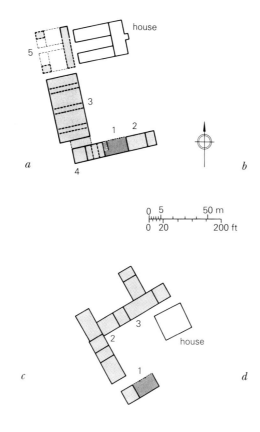

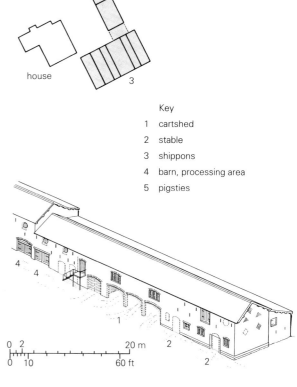

Key

1 cartshed
2 stable
3 shippons
4 barn, processing area
5 pigsties

looking the main farmyard (not usually in the back wall, probably for reasons of security).

The cartsheds below the granaries provided accommodation for a small number of carts or large implements – though fewer than in predominantly arable areas, reflecting the smaller amount of fieldwork. On the L-shaped farmsteads of the mid and late 19th century, the cartsheds almost always form part of the range at right angles to the shippons, and consist of a varying number of bays open to the farmyard. The placing of cartsheds is less consistent in the earlier farmstead, but they almost always still formed part of one of the main ranges of buildings, rather than being detached.

Poorer integration in the early 19th-century farmsteads is also reflected in the placing of the stables, which were usually accommodated in two-storey buildings or sections of buildings, with a hayloft on the first floor. At the Daintry's home farm in North Rode (Bell Farm, formerly The Grange), the stables were placed in the west wing of a U-shaped farmstead, but there is little consistency in the siting of stables on the other farmsteads of similar date built by the same estate. By the middle of the century, however, the stables were usually placed adjacent to the cartshed/granary. In most cases, they lay at the

above the ground. On some of the earlier farmsteads, the granaries were placed in other parts of the complex, though still usually above the cartsheds (Fig 6.19).

Some granaries were reached by external steps, but many had an enclosed stairway within one end bay of the cartshed; in some instances, such as Burland Farm, Burland, there were pitching doors to facilitate loading, and one or more trapdoors in the floor to enable grain to be lowered directly into carts below. Ventilation was provided by means of various kinds of slit vent, or by windows in the front wall over-

Fig 6.20 Stables. The stable is often separated from the processing room and shippon by the cartshed (the wide opening has been blocked), and placed conveniently for horses being taken to and from the fields, as at Haycroft Farm, Spurstow (a; BB94/6065). The main features of Cheshire stables at Brindley Lea Hall Farm, Brindley (b), are a sett floor with a drain behind the stalls, and the hay rack and manger. The first floor above the hay rack is unboarded so that hay could be dropped into the rack from above. Fittings rarely survive, but at Sunnyside Farm, Spurstow (c; BB93/21465), the floor and drain are largely intact, as is the 'pigeon ladder' to the loft and, to its right, tack hooks. There was no drop-feed system here; instead of hay racks there were iron hay baskets in the corners of the stalls: this may have been quite common in the late 19th century.

a

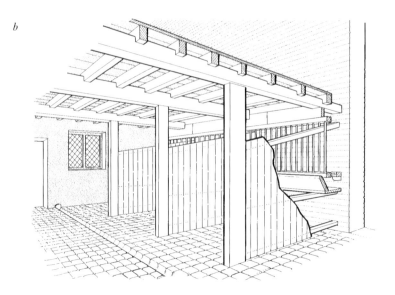

b

c

outer end of the range (Fig 6.20*a*), probably to separate the horses from the disturbance of the fodder preparation, but in a minority of instances they are set between the processing area and the cartshed.

The fittings of stables very rarely survive: one reason for this is that the moment at which tractors rendered stables unnecessary (the early 1950s) was approximately the same as that at which modern electrically powered milking and cooling machinery was introduced. Consequently, the stable was often converted to the new dairy, with the adjacent cartshed (also obsolete) made into the milking parlour. The few examples – of whatever date – which do remain reasonably intact show that there was a drop-feed system whereby hay, which was loaded into the vented loft above through pitching eyes, could be dropped (through trapdoors or slots in the floor) directly into hay racks in the stable below (Fig 6.20*b*). Human access to the loft was internal, and was arranged by means of a Jacob's ladder (sometimes a pigeon ladder), rising though a trap. The horses were stalled in a single line, either opposite the doorway, or at right angles to it, with a drain in the floor behind and ventilation supplied by means of one or more vented window.

Milk-processing

In the age of farm-produced cheese, the milk was processed in the house by the farmer's wife, who, according to at least one leading commentator on mid 19th-century agriculture, was the most important person on the farmstead.[50] The dairy and cheese room(s) were situated at the rear of the house, and once contained fixtures such as whey vats, cheese ovens and, when the cheese room was on the first floor, cheese hoists for lifting them through trapdoors in the floor (Fig 6.21).[51] Such fittings rarely survive, however, since, although the buildings still exist, the rooms once used for cheese production

Fig 6.21 Fixtures for cheese-making. The dairies where cheese was made were in the house: although they have often been converted to fully domestic accommodation, fixtures – such as the whey vats at Lower Hall, Spurstow (a; BB94/3729), the cheese oven at Manor Farm, Peckforton (b; BB94/6072), and the cheese hoist at Brindley Hall Farm, Brindley (c; BB94/6103) – occasionally remain.

have been largely converted to more fully domestic use.

Most of the houses associated with the farmsteads recorded during the course of the survey are of 19th-century date, like the farm buildings. In many instances, the houses were built at the same time as the main phase of the farmstead, indicating that they formed part of the same scheme of development. This is particularly true of the farms on the Daintry estate in North Rode and of those on the Tollemache estate in the western survey area, which were entirely new farmsteads produced as part of a policy of estate rationalisation (see above). This is of some significance, since the position of the house in relation to the rest of the farmstead was a matter of practical concern.[52] It was clearly advantageous for the dairy to be fairly readily accessible from the shippons where the cattle were milked, and also for the pigsties, which received much of the waste products from cheese-making, to be placed nearby.[53]

Piggeries

Writing in 1843, William Palin observed that the breeding and fattening of pigs was widespread in Cheshire;[54] given the fact that pigs were fed on the whey and skimmed milk which were by-products of the cheese-making process, this is not unexpected. Despite this, and despite the fact that dairying had for long been the dominant feature of Cheshire agriculture, there is very little physical evidence for the existence of large numbers of pigs before the middle of the 19th century, even on farmsteads, such as those on the North Rode estate, on which the other buildings were constructed earlier. That this is not a reflection of later rebuilding is suggested by the absence of large numbers of piggeries on the tithe maps and by a lack of widespread evidence for large numbers of pigs in the documentary sources for the century after 1750.[55]

The reasons for the relative lack of permanent pigsties before the mid 19th century may be twofold. First, as with the housing of cattle (in areas such as Lincolnshire – see Chapter 3), ideas on how pigs should be kept changed during the 19th century: before the middle of the century they were outdoors for a greater proportion of the time than was later thought desirable, and the only accommodation required for them took the form of temporary shelters. Secondly, there may have been an increase in the number of pigs on many farmsteads after the first third of the century, mirroring larger numbers of cattle and the greater intensification of agriculture.

Piggeries consisted of small structures: they are difficult to convert to other uses (agricultural or otherwise), and are easy to demolish, since they are usually detached from the other farm buildings. Combined with their proximity to the house, this has meant that survival is relatively poor, though the basic form of demolished complexes can often be deduced from early editions of the large-scale Ordnance Survey plans.

On the few early 19th-century farmsteads, such as Dobford, North Rode (Fig 6.22a), on which pigsties were provided initially, they seem to have taken the form of small enclosed rooms, probably with no yards outside. Later, provision became not only more extensive, but also more sophisticated, with sties arranged on a linear or U-shaped plan, often with associated meal houses, feeding passages and provision for poultry (Fig 6.22b–d). One of the simplest arrangements was for a series of pigsties, each with a small yard outside, to be set in a single line, as at Moss Bank Farm, Marton (Fig 6.22c). Yards usually had drains to remove liquid manure, gates in their front walls, and feeding troughs filled through chutes in the front walls.

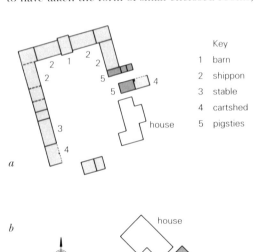

Key
1   barn
2   shippon
3   stable
4   cartshed
5   pigsties

house

a

e

Fig 6.22 Pigsties. In the early 19th century pigsties were rarely extensive, but, where they survive, they are usually at the rear of the house, as at Dobford, North Rode (a). Later sties might be more numerous and/or larger, and on a linear plan, as at Stonehouse Farm, Peckforton (b), and Moss Bank Farm, Marton (c), where there is a fowl house above, and feeding chutes in the yard walls (as at Sunnyside Farm, Spurstow – e; BB93/21463). On some farmsteads provision for pigs was on an even larger scale, as at Haycroft Farm, Spurstow (d).

house

b

0 5   50 m
0 20   200 ft

3

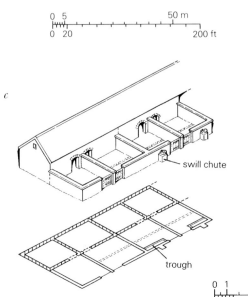

c

swill chute

trough

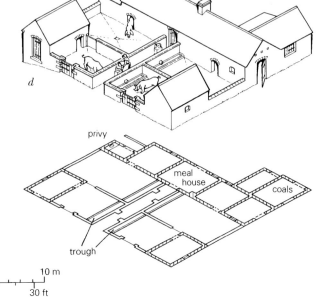

d

privy

meal house

coals

trough

0 1   10 m
0 5   30 ft

143

Fig 6.23 Covered manure store: Dairy Farm, Haughton. Despite widespread recognition that manure was best protected from rain, covered manure stores such as this one are very rare, even in such a damp area as Cheshire (BB93/34744).

Fodder was prepared in the back of the house, near to the dairy, from where it was carried to the sties and tipped into the chutes. Sometimes there was a low loft above the sties in which poultry were housed. There are also more complex examples of linear plans, such as that which formerly existed at Manor Farm, Peckforton, where fodder was prepared in a meal house in the centre of the range, rather than in the domestic buildings. Where this was the case, a feed passage led from the meal house between the central yards, the walls of which were supplied with chutes exactly as described above. The largest piggeries were not linear, but were U-shaped or nearly so. The yards associated with pig units of this sort were sometimes later roofed over (like miniature covered cattle yards), and the sties themselves were associated not only with poultry and meal houses, but also with coal and/or ash houses and privies.

Manure

In addition to using the waste products from cheese-making and thereby producing meat – both for consumption on the farm and as a minor cash crop – pigs, like the cattle and horses, produced manure, which was used to improve the quality of the grassland. Before being taken to the fields, however, the manure had to be stacked in a midden, which was usually placed in the centre of the farmstead, where manure could be taken to it with equal ease from all the animal accommodation, and whence it could be removed easily by cart either round the end of the buildings or through the drift house. Despite the wet climate, almost all middens in Cheshire were uncovered: this was not in accordance with best practice, since it meant that the quality of the manure was

reduced by the leaching effect of rain. Better practice was for the manure to be accommodated under a roof, though with plenty of side ventilation: examples of covered middens are extremely rare, the only one found within the survey area being that at Dairy Farm, Haughton, built in about 1900 (Fig 6.23).

A Continuing Tradition

Even though Dairy Farm was constructed at such a late date, and at a time when few other new farmsteads were being built, and even though it was constructed by an estate (probably that of the Brocklebanks, based at Haughton Hall) as a small model dairy farm with minor architectural embellishments, its fundamental plan would have been recognised by farmers from two generations earlier (Fig 6.24a). The main block of buildings is L-shaped and of two storeys, with haylofts and a granary on the first floor. The ground floor has been substantially altered, and not all of its original plan can be recovered with certainty, but it is clear that the angle between the two ranges was occupied by a fodder-preparation room, and that the east range contained shippons, one of which was arranged as a double cross shippon with a central manure passage. Apart from the covered manure store, the remainder of the site was also fundamentally traditional, including a range of pigsties, and a detached steel hay barn (which may have been erected a few years after the main buildings).

Although few new farmsteads were constructed during the early 20th-century agricultural depression, one of the means by which governments sought to encourage new farmers was the creation of smallholdings of up to

a

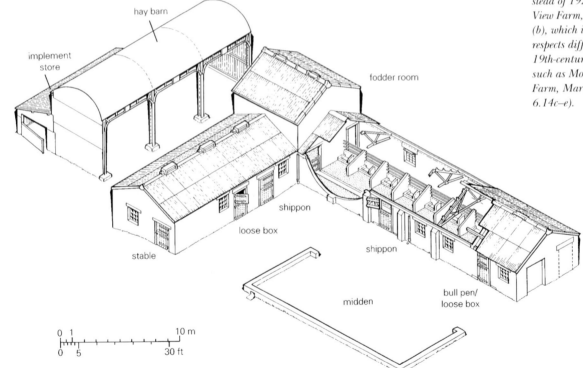

b

Fig 6.24 Late farm-steads: a continuing tradition. The architectural form of the model farmstead of c 1900 at Dairy Farm, Haughton (a; BB93/34741), may appear unfamiliar, but the plan is traditional. This is also true of even more recent farmsteads in the area, such as the County Council farmstead of 1929 at Cloud View Farm, North Rode (b), which in many respects differs little from 19th-century farmsteads such as Moss Bank Farm, Marton (Fig 6.14c–e).

20 hectares (50 acres). Sometimes such small farms were centred on earlier sets of buildings, but in many instances new farmsteads were required: such farmsteads were built to fairly standardised plans, but they were essentially traditional, as exemplified by Cloud View Farm, North Rode, built in 1929 (Fig 6.24*b*). The L-shaped block is retained: the angle between the ranges contains a fodder room with direct access to a lengthwise shippon in one of the ranges and a smaller shippon in the other.

Above the fodder room is a loft, hay being stored in an iron hay barn on the back of which is a large lean-to for carts and large implements, and there is a concrete midden stead in the yard between the ranges. The fact that even such a late farmstead as this, built as part of a government initiative, housed the same processes as its 19th-century predecessors, and in a broadly similar fashion, demonstrates how little Cheshire agriculture had changed during the preceding hundred years.

7 National Models and Regional Diversity

Each of the preceding chapters has sought to present an account of the development of farmsteads in a different region. While the buildings have been set against a summary of the main topographical, social and agricultural features which helped to determine their function, form and date, and reference has been made to the 19th-century literature concerning building design and farmstead layout, the context has largely been internal. In this chapter, by contrast, the pattern of development in each region will be set in a wider, national, context, and some suggestions will be made concerning the historical significance of the farmsteads which form so widespread and distinctive a feature of the English countryside.

The farmsteads recorded can be divided into two broad categories: those which were planned as a whole, including 'model' farmsteads, and those which reached their mature form through a process of evolution. The former, whether built primarily as showpieces or as efficient working farms, are readily set in a context derived from the contemporary literature. Landlords building for show wished to demonstrate how advanced they were, and so employed leading architects or adapted ideas from the writings of other designers; in turn, any innovations for which they were responsible found their way into the literature, and might be imitated elsewhere. New farmsteads which were planned on more utilitarian lines also tend to reflect the advanced thinking of their day, and they too may readily be related to the literature. What is much more difficult is to make sense of the vast majority of farmsteads – often of little strictly architectural merit – which reached their mature form through a process of evolution, which in many cases may have begun before the period at which the earliest extant structures were erected. Such a task is, however, of the greatest importance, since it is only by means of understanding the way in which those 'ordinary' farmsteads relate to their more scientifically planned counterparts that it is possible to assess the actual impact of new ideas: a history of farm buildings written solely from documentary sources, and study of model farms, may yield valuable indications of when innovations were made, but cannot accurately chart their success or the speed with which they were adopted. Without such an assessment, the regional structure of the agricultural economy upon which the Industrial Revolution depended for the feeding of a rapidly expanding population cannot adequately be appreciated. This is not the place to address all the issues this raises in terms of social and economic history,[1] and what is attempted is the more limited objective of providing an indication of some of the ways in which buildings reflect the development of agriculture over the century and a half after 1750.

Pre-1750 Farmsteads

Within the survey areas, no farmstead layouts and few individual buildings (none in Cornwall or Northumberland) have survived from before the middle of the 18th century. To some extent this was expected, particularly in relation to overall layouts, but it was anticipated that Berkshire, and perhaps also Cheshire, would have yielded a greater number of buildings dating from the 17th and early 18th centuries. Some of the reasons for this are peculiar to each region, and are discussed below, but some recur in a number of regions, and are likely also to have a wider application. Chief amongst these is the inadequacy of earlier buildings in face of the major developments in farming in the period between about 1750 and 1820: in areas affected by new enclosure, older buildings were often wrongly sited in relation to newly laid-out farms. In addition, many of the earlier buildings have fallen victim to the natural process of attrition by age: fewer buildings are likely to have survived from more remote periods than from the relatively recent past.

Turning to the specific areas chosen for survey, the poverty of Cheshire in terms of pre-1750 buildings may be attributed to the increasing scale and intensification of farming during the 19th century, which was related to the rise of industrial centres, with their increased demand for cheese and, more particularly, liquid milk. Although the emphasis on dairying was long-standing, buildings erected in earlier periods were simply too small or inefficient – in terms both of providing the cattle with the highest possible standard of accommodation, and of labour – to have been worth retaining in significant numbers. A further factor is that in many parts of Cheshire, including those parts of the survey areas which lay on the Peckforton and Daintry estates, landowners engaged in large-scale reorganisations of their holdings during the 19th century, often creating completely new farmsteads. The precise positioning of the survey areas (which are quite small) within the county may mean that areas of better survival have been missed, but casual observation over the rest of the Cheshire plain suggests that the general picture of 19th-century redevelopment holds true over a wider area.

In Cornwall, although the pattern of building is very different (in terms of both timing and type), it may also have been an intensification of agriculture which led to the rebuilding of farm-steads in the early 19th century. Archaeological evidence and some of the surviving houses show that both Bodmin Moor and the Lynher Valley have been farmed continuously since the Middle Ages. The earlier buildings were probably simply too inconvenient to have allowed for the intensi-fication of agriculture witnessed during the 19th century; by contrast with Cheshire, the size of the buildings is unlikely to have been a factor, since many of the 19th-century farmsteads are of small proportions.

Slightly different factors may account for the lack of early buildings in the parts of Northumberland and Lincolnshire which were studied. In Northumberland, the uncertain conditions attendant upon its border position meant that the county was agriculturally back-ward until well into the 18th century, for not even the Act of Union (1707) fully stabilised the region. Once the area was opened up, invest-ment had to be on a large scale if its agricultural potential was to be realised. Estates divided their lands into large new farms which required buildings on an unprecedented scale; older, smaller, buildings were so inappropriate that they were completely swept away. As in Cheshire, the pattern observed in the survey area is probably a fairly accurate reflection of much of the county. In terms of lowland farm-steads, the only exception to this is that some later farmsteads outside the survey area are known to incorporate bastles, though many more – including some (such as Hethpool, Kirknewton) which were recorded – were built a short distance from the pre-existing bastles. Upland farmsteads are more difficult to assess, since the range of buildings required for sheep-farming has changed little over the years. It is possible that the fact that much of the Cheviot survey area lay within a single estate has given an atypical picture of 19th-century rebuilding, and detailed examination of an area such as Coquetdale might reveal that some of the houses (if not the farm buildings) survive from a rather earlier period.

The greater part of the fenland section of the Lincolnshire survey area was as devoid of useful earlier farm buildings as was north Northumberland. The draining of the fens during the late 18th and early 19th centuries allowed for the expansion of agriculture into areas hitherto unexploited. This led to the establishment of many new farms, while old farmsteads were expanded, and the nature of their agriculture sometimes changed, with the result that buildings of new scale and type were required. Exploitation of the clays nearer Grantham also appears to have been relatively restricted before the second half of the 18th century, for reasons of inaccessibility, as well as those connected with the generally poor quality of the land. As in the fenland area, many earlier farm buildings are likely to have proved inade-quate soon after agricultural improvement began in the 18th century. The great variety of agricultural conditions within Lincolnshire, however, makes it less certain that the pattern observed within the survey area is typical. The Wolds are unlikely to contain large numbers of pre-1750 buildings, since much of the area was turned from sheep runs to arable only in the 19th century, but study of other parts of the county might produce a modest number of buildings from the 17th or early 18th centuries.

The most unexpected finding was the small number of early buildings found within the Berkshire survey area, while many of the build-ings erected during and after the late 18th century were traditional (if not archaic) in form. The 18th century does not appear to have witnessed a dramatic change in the type of arable farming practised in the region, though enclosure during that century may have involved the creation of a significant number of new farmsteads, and the expansion of arable acreages associated with old ones. However, it is known that in some parts of south-east England a significantly larger number of early buildings (especially barns) does survive.[2] One factor which may have been at play in Berkshire is that the buildings (which were timber framed) seem to have been poorly constructed – perhaps to a greater extent than in some other south-eastern counties. Certainly many examples of Berkshire barns built after 1800 are now in precarious condition, and several have been strengthened at more than one time in the past two centuries;

anecdotal evidence supplied by farmers in the area also indicates that the timber-framed buildings have for long been subject to a high rate of collapse.

Post-1750 Farmsteads

While it is likely that some parts of the country – particularly, as mentioned above, the south east – do contain larger numbers of early farm buildings than were discovered in any of the survey areas, the regions studied in this book accurately reflect the fact that the vast majority of farm buildings across England are of later date, and it is likely to be a rare farm anywhere that still preserves enough pre-1750 structures for it to be understood as a whole. This is to a large extent a product of the changes in agriculture which began in the 17th century, saw the introduction of new types of crop, and led to increased yields: these changes may have necessitated the creation of new farmsteads or the expansion of older ones. The later phases of the Agricultural Revolution witnessed the expansion of the area under cultivation (by enclosure and drainage) followed by the intensification of agriculture and the integration of the arable and livestock economy. Not only did this lead to the creation of many new farmsteads in some areas, but over much of the country it demanded buildings on a new scale and of novel types: older structures – even those erected as recently as the first half of the 18th century – must often have proved inadequate to meet the new demands, particularly those generated by the advent of new and large machines and implements. It was not only individual buildings which were affected by the changes of the 19th century, but also farmstead layouts which were simply too inefficient to survive in an era when maximum production was required at minimum cost.

The farmsteads which were erected during and after the second half of the 18th century are here divided into two broad categories: planned farmsteads, and complexes which reached their mature form by a process of evolution. As will become apparent, these two groups may provide rather different, and complementary, kinds of information concerning the nature and timing of innovations in building design and farmstead plan.

PLANNED FARMSTEADS

The first book which was solely concerned with the design of farm buildings was published in 1747,[3] and in the seventy years which followed its appearance many landowners constructed new home farms which were based on principles derived partly from the early stages of scientific thought as it affected agriculture, but were also influenced by the architectural ideas of the age. Such farmsteads were designed and built in a single phase, and represent the best practice of their era mixed with a degree of experimentation. Ideas were communicated not only – or even, perhaps, mainly – by the printed word, but also by correspondence between the landowners and their agents, who also often personally visited 'advanced' farmsteads before embarking on building their own.

During the 19th century, the printed word gradually became more important (as it did in relation to all branches of agriculture), allowing for a wider diffusion of knowledge. This is reflected not only in the large number of books devoted to the design and proper management of farmsteads, but in the papers submitted to the *Journal of the Royal Agricultural Society of England*, founded in 1838, and the agricultural press;[4] the significance attached to the subject is witnessed by the decision of the Society to hold competitions for farm designs. The result of this, combined with the requirements for new buildings engendered by the intensification of agriculture during the 19th century, was that a greater number of planned farmsteads were built in the middle of the century than before. Although they were planned, however, the majority of them were not so showy as their earlier counterparts, and a large proportion were not home farms. Instead, they were designed to be efficient working farmsteads: in a sense, this reflects the shift from 'big' farming being the pursuit of gentlemen to it being a business geared for production and profit. These later farms are, therefore, of a slightly different character from the earlier 'model' farms, and, although the two categories inevitably overlap, discussion of their manifestation within the survey areas may be separated.

Fig 7.1 The 18th-century model farmstead: Demesne Farm, Doddington, Cheshire. A large architect-designed home farmstead of a scale, and refinement typical of the late 18th century (BB91/21844).

Model Farms, 1750–1820

It was only the wealthy who could afford to indulge in the construction of model home farmsteads in the late 18th and early 19th centuries, and, of the total number of farms in existence at the time, such farmsteads only ever represented a very small proportion. This does not mean that they are an unimportant part of the history of agriculture, since it was with them that the idea of scientific planning began, and from them that ideas about design gradually filtered down to more 'ordinary' farms.

The small number of these model farms means that many of them are relatively well known, and that the principles which underlay their design are fairly well understood;[5] in addition, the small dimensions of the survey areas meant that such farms were never likely to form a major component of the recording programme. In fact there are almost no planned farmsteads of this date in the areas chosen: a few in Cheshire, none in Cornwall, Berkshire, Lincolnshire or Northumberland. However, many of the principles upon which these model farmsteads were designed have little regional significance, beyond that of the precise processes which required to be accommodated, and they have to be considered in a national context.

The type of farmstead concerned may be exemplified by Demesne Farm, Doddington, in Cheshire (Fig 7.1) which, although not within the survey area, was recorded prior to alterations. The farmstead (built in the 1780s) was designed by Samuel Wyatt, who was employed by landowners as far afield as Norfolk, where he worked on the Holkham estate – one of the most advanced estates in England in the late 18th century.[6] As seen in Chapter 6, the buildings were planned with convenience in mind, and represented a vast improvement on anything built earlier: working farm though it was, however, it was meant to be a talking point amongst other landowners (and not only local ones), and to impress those who visited the estate either to gain ideas for their own estates, or in the course of the social round.

Broadly similar is Bell Farm (c 1810), the home farm of the Daintry's North Rode estate in the eastern Cheshire survey area (Fig 7.2). The scheme is less overtly ostentatious, but the farmstead was attached to the house and was built in the same style. Again, the plan is advanced in agricultural terms (see pp 130, 132 above), but the scale and decoration of the building nevertheless indicate a desire to impress. The Daintrys represented new money, made in the Macclesfield textile and banking industries, and they clearly wished to announce their arrival to the regional community. Not

only did they build a new home farm, but they also constructed planned farmsteads for their tenants. Although dairy farming was practised on all, the plans vary in detail, perhaps indicating a genuine interest in agriculture and an experimental approach, but all the farmsteads share a common architectural style which, while not ostentatious, was clearly intended to be the hallmark of Daintry property (Fig 7.3).

Despite the fact that Demesne Farm, Doddington, was designed by a leading farmstead architect, it does not conform to the 'typical' Hanoverian kind of farm plan most frequently found in the literature, in which the buildings are laid out in a south-facing U-shape with tall barn ranges at the north and open cattle yards to the south.[7] Demesne Farm is not unique in this[8] and may deliberately have been designed on experimental principles, but it is also probable that the Hanoverian model was less applicable to the kind of dairy farm required in Cheshire than to mixed farms more typical of arable areas. The Daintry's North Rode farmsteads, by contrast, are less innovative, and try to apply the national principle of the courtyard plan to the particular needs of the local agricultural economy. As will be seen later, similar adaptations are found throughout the 19th century.

Planned farmsteads, 1820–1914

Model farmsteads continued to be built throughout the 19th century, alike in times of prosperity and depression, when the construction of an efficient set of buildings may have been seen as a way of overcoming economic difficulties: in the late-century depression, many planned farmsteads were built as late as the

Fig 7.2 The home farmstead, c 1800: Bell Farm, North Rode, Cheshire. The model home farmstead built by the Daintry family shortly after they acquired the North Rode estate, in c 1810. Although not ostentatious, the buildings are well designed and impressive (BB94/13565).

149

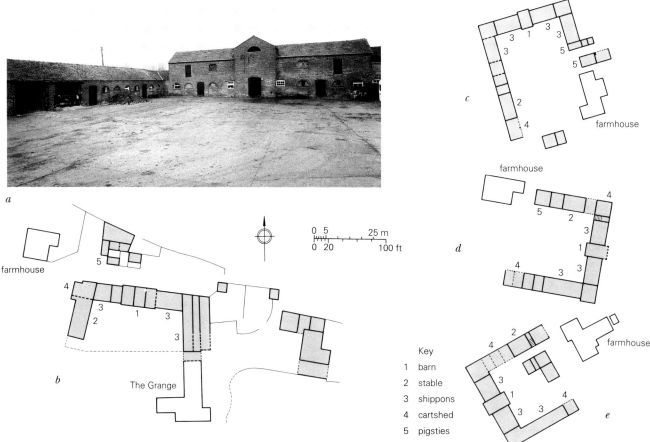

Key
1 barn
2 stable
3 shippons
4 cartshed
5 pigsties

Fig 7.3 Tenant farm-steads, c 1800: the North Rode estate, Cheshire. At the same time as Bell Farm (Fig 7.2) was built, the Daintrys provided their tenants with new farmsteads (such as Dobford, North Rode (a; BB94/13553)) which, although plainer than the home farm-stead, were of the same architectural style. In terms of plan, the tenant farmsteads were also simpler than Bell Farm (b), but all share some of its characteristics and are variations on a theme (c: Dobford; d: Rode Hall Farm; e: Bank Farm). The similarity of plan and architectural form helped to stamp the Daintry's identity on the parish.

early 1880s, though thereafter the number drops significantly.[9] Many more of the model layouts of the 1820s and later were on tenant farms (see below) than was the case in the earlier period, but there were also new planned home farmsteads; on the whole, however, the latter were rather plainer and more functional in design than was the case in the 18th century. This does not mean that the element of ostentation was entirely lost, nor that there was not still a degree of experimentation, but the emphasis was often more on functional simplicity and efficiency than on architectural embellishment.

The principles may be illustrated by Hareby Farm, Hareby (Bolingbroke parish) outside the survey area in Lincolnshire (Fig 7.4). The farmstead is set a short distance from the house, from which it is not visible, at a road junction. The main block of buildings provides sophisticated accommodation for mixed farming: it is large and imposing, but almost entirely plain. The overall plan adheres to many of the principles set out by the commentators of the time: the barn (here specifically a threshing barn), one of the tallest buildings, is on the north side, protecting the cattle from the cold winds; the remainder of the north range contains chaff

houses and cartsheds (facing north) above some of which is the granary. Dividing the area to the south into two equal portions is a two-storey north–south range which appears to have served as a straw and hay barn and fodder-preparation area: this was conveniently placed for the distribution of prepared feedstuffs to cattle in the flanking yards. The sides of the farmstead contain cake houses, tool stores and loose boxes, while each of the two main yards was originally divided by an east–west shelter shed. This farmstead was clearly designed to reflect the best practice of its age: the barn was designed for portable steam power, which was quite new in the years around 1850, and part of the cattle accommodation incorporated a sophisticated feeding system which was designed to hold the beasts still while they fed to ensure that each obtained a fair share of the fodder. Physical evidence for the system has been removed, but details are known because it attracted the attention of J A Clarke, who published a description of it in the *Journal of the Royal Agricultural Society of England* so that others could emulate it.[10] Another feature of the farmstead is that the loose boxes have timber thresholds, like those sometimes found

a

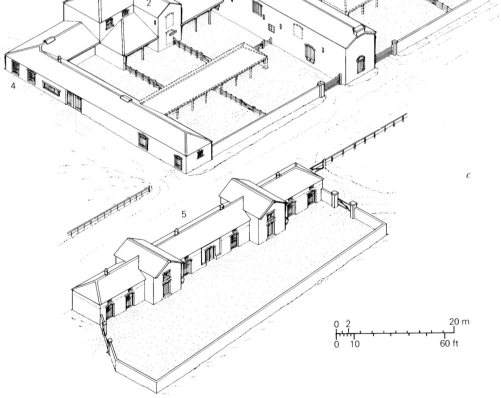

b

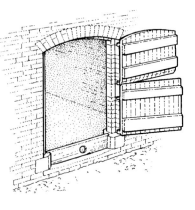

c

Fig 7.4 The model home farmstead, c 1850: Hareby Farm, Hareby, Bolingbroke, Lincolnshire. The buildings are much plainer than those of the Daintrys, but are imposing by their scale (a; BB95/9486). The cattle yards were disposed around the threshing barn (at the rear) and central straw barn/fodder rooms, so as to facilitate the distribution of litter and fodder, and the yards, which faced south, were given shelters, but were largely open (b). The farmstead was advanced for its day, and included experimental features such as timber thresholds in the loose boxes (c), designed to retain the litter which built up during the winter.

Key

1   barn
2   chaff house
3   fodder storage, preparation area
4   loose boxes
5   stable range

a

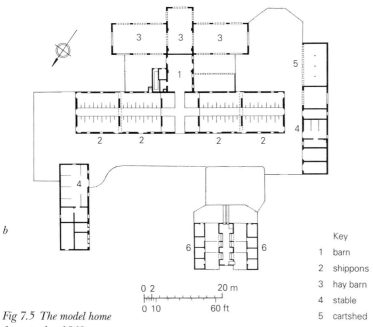

b

Key

1 barn
2 shippons
3 hay barn
4 stable
5 cartshed
6 pigsties

Fig 7.5 The model home farmstead, c 1860: Tattenhall Farm, Tattenhall, Cheshire. As at Hareby, the farmstead impresses more by its scale than by architectural refinement (a; BB93/34748), but the plan (b) was designed for ease of working, and was included in J B Denton's The Farm Homesteads of England *(1st edn, 1863) (here redrawn in simplified form).*

but recorded before alterations) (Fig 7.5). The latter was largely built in 1860, and within a few years its plan had been published by J B Denton as one of the model plans in his *The Farm Homesteads of England* (1st edn, 1863), which were held up for emulation.[12]

Some of the features of the home farmsteads are shared by the significant number of tenant farms which were built, or rebuilt, with landlords' capital, though the tenant farms were often even more plain, and rarely incorporated 'experimental' features (such as the loose-box thresholds of Hareby Farm) until their worth was proven. The point is well illustrated by Northumberland, and particularly by the farmstead at Thornington, Kilham (Fig 7.6), which lay on the Earl of Tankerville's estate. Map evidence shows that there was a farmstead on the site from at least the 1840s, and that between that date and 1860 a number of new buildings were constructed piecemeal: the overall plan, however, lacked coherence, and, shortly after 1879, the farmstead was completely replaced. Even though this was not the home farm – and was some kilometres from the estate centre – the new farmstead was absolutely up to date, as it followed (in all except minor details) a plan which J B Denton had submitted to the Royal Agricultural Society's farm-building competition in 1879.[13] The following of such a nationally known plan was exceptional, but other tenant farmsteads in the region – notably those on the Pallinsburn estate at Crookham Eastfield and Crookham Westfield, both in the parish of Ford – were almost completely reconstructed as sophisticated planned units in the late 19th century.

Developments of the same kind occurred in the other survey areas, though in varying degree. Planned farmsteads are relatively rare in Cornwall, although the buildings at Trebartha Barton, North Hill, are a slightly earlier manifestation of the same kind of development. Cheshire, on the other hand, is rich in planned farmsteads of the middle of the century, particularly in the western survey area, where the occasion for large-scale rebuilding was provided by the reorganisation of the Tollemache estate from the 1820s to the 1860s. The new tenant farmsteads were designed in accordance with best contemporary practice, as may be reflected by the forms of the shippons. The majority of the farmsteads, which were built in the middle of the 19th century, had cross shippons, but the slightly later farmstead at Haycroft Farm, Spurstow, was built with the kind of lengthwise shippon which was by then thought superior, and was used *c* 1860 at the model home farmstead of Tattenhall Farm a few miles away (see above). All the Tollemache farmsteads are more soundly

in barns: the reason seems to have been to hold in the litter, which became quite deep during the winter. Although this did not attract comment, it is an unusual phenomenon, and may represent something of an experiment, perhaps as an alternative to the practice of sinking the floors of loose boxes below ground level which was later advocated by J B Denton.[11]

Similar characteristics are in evidence at Bradford's Farm, Speen, in Berkshire (see Chapter 2), which was also built in the mid 19th century, and formed the home farmstead of the Sutton estate, and at Tattenhall Farm, Tattenhall, Cheshire (outside the survey area

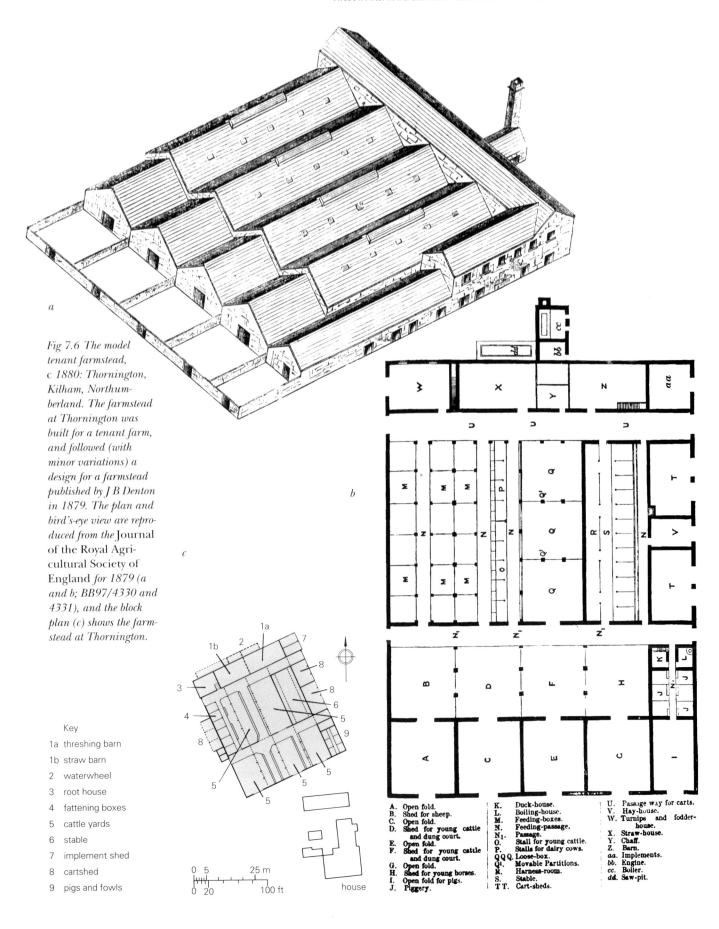

a

Fig 7.6 The model tenant farmstead, c 1880: Thornington, Kilham, Northumberland. The farmstead at Thornington was built for a tenant farm, and followed (with minor variations) a design for a farmstead published by J B Denton in 1879. The plan and bird's-eye view are reproduced from the Journal of the Royal Agricultural Society of England *for 1879 (a and b; BB97/4330 and 4331), and the block plan (c) shows the farmstead at Thornington.*

b

c

Key

1a threshing barn

1b straw barn

2   waterwheel

3   root house

4   fattening boxes

5   cattle yards

6   stable

7   implement shed

8   cartshed

9   pigs and fowls

0 5   25 m

0 20   100 ft

house

A.	Open fold.	K.	Duck-house.	U.	Passage way for carts.
B.	Shed for sheep.	L.	Boiling-house.	V.	Hay-house.
C.	Open fold.	M.	Feeding-boxes.	W.	Turnips and fodder-house.
D.	Shed for young cattle and dung court.	N.	Feeding-passage.	X.	Straw-house.
E.	Open fold.	N1.	Passage.	Y.	Chaff.
F.	Shed for young cattle and dung court.	O.	Stall for young cattle.	Z.	Barn.
		P.	Stalls for dairy cows.	aa.	Implements.
G.	Open fold.	Q Q Q.	Loose-box.	bb.	Engine.
H.	Shed for young horses.	Q¹.	Movable Partitions.	cc.	Boiler.
I.	Open fold for pigs.	R.	Harness-room.	dd.	Saw-pit.
J.	Piggery.	S.	Stable.		
		T T.	Cart-sheds.		

Fig 7.7 Estate farmsteads in Cheshire. The farmsteads built by the Tollemache estate in the middle of the 19th century (such as Manor Farm, Peckforton) were not flamboyant, but were well constructed. The circular pitching eyes and timber framing in the gable are part of the estate style (BB94/5984).

constructed than architecturally flamboyant, though, as on many estates, there is an estate style (Fig 7.7). This was partly for reasons of economy, since the same solutions to the same problems could be adopted on more than one farm. There was probably also an element of giving the estate a readily identifiable character of its own, of the same kind as that which was often provided by estate cottages and estate villages.

The Cheshire survey area contains a relatively large number of planned tenant farmsteads for the reason given above; similar reorganisations occurred elsewhere in Cheshire during the first half of the 19th century, as there was an active land market. In the other survey areas the numbers are more variable, ranging from almost none in Cornwall and Berkshire to a few in Lincolnshire and a rather larger number in Northumberland. Part of the reason for such differences may be related to estate and farm size: in the Lincolnshire fens estates were small, as were farms, many of which were owned by independent freeholders who may not have had the means to invest in completely new farmsteads. Such a hypothesis may be strengthened by the fact that the one relatively large estate with property in the fenland survey area – that of the Marquis of Bristol – did build new farmsteads in the late 19th century, notably at Grange Farm, Little Hale.[14] Similar factors may have affected Cornwall, whereas Northumberland farms and estates may have been of a size to be able to sustain much higher levels of investment. The picture is not, however, as simple as that, for Berkshire was also a county of great estates: other factors must have been involved, one of which may have concerned the earlier development of the farmsteads themselves. It is possible, for example, that the large Berkshire barns were of sufficient size to have been adapted to new

uses as the 19th century progressed, while a greater proportion of the buildings in Northumberland were too small and inconvenient to have been worth retaining. Like the question of farm and estate size, however, this can only be a very partial explanation, for it is clear from sites such as the Crookhams (discussed above) that some of the planned farmsteads of Northumberland replaced complexes which were probably no less convenient than many which survived in Berkshire.

One factor which is likely to have been of significance is the cost of labour. As suggested in Chapter 2, this was clearly of importance in relation to the rate at which mechanisation was adopted, and it may be that in areas where labour was relatively cheap there was less need to spend large capital sums on the provision of buildings designed to streamline flows of processes and thereby to reduce labour costs. A further influence may have been the agrarian history of an area: Berkshire had for long been a prosperous farming county in which both agricultural practice and farmsteads had historically evolved slowly, whereas until the late 18th century Northumberland and parts of the Lincolnshire survey area had not been prosperous. In those areas, major investment was required in the years around 1800 in order to bring both farming practice and farmsteads up to standard; when, later in the century, agriculture was placed under pressure by the developing global economy, estates which had already invested their way to prosperity may have thought they could do the same again.

Although the balance of the factors discussed above – and probably others – varied between regions, the circumstances of each estate or small landowner differed. Nor were all the influences purely economic: family fortunes and personalities were probably often as important as statistics in determining whether an estate built new farmsteads or added to existing ones, and in determining the timing of such investment. As a result, the incidence of planned farmsteads differs radically not only between the main agricultural regions (not only those which were surveyed), but also within individual counties.[15]

REGIONAL BUILDINGS FOR A NATIONAL INDUSTRY

Farmsteads which were planned as a single phase show what best practice was considered to be at the time at which they were built for the type of agriculture for which they were designed (Fig 7.8). The same is largely true of the new buildings erected on old farmsteads during the 19th century, though the final plan of such farmsteads

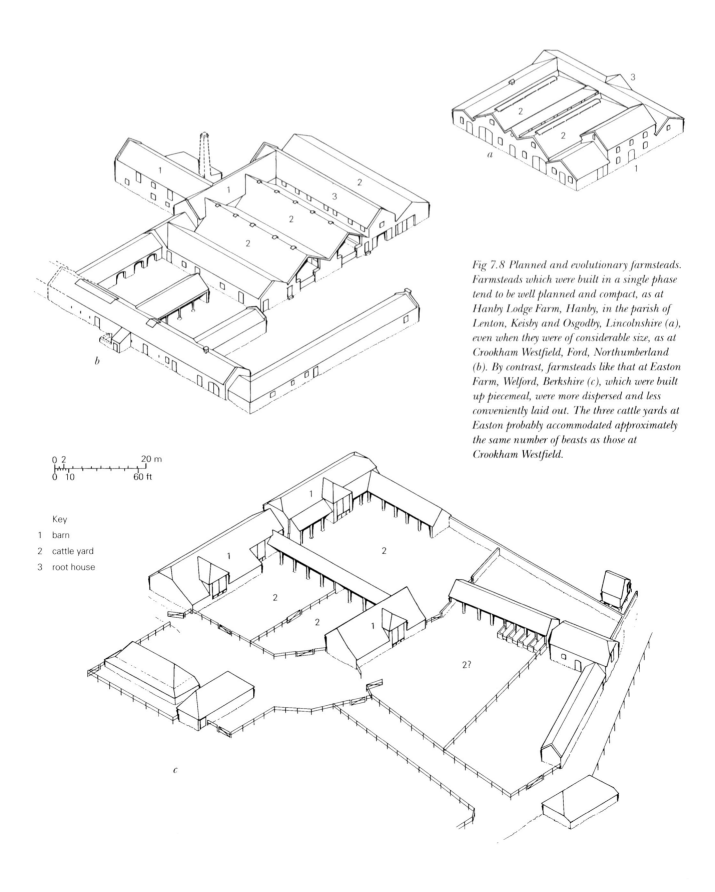

Fig 7.8 Planned and evolutionary farmsteads. Farmsteads which were built in a single phase tend to be well planned and compact, as at Hanby Lodge Farm, Hanby, in the parish of Lenton, Keisby and Osgodby, Lincolnshire (a), even when they were of considerable size, as at Crookham Westfield, Ford, Northumberland (b). By contrast, farmsteads like that at Easton Farm, Welford, Berkshire (c), which were built up piecemeal, were more dispersed and less conveniently laid out. The three cattle yards at Easton probably accommodated approximately the same number of beasts as those at Crookham Westfield.

0 2   20 m
0 10   60 ft

Key
1 barn
2 cattle yard
3 root house

Fig 7.9 Regional variation: barns. The traditional 'southern' barn (a: Elm Farm, Hamstead Marshall, Berkshire) was a timber-framed structure with storage bays flanking threshing floors which had wide and tall doorways. Although built for hand threshing, the type could still be used for storage when threshing moved outside in the era of mechanisation. Similar barns – though built of brick – were also built in Lincolnshire until the early 19th century (b: Manor Farm, Walcot), though the advent of mechanisation there led to the barn becoming smaller, as threshing was conducted in the open air and straw was stacked outside. In addition to becoming smaller, barns were often partially (c: Rookery Farm, Great Hale) or fully floored (d: Hanby Lodge Farm, Hanby, Lenton, Keisby and Osgodby), the first floor being used as a granary, and the ground floor for the storage of bought-in oil cake. In Northumberland, by contrast, the use of fixed machinery inside the barn led to the evolution of a very different kind of building, with a two-storey threshing barn attached to a straw barn (e: Westnewton, Kirknewton). In Cornwall, where farms and arable acreages were considerably smaller, the barn did not form a separate building, but lay on the first floor of a two-storey structure, above cattle accommodation (f: Trefuge, North Hill); barns of this kind could be used for hand threshing or could have machines installed within them. As in Cornwall, there was little arable land in Cheshire, and the barn was little more than a processing room: in the early 19th-century example at Hill Side Farm, Peckforton (g) it lay between two shippons, so that fodder could be passed straight to the cattle.

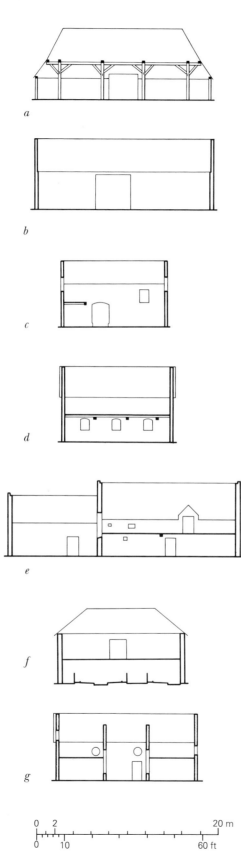

frequently fell short of the commentators' standards, often on account of the need to work round existing buildings. In general terms, therefore, evolutionary farmsteads tend either to have dispersed plans, as is often the case in Berkshire, or, as in much of Lincolnshire, plans which are more compact, but with individual buildings not always standing in the best relationships to each other in terms of flows of processes, as at Village Farm, Swaton (see p 46 above). This is true even in terms of individual buildings: the commentators frequently recommended that cartsheds should face roughly north in order to protect wooden vehicles from drying out in the sun, but fewer than half the cartsheds within the Lincolnshire survey area adhere to the principle.

It is, in fact, in such deviations from best practice that much of the historical significance of evolutionary farmsteads lies, for they show, in a way which neither the literature nor the planned farmsteads can, what was actually happening on the ground. At one level, much of the national literature is concerned with what was regarded as the best farming system of the 19th century – High Farming – in which livestock and arable husbandry were of equal importance, and were managed (with the aid of bought-in fertilisers) in an integrated fashion. While such a system was appropriate to Lincolnshire, Northumberland and Berkshire (at least at some points in the 19th century), it was unsuitable for Cheshire and Cornwall. There is a small volume of specialised literature on dairy farming as practised in Cheshire, but almost nothing on the type of cattle husbandry appropriate to the fringes of Bodmin Moor. Using the 19th-century literature on farm buildings alone, therefore, risks giving a distorted and over-uniform picture of agriculture in England.

The same is also true of the rate of agricultural change: in Northumberland there was a marked shift from cereal production to fatstock, which is mirrored, to a lesser extent, in Lincolnshire, while in Berkshire the shift was from arable to milk cattle; in Cheshire and Cornwall, by contrast, the agricultural emphasis remained stable throughout the 19th century. Some of the issues related to this are directly reflected in the buildings, three aspects of which have been selected for illustration.

The mechanisation of barn processing
One of the most significant of the developments of the 19th century which affected the organisation of the buildings of the farmstead was the application of mechanical power to barn processing. Fixed threshing machines were available from the time of Meikle's patent in 1786; portable engines (both steam and horse driven)

became available in the early 1840s. The date of invention, or even of introduction, is not, however, the same as that of widespread adoption: the type of power used, and the rate at which it was adopted, vary radically across the country. Since the emphasis in the literature is often understandably on the latest and most efficient mechanical aids, it is often only the physical evidence which allows the situation on the ground to be assessed.

The most rapid adoption of mechanisation was in Northumberland, where fixed engines and machines were used from the early years of the 19th century and were common by the 1830s. There are several reasons for the rapid take-up of mechanical power in the area: labour was relatively scarce and expensive; farms and estates were large, and there was a high proportion of arable land, making investment in barn machinery worthwhile; agriculture was relatively backward before the end of the 18th century, and its organisation required radical change and large-scale investment if it was to become profitable. In Berkshire, by contrast, the adoption of mechanical power was slow, largely because labour was plentiful and cheap. This meant that, when machines were adopted later in the 19th century, they were of the more advanced portable type. The same was also true of the part of Lincolnshire which was recorded, though there the reason may have had less to do with labour costs than with the small scale of many of the farms, particularly in the fens. Cheshire, on the other hand, seems to have been slow to mechanise for a different reason: dairy farms had little arable land, making the investment in expensive fixed engines and processing machines less worthwhile, with the result that cheaper portable horse wheels were favoured even after mobile steam engines became available. That the size of farm and the type of agriculture practised were major factors in the choice of power source may be confirmed by Cornwall, where farms were largely devoted to cattle-breeding, and had proportionately small arable acreages. The larger farms were equipped with fixed machines, driven by horses or, more frequently within the survey area, by water; but the smaller farms were adequately served by small portable horse-driven machines, which continued in use throughout the 19th century.

Barns

The different kinds of powered processing are to some extent reflected in the design of barns, but the buildings may also have been influenced by other factors which gave rise to local types (Fig 7.9). Even in the era of hand threshing, barns had varied from one region to another: in Cornwall, for example, where the topography lent itself to the form, the bank barn was adopted. The form became so widespread during the first half of the 19th century as to be almost universal: bank barns were built for powered threshing (both internal and external, and for both horse and water power) as well as for hand threshing, and could be adapted as the type of power changed. The form was so embedded in local practice that it was adopted even on level sites on which access to the first floor had to be contrived by steep stone steps, and continued to be used in the few farmsteads built after the 1840s. A similarly strong regional identity is represented in Berkshire, where 'traditional' aisled threshing barns were still built well into the 19th century. To some extent that reflects the slow adoption of powered processing, while earlier examples, such as that at Folly Farm, Eddington, Hungerford, proved adaptable to horse power. Once powered processing became widespread in the area, it was generally performed in the open air by portable engines: as a result there was little need to build new barns later in the century, and novel designs of building are lacking.

The position in Northumberland was almost entirely different, since the pre 19th-century farmsteads (and agricultural techniques) were so wholly inadequate that they were swept away, with the result that all the surviving barns were built for mechanical processing. Much of the redevelopment took place in the early 19th century, when only fixed machinery was available, and a highly distinctive form of barn was developed to accommodate it. Once perfected, the type remained in fashion for as long as similar machinery was employed – that is, until the end of the 19th century, as demonstrated by Thornington, Kilham (see Fig 7.6), which was built after 1879.

By contrast with the relative uniformity of Cornwall, Berkshire and Northumberland, Lincolnshire barns were subject to considerable typological change. Barns built for hand threshing early in the 19th century contained traditional threshing floors flanked by storage bays. In the middle of the century, when portable power became available and threshing was conducted outside, the barn was reduced to a small storage room, but new barns built after about 1870 were of a third type, with a first-floor granary over a processing room. Part of the reason for the differing kinds of barn in Lincolnshire is that there was no single predominant phase of rebuilding: some barns were built before the adoption of mechanical power, others afterwards. That cannot, however, be the whole explanation, since the second change in barn type does not correspond to a further change in machinery: either the mid-century buildings were found inadequate or some other factor was involved.

Cattle-housing

Regional diversity is also evident in the development of cattle-housing. There is a clear national trend towards increasing numbers of cattle from the 1830s onwards, and a high proportion of the contemporary literature concerning farm buildings is devoted to the propounding of best practice in relation to their accommodation (and not always agreeing). During the 1850s, for example, there was a debate concerning the merits of fattening cattle in boxes or yards, and later in the century the covering of yards was widely advocated, particularly from the 1860s. The latter is reflected in some of the planned farmsteads of the last third of the 19th century, as, for example, at Crookham Westfield, Ford, in Northumberland, and Hanby Lodge Farm, Hanby, in the parish of Lenton, Keisby and Osgodby, in Lincolnshire.

Despite the impression created by the national literature and many of the planned farmsteads, the rate at which covered yards were widely adopted is much more varied than the literature suggests. Covered yards were primarily advocated for fatstock, but, even in areas – such as Lincolnshire and Northumberland – where such animals formed an important part of the agricultural economy, covered yards were in reality seldom added to pre-existing farmsteads much before 1900. In Lincolnshire the commentators noted the reluctance to add roofs to the yards, giving as the reason the dry climate which meant that the manure was less damaged by rain than in wetter parts of the country. Even in the damper Northumberland, however, fully covered yards were only infrequently added to evolutionary farmsteads during the 19th century. The majority of farmers in both Lincolnshire and Northumberland worked with the compromise provided by shelter sheds (in Northumberland associated with sophisticated feeding systems) – yet this is hardly accorded any recognition in the national literature.

In areas where fatstock were less important, covered yards were probably simply inappropriate. Hence, for example, in Cheshire, where the cattle were kept for milk and cheese production, they were accommodated in cow houses at times when they could not be kept in the fields. A broadly similar method was adopted in Cornwall, where cows were largely kept for breeding (which is intimately related to milk production), but the type of cow house associated with that area is hardly touched upon by the national commentators. The picture in Berkshire, where the 19th century saw a shift in agricultural emphasis towards dairying, is more complex: during the mid 19th century the open yards surrounding the barns were furnished with shelter sheds, but later, as the emphasis moved towards dairying, the barns themselves were sometimes converted into cow houses of a plan not wholly dissimilar to Cheshire shippons; covered yards are practically unknown.

All areas (even Cornwall, where the main rebuilding occurred early in the period) saw some degree of increased sophistication in the housing of cattle during the 19th century, and some of the planned farms of Northumberland and Lincolnshire reflect the type and rate of change suggested by the national literature. The reality faced by most farmers was, however, very different: not only did each region develop at a different speed and in a way appropriate to its own agricultural system, but new methods were only slowly adopted on evolutionary farmsteads.

Conclusion

For all that the 19th century saw the beginnings of the industrialisation of farming, and of a shift away from local economies to regional, national and even international ones, agriculture remained far from uniform. Cornish cattle were sold to lowland farms in Somerset for fattening prior to being sold again on what was effectively a national market; Cheshire, traditionally dominated by cheese production, retained its regional emphasis on dairying though with a shift away from cheese to liquid milk production, which was as much engendered by the requirements of the new industrial cities of the region as by the competition from imported cheeses. To a greater or lesser extent, the other three survey areas all witnessed a shift from arable to livestock farming, though, in contrast to Lincolnshire and Northumberland, dairying (for the London market) became important in Berkshire. These variations, both between areas and, through time, within them, are all to a large extent reflected in the buildings. Even the planned farmsteads show this, for, while there are some similarities between those erected in areas of similar agricultural emphasis (such as Northumberland and Lincolnshire), the types of planned farmstead found in Cheshire and, especially, Cornwall, represent the application of the principles of improvement to local farming systems.

The relationship between the local and wider economies is illustrated by one further feature of the buildings of the farmstead – the

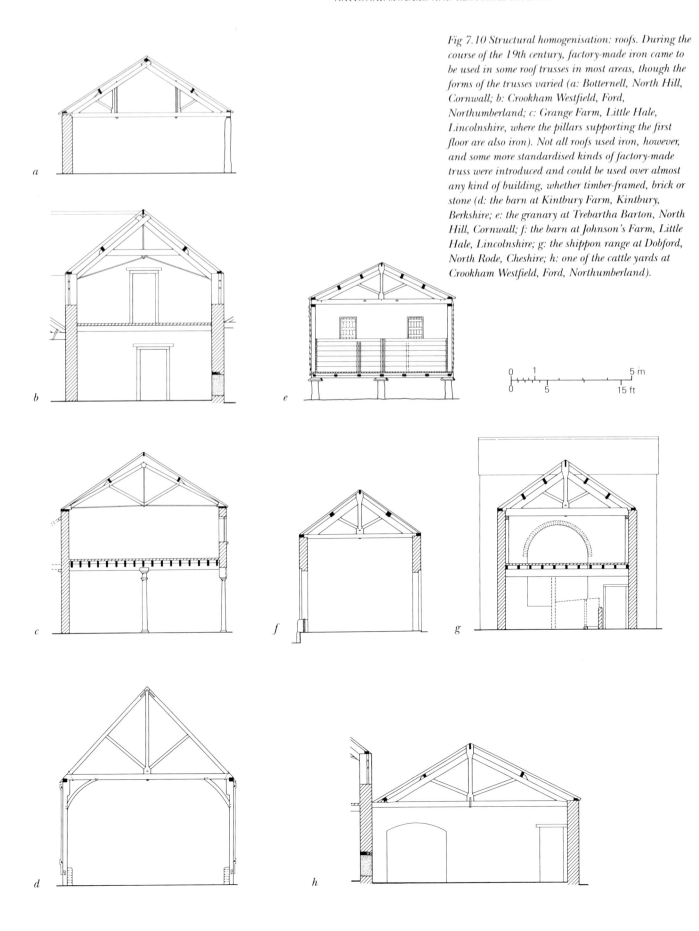

Fig 7.10 Structural homogenisation: roofs. During the course of the 19th century, factory-made iron came to be used in some roof trusses in most areas, though the forms of the trusses varied (a: Botternell, North Hill, Cornwall; b: Crookham Westfield, Ford, Northumberland; c: Grange Farm, Little Hale, Lincolnshire, where the pillars supporting the first floor are also iron). Not all roofs used iron, however, and some more standardised kinds of factory-made truss were introduced and could be used over almost any kind of building, whether timber-framed, brick or stone (d: the barn at Kintbury Farm, Kintbury, Berkshire; e: the granary at Trebartha Barton, North Hill, Cornwall; f: the barn at Johnson's Farm, Little Hale, Lincolnshire; g: the shippon range at Dobford, North Rode, Cheshire; h: one of the cattle yards at Crookham Westfield, Ford, Northumberland).

Fig 7.11 (right) Imported building materials: Grange Farm, Little Hale. Much of the timber used in the second half of the 19th century was imported, as Baltic pine was straighter and less prone to warp than British timber. Evidence for this is sometimes found in the form of marks scratched onto the timber by traders. (Based on a photograph by John Severn.)

Fig 7.12 (far right) Regional types of window. As factory-made products became available, there was a certain amount of stan-dardisation in fittings such as windows, but regional identity was not entirely lost. The iron vented windows at Grange Farm, Little Hale, Lincolnshire (a), are of a kind referred to in the national litera-ture, as might be expected in a planned farmstead of the 1880s. In Northumberland, by contrast, timber windows, such as those at East Moneylaws, Carham (b), continued to be used throughout the period. Cheshire farm-steads had a distinctive kind in the second half of the 19th century (as at Brindley Hall Farm, Brindley (c)), which could be made of either timber or iron.

materials of which they are constructed. Until the mid 19th century, farm buildings (apart from some of the great model farmsteads) were built entirely of local materials and often followed local building traditions. This is perhaps best exemplified in the survey areas by the timber-framed barns of Berkshire and the few surviving fragments of timber-framed build-ings in Cheshire. During the course of the 19th century, as agriculture became more scientific and buildings were influenced by national models, more sophisticated materials began to be used.

During the second half of the 19th century, iron began to be used for structural members in roofs, largely under the influence of a growing body of literature recommending it as a cheap and reliable material (Fig 7.10).[16] This was not a regional phenomenon, but occurred in areas as divergent as Lincolnshire and Northumberland. Despite the fact that such structural components were rarely made locally – they were standard-ised factory-made products rather than those of the local blacksmith – there is still a degree of regional variation in the kind of roof truss, though some kinds of truss, whether incorpor-ating iron or not, were more widely adopted. No matter how much iron was used, structural timber work was still required: like iron, however, an increasing proportion of the raw material was not local, as it was recognised that Baltic pine was of better and more even quality than home-grown timber.[17] The straightness of much of the timberwork in farmsteads built from the middle of the century onwards suggests that the injunc-tion to use foreign timber was generally heeded, and in a few cases, such as Grange Farm, Little Hale, in Lincolnshire (built in 1882), importers' marks can be seen scratched onto the surface of the timber (Fig 7.11).

Many of the smaller components of the buildings, such as roof vents and windows, might also be bought in. At Grange Farm, Little Hale, the columns separating the open bays of the cartshed are iron (Fig 7.10*c*), while the

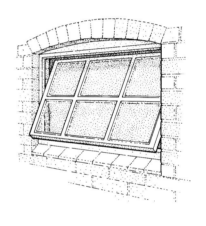

a

b

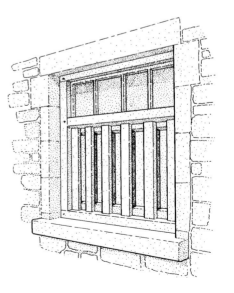

c

a

b

c

d

e

f

Fig 7.13 The regional character of buildings. The distinctiveness of each of the barns illustrated here derives as much from its style and the materials from which it is built as from its form. Northumberland (a): stone threshing barn (left) and straw barn at Crookhouse, Kirknewton (BB94/19583). Cheshire (b): brick barn and fodder-processing range at Brindley Hall Farm, Brindley (BB94/6096). Lincolnshire fen (c): *brick barn and chaff house (left) at Village Farm, Swaton (BB93/21322). Lincolnshire clays (d): stone barn at Moat Farm, Haceby, Newton and Haceby (BB93/6102). Berkshire (e): timber-framed threshing barn at Prior's Farm, Peasemore (BB95/12213). Cornwall (f): stone bank barn at Great Hammett, St Neot (BB95/412).*

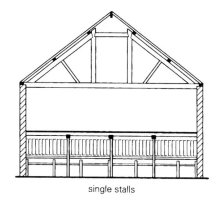

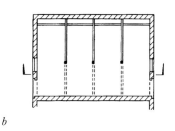

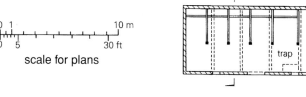

scale for sections

a

single stalls

b

scale for plans

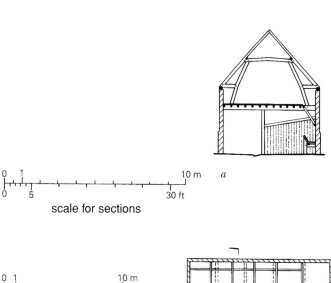

trap

a

b

Fig 7.14 (below) Regional variation: livestock shelters. The Lincolnshire shelter shed, of timber and brick, with a tile roof (a: Woodside Farm, Newton, Newton and Haceby; BB93/24147) served much the same purpose as the Northumberland hemmel, which was built of stone and was more enclosed (b: Crookhouse, Kirknewton; BB94/19585).

vented windows were made at a foundry in Grantham, and conform to a general type of design favourably commented upon by J B Denton (Fig 7.12*a*).[18] Less sophisticated iron windows, also made in Grantham, are found elsewhere within the Lincolnshire survey area, reflecting the relative proximity of engineering works; in Northumberland, however, vented windows of similar type and date continued to be wooden (Fig 7.12*b*), while in Cheshire windows tended to be of a different kind, and might be made of either wood or iron (Fig 7.12*c*).

It is likely that the ability to import materials from other parts of the country was enhanced by the arrival of cheap transport in the form of canals and railways. In Cheshire, it was recommended that slate – which was quarried in Wales – was used as a roof covering (in place of thatch) from shortly after 1800, and the local commentators consistently refer to its use on the improved buildings of the late 18th and early 19th century. Similarly, John Grey, writing in 1841, noted that slate from Wales and Westmorland was widely used in Northumberland by 1841 – before the advent of the railway.[19]

a

b

double stalls

c

d

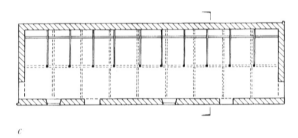

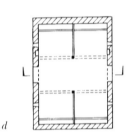

c

d

For all the use of building materials brought in from the Baltic and other parts of Britain, and despite the purchase of factory-made components, farmsteads retained a strongly regional and local character (Fig 7.13). Where good building stone was available, as in Cornwall and Northumberland, it continued to be used, while on the Cheshire plain, where building stone is in poor supply, brick was employed. The favoured material changes rapidly with the geology, since the Pennine farmsteads of east Cheshire (outside the survey area) are built of stone, while in Lincolnshire farmsteads of the clayland area around Grantham are almost all built of local limestone (with brick dressings), but those only a few miles away in the fens are brick. That this was not simply an economic matter, but to some extent represents a continuation of local building traditions, may be illustrated by the case of Berkshire, where timber-framed structures continued to be erected throughout the 19th century, even for high-class buildings such as the Stud Farm at Marsh Benham in Speen.

The variety reflected in the continued use of local materials is mirrored in some of the forms of structure adopted. Hence, for example, although the open-sided shelter shed of Lincolnshire and the Northumberland hemmel perform near-identical functions, their construc-

tion is very different and is in each case drawn from local or regional traditions (Fig 7.14). Both were adequate, and there was little to be gained from adopting new forms. The same is true of stables in some areas (Fig 7.15). The Berkshire stable, for example, retained its local characteristics for much of the 19th century. On the other hand, where local types were found wanting, as in the case of the earlier Lincolnshire variety (in which horses stood in two rows in dark and ill-ventilated conditions), new forms of stable were devised under the influence of the ideas of the national commentators.

Much of this kind of regional variation, which forms such an important part of the English landscape, is as true of many 19th-century planned farmsteads – no matter how industrial in character – as of the mass of sites which evolved in more piecemeal fashion. While the use of imported materials and ideas means that the buildings cannot be described as 'traditional', any more than can 19th-century farming, local and regional character was not entirely lost. In this, as in terms of the general types of building described earlier, and of farmstead layout, farmsteads reflect the continued regional nature of English agriculture in a way which can only rarely be revealed by the national literature.

Notes

Introduction

1 The results of this fact-finding exercise, carried out by Janet Atterbury, were set out in an internal report for the Survey of Surveys. A copy is available for reference in the NMRC.

2 See Barnwell and Adams 1994 for a detailed description of the survey methodology; for sources, see Short 1989; Barnwell 1993 and Short and Watkins 1994.

1 English Agriculture, 1500–1914

1 The summary of historical development provided in this chapter is derived entirely from secondary sources. Among the most important works consulted are Thirsk 1967a; Harvey 1984; Grigg 1989; Mingay 1989a; and Beckett 1990. General statements are not referenced when drawn from these sources.

2 Thirsk 1967b, 3. See Thirsk (1967b, 4) for a map of farming regions.

3 Defoe 1724–6, 493, 49.

4 Punchard 1890a, 522–4; Punchard 1890b, 814–19.

5 Squires 1987; most of the light railways were built after the First World War, but many schemes were drawn up, and a few executed, before 1914.

6 Brown 1991, 8.

2 West Berkshire

1 Spearing 1860, 5.

2 Mavor 1813, 16–18; Spearing 1860, 7–12.

3 Mavor 1813, 196.

4 Ibid, 458; Kelly 1869, 662–3.

5 Pearce 1794, 38; Mavor 1813, 198, 455.

6 Return of Owners of Land 1874, pt 1, vol 1; Thompson 1971, 32, 113.

7 Kelly 1869, Return of Owners of Land 1874, pt 1, vol 1; Berkshire Record Office, Parish Tithe Records D/D1.

8 Mavor 1813, 50; Berkshire Record Office, D/D1, 76/1, 21/1.

9 Pearce 1794, 17; Mavor 1813, 52; Spearing 1860, 2.

10 Mavor 1813, 498–9.

11 Ibid, 62–3.

12 Spearing 1860, 25–9; Lake 1989, 122–3.

13 Denton 1865, 50–2.

14 Pearce 1794, 49; Mavor 1813, 492.

15 Pearce 1794, 59.

16 Mavor 1813, 324.

17 T Hughes, The Scouring of the White Horse (1857), quoted in Orr 1918, 27.

18 Spearing 1860, 33.

19 Pearce 1794, 44; Mavor 1813, 380; Spearing 1860, 37–40.

20 Orr 1918, 200–4.

21 Kain 1986, 139.

22 Pearce 1794, 24, 28–9; Mavor 1813, 170, 175, 220, 283, ch 12; Spearing 1860, 15–16.

23 Orr 1918, 187.

24 PRO, MAF 68, Parish Crop Returns.

25 Pearce 1794, 44–8; Marshall 1818, vol 5, 57; Caird 1852, 99.

26 Mavor 1813, 283; Spearing 1860, 16.

27 Spearing 1860, 36.

28 Orr 1918, 32, 46, 186–8; Taylor 1987, 47, 57–8; PRO, MAF 68, Parish Crop Returns.

29 Lake 1989, 58–60; Pevsner 1966, 117.

30 Pearce 1794, 20; Mavor 1813, 65–7.

31 Caird 1852, 115.

32 Mavor 1813, 65.

33 Caird 1852, 116.

34 Spearing 1860, 25–32; Lake 1989, 122–3.

35 Berkshire lay in Caird's low wage zone, and in the mid 19th century the average weekly wage for a male labourer was about 10s, compared to 14s with house and coal in Northumberland. Caird 1852, map opposite title-page; Colbeck 1847, 436; Spearing 1860, 42.

36 Spearing 1860, 16–17, 21–2.

37 See Hayfield 1991 for the 'high barns' of the Yorkshire Wolds.

38 Grey 1843, 5.

39 Mavor 1813, 129–36.

40 Collins 1972, 17.

41 Mavor 1813, 129–36.

42 Collins 1972, 20–9.

43 Ibid, 18–19.

44 Armstrong 1989, 829; Hobsbawm and Rudé 1973.

45 Hobsbawm and Rudé 1973, 104–10, 167.

46 Collins 1972, 19–20, 28–9.

47 Spearing 1860, 41.

48 For example, Haines Hill Farm, Twyford, Flemish Farm, Windsor, and Chalkpit Farm, Englefield: Spearing 1860, 26, 31; Denton 1865, pl. 53.

49 Mavor 1813, 67.

50 Spearing 1860, 41.

51 Mavor 1813, pl. 1, 403.

52 Spearing 1860, 17.

53 Mavor 1813, 64–5.

54 Caird 1852, 103; Spearing 1860, 38.

55 Caird 1852, 100.

3 South Lincolnshire

1 Kelly 1855, 110, 116–17.

2 Clarke 1851, 303 note.

3 Caird 1852, 186.

4 Clarke 1851, 298–302, 306–7; Clarke 1847, 122–3; Grigg 1966, 28–9, 139–40; Thirsk 1957, 210.

5 Clarke 1851, 379–80.

6 Grigg 1966, 83.

7 Ibid, 88, 106.

8 Manuscript of John Cragg's 'Topographical Dictionary', cited in Grigg 1966, 69.

9 See also Thirsk 1957, 299–300; Grigg 1966, 67–9, 105–6.

10 Thirsk 1957, 225, 299–300; Grigg 1966, 108, 117, 163, 164–5.

11 Clarke 1851, 380.

12 Thirsk (1957, 320–1) discusses the main trends of the period.

13 Marshall 1796a, 177–8; cf Caird 1852, 180, and Clarke 1851, 390.

14 Pusey 1843, 305.

15 NMR Buildings Index no. 91511.

16 The alterations are shown on architect's plans for alterations to the barn on the occasion of the construction of a new farmstead around it (Lincolnshire Archives Office, 3 Anc 5/82).

17 NMR Buildings Index no. 91570.

18 Ewart 1850, 238–9; Sturgess 1850, 294; Denton 1865, 154.

19 Young 1799, 379; cf Brown 1991, 50–1.

20 Denton 1865, pl. 63.

21 NMR Buildings Index no. 91511.

22 See, for example, Dean 1850, 563; Ewart 1850, 241; Tancred 1850, 193; Thompson 1850, 190; Moscrop 1865 and 1890.

23 Denton 1865, 129–30; Moscrop 1865 and 1890.

24 See Denton 1865, 129–30.

25 Lincolnshire Archives Office 3 Anc 5/82 and 5/83.

26 Clarke 1851, 402–3.

27 NMR Buildings Index no. 91511.

4 North Northumberland

1 Pawson 1961, 51; Bailey and Culley 1805, 4.

2 Pawson 1961, 46.

3 Bailey and Culley 1805, 4.

4 Little 1887, 588–9.

5 Pawson 1961, 13–14.

6 Bailey and Culley 1805, 3; MacKenzie 1825, 70–1.
7 Rowe 1971, 159.
8 Bailey and Culley 1805, 128.
9 Grey 1841, 159.
10 Colbeck 1847, 423 and 437, respectively.
11 Bailey and Culley 1805, 60.
12 Ibid, 23.
13 McCord 1979, 28.
14 Little 1887, 589.
15 Bailey and Culley 1805, 23.
16 Figures for estate size taken from the Return of Owners of Land 1873, vol 2.
17 Grey 1841, 157–8; cf Pawson 1961, 50.
18 Bailey and Culley 1805, 29.
19 In the first half of the 19th century the cottages attracted much opprobrium. See MacKenzie 1825, 129, and Caird 1852, 389–90, where they are described as 'most discreditable' and likened to the worst in Ireland.
20 Bailey and Culley 1805, 32; Grey 1841, 156.
21 Colbeck 1847, 429.
22 Ibid, 423.
23 Bailey and Culley 1805, 24–5.
24 Caird 1852, 387–8.
25 Little 1887, 591.
26 Young 1771, vol 3, 70–1 and, more generally, 92; cf Grey 1841, 151–3.
27 MacKenzie 1825, 303.
28 Bailey and Culley 1805, 23.
29 Colbeck 1847, 436–7.
30 Brassley 1985, 142–50.
31 Rowe 1971, passim; Hellen 1972, 148; Hepple 1976, 90.
32 Bailey and Culley 1805, 130–1, 184–7.
33 Ibid, 68–71.
34 Grey 1841, 168.
35 Colbeck 1847, 427–8.
36 Grey 1841, 168; Pawson 1961, 51.
37 Colbeck 1847, 429–31; Caird 1852, 379.
38 Grey 1841, 156, 160–1, 182; Colbeck 1847, 422.
39 Colbeck 1847, 429–31.
40 Caird 1852, 385–6.
41 Ibid, 376–7. Despite his general praise for the management of the farm, Caird thought that the buildings were very poor – the ones which exist today, and were recorded during the course of the survey, were built almost immediately after he wrote.
42 Pawson 1961, 57.
43 Little 1887, 593–4.
44 Hellen 1972, 151.
45 Little, 1887, 593–4.
46 Pawson 1961, 46–7.
47 Bailey and Culley 1805, 26.

48 MacKenzie 1825, 129.
49 Grey 1841, 154, 191; Colbeck 1847, 423.
50 Grey 1841, 191.
51 Caird 1852, 377.
52 Grey 1841, 163.
53 Denton 1865, 138.
54 Ibid, 172–3.
55 Grey 1841, 163.
56 Beatson 1797 pt 1, 9–13; Ewart 1850, 231; Grey 1843, 5; Denton 1865, 152.
57 The single exception to this pattern is Housdenhaugh, Kilham, which was only 20 hectares (48 acres) in extent during the 19th century, some of that being pasture; the farmstead shares more characteristics with those of the Cheviots than with the other sites discussed here.
58 Bailey and Culley 1797, 46; 1805, 49–50.
59 Bailey and Culley 1805, 52; wind power did not become popular, owing to its uncertainty (see Grey 1841, 154), and no surviving examples are known within the survey area, though at Chollerton Steading in the south of the county (Chollerton parish, near Hexham), there is a windmill which is reputed to have been used to power a threshing machine.
60 Grey 1841, 154, 178; cf Colbeck 1847, 424, and Tancred 1850, 194.
61 MacDonald 1978.
62 Hellen 1972, 146.
63 MacDonald 1978, 176.
64 Cookstead and Reedsford, at 42 and 85 hectares (103 and 211 acres), respectively, in 1910.
65 Cheswick Cottage, Ancroft, at 230 hectares (569 acres), and Lanton, Ewart, at 258 hectares (637 acres) in 1910.
66 Denton 1865, 91, 163.
67 Ewart 1850, 219, comments that, while water power was cheaper, steam allowed greater flexibility in the choice of site.
68 Bailey and Culley 1805, 16.
69 That these instances are not entirely isolated may be illustrated by the case of Chollerton Steading (Chollerton parish) near Hexham: as mentioned in n. 59, threshing at one stage appears to have been powered by a windmill; during the first half of the 19th century that seems to have been replaced first by a waterwheel and then by a fixed steam engine.
70 Colbeck 1847, 485; Little 1887, 590.
71 Grey 1841, 191–2; Denton 1865, 143,

citing C E Scott Burn, *Book of Farm Buildings*, 6.
72 Colbeck 1847, 435; cf Caird 1852, 381.
73 Ewart 1850, 236; Denton 1865, 143, citing C E Scott Burn, *Book of Farm Buildings*, 6.
74 For the siting of cattle units in relation to the pre-existing buildings, see p 72 above.
75 eg Ewart 1850, 241–2; Tancred 1850, 202–3; Thompson 1850.
76 McCord 1979, 33–4.

5 EAST CORNWALL

1 Sharpe 1993, 4–6; Johnson and Rose 1994, 2–3.
2 Karkeek 1845, 401; Cornwall Record Office, Tithe Surveys, TA32, TA125, TA162, TA166.
3 Fraser 1794, 31.
4 Karkeek 1845, 434–8.
5 Punchard 1890a, 516.
6 Karkeek 1845, 402.
7 Worgan 1811, 53.
8 Marshall 1796b, 6.
9 Worgan 1811, 146–7.
10 Karkeek 1845, 403.
11 Kain and Holt 1981, 150.
12 Worgan 1811, 138.
13 Fraser 1794, 45.
14 Worgan 1811, 140 *et seq*.
15 Marshall 1796b, 16.
16 Worgan 1811, 55.
17 Karkeek 1845, 414, 433.
18 Worgan 1811, 146–7.
19 Karkeek 1845, 400.
20 Ibid, 402–3.
21 Punchard 1890a, 516–17.
22 Whitley 1861, 17.
23 Fussell 1960, 344; PRO Crop Returns.
24 Austin, Gerrard and Greeves 1989, 54–61; Johnson and Rose 1994, 83–90.
25 Chesher and Chesher 1968, 103, 122; Johnson and Rose 1994, 98–100.
26 Johnson and Rose 1994, 89–90.
27 Worgan 1811, 23.
28 Karkeek 1845, 461.
29 Punchard 1890a, 516.
30 Worgan 1811, 146–7.
31 Cornwall Record Office, CY6567.
32 Worgan 1811, 24, pls II–IV.
33 Denyer 1991, 134–41.
34 The 1755 building is at East Peek, Ugborough, Devon (Laithwaite 1989, 11).
35 Worgan 1811, 43.
36 Ibid, 44.
37 Ibid, 43.
38 Harvey 1984, 112; personal note from Professor Charles Thomas.

39 Harvey 1984, 94.
40 Robertson and Gilbert 1979, 14–16, Map 6, 46–7.
41 Cornwall Record Office, RD766.
42 Harvey 1984, 175–6.
43 See Peters (1969, 175–6) for 19th-century views on the advantages of dark but ventilated housing for cattle.
44 Terminology derived from Laithwaite 1990, 126.
45 Child 1990, 71–2.
46 Karkeek 1845, 433; Punchard 1890a, 524–6.
47 Robertson and Gilbert 1979, 4, Map 1, 35–7.

6 CENTRAL CHESHIRE

1 Fussell 1954.
2 Holland 1813, 5–6.
3 Ibid, 210–11; Palin 1845, 77–8; Caird 1852, 256; see also Davies 1960, 107–10.
4 Mercer 1963, 42.
5 Holland 1813, 79–80.
6 For a general discussion of landownership, see Scard 1981, esp at 15–19.
7 Holland 1813, 79–80.
8 Davies 1960, 13; de Figeurido and Treuherz 1988, 131–4.
9 Davies 1960, 54–7.
10 Holland 1813, 91–3.
11 Wedge 1794, 13; Holland 1813, 81, 108–11; Palin 1845, 84; Young 1924, 161–2.
12 Davies 1960, 14, 16.
13 Holland 1813, 101–3; Caird 1852, 259.
14 Holland 1813, 101–3.
15 Defoe 1724–6, 394–5.
16 Porter 1976, 141–2.
17 Mercer 1963, 21.
18 Taylor 1987, 57.
19 Sylvester and Nulty 1958, 59.
20 Porter 1976, 144–5; Taylor 1987, 48–50.
21 Harvey 1984, 136.
22 Grigg 1989, 218.
23 Holland 1813, 125; cf Davies 1960, 52.
24 Kain and Holt 1983, 28, cf Caird 1852, 253; but see the cautionary remarks in Phillips 1987.
25 Mercer 1963, 18.
26 Holland 1813, 129–30; Palin 1845, 58–70; cf Young 1915, 100.
27 Davies 1960, 128.
28 Kain and Holt 1983, 40.
29 Davies 1960, 128, on the first half of the 19th century, and Young 1915, 100, for later.
30 Palin 1845, 58, 102–3.
31 Davies 1960, 99–100.
32 Young 1924, 161.
33 Porter 1976, 139.

34 Young 1771, vol 3, 224.
35 Marshall 1818, vol 2, 7; for later comments, see Carrington 1865, 344–5.
36 Davies 1960, 52.
37 Palin 1845, 58, 89–90, 98–9; Caird 1852, 257–8.
38 Palin 1845, 90; Davies 1960, 119.
39 Wedge 1794, 2–3.
40 Holland 1813, 82–3.
41 Davies 1960, 93.
42 For a similar arrangement in Staffordshire, see Peters 1969, 80–3.
43 For criticisms of the system, see Denton 1865, 141, 169.
44 For the advantages of this kind of shippon, see Young 1924, 163.
45 Young 1924, 163.
46 Holland 1813, 191–2; Denton 1865, 141.
47 Harvey 1984, 176.
48 Beatson 1797.
49 PRO, IR 58/24207, no. 78.
50 Caird 1852, 252.
51 For the processes involved in cheese-making, see Cheke 1959, ch 2.
52 Denton 1865, 140.
53 Ewart 1850, 259.
54 Palin 1845, 73–4.
55 Davies 1960, 137.

7 NATIONAL MODELS AND REGIONAL DIVERSITY

1 For a tentative attempt to do this in relation to Lincolnshire, see Barnwell forthcoming.
2 In Sussex, for example – see Martin and Martin 1982, esp chapter 4; a similar pattern may exist in Kent, and lectures by Philip Aitkin at the 1994 Cressing Temple Conference, and at a joint conference of the Historic Farm Buildings Group and the Society for Landscape Studies, suggest that quite a large number of 17th-century farm buildings (not only barns) survive in parts of Suffolk.
3 Garret 1747.
4 The most important of the books are conveniently listed in Harvey 1984, 271; on the diffusion of knowledge more generally, see Wilmot 1990, and Goddard 1991.
5 See Robinson 1983.
6 See Wade Martins 1980.
7 See Harvey 1984, 115–19, for a concise discussion of such plans.
8 See Robinson 1983 for other individual designs.
9 Of the 1880s, for example, are Hanby Lodge Farm, Hanby, and Hanby Grange Farm, Hanby, both in

Lenton, Keisby and Osgodby, Lincolnshire, Grange Farm, Little Hale (also Lincolnshire), and Thornington, Kilham, Northumberland. Later farmsteads include Dairy Farm, Haughton, Cheshire, Botternell, North Hill, Cornwall, and Moat Farm, Newton and Haceby, Lincolnshire.
10 Clarke 1851, 390; Caird (1852, 180) describes a similar system on the Duke of Bedford's estate, at Thorney in Lincolnshire.
11 Denton 1865, 61.
12 Ibid, 70–3.
13 Denton 1879, 796–800.
14 Also, on a smaller scale, at Car Dike Farm, Little Hale, and Mastins Farm, Great Hale.
15 For an example of this kind of variation between estates within a single county, see Wade Martins 1991.
16 For example, Denton 1866; Tuckett 1866, esp 140–3.
17 See, for example, Denton 1866, 122–3; Tuckett 1866, 141.
18 Denton 1865, 155.
19 Grey 1841, 190–1.

BIBLIOGRAPHY

In addition to a complete list of works cited in the text, the bibliography includes a few works of a general nature which may prove useful to readers who wish to pursue the subject further.

Armstrong, W A 1989. The Position of the Labourer in Rural Society. In Mingay 1989a, 810–35

Austin, D, Gerrard, G A M and Greaves, T A P 1989. Tin and Agriculture in the Middle Ages and Beyond: Landscape Archaeology in St Neot Parish, Cornwall. *Cornish Archaeology* **28**, 5–251

Bailey, J and Culley, G 1797. *General View of the Agriculture of Northumberland*

— 1805. *General View of the Agriculture of Northumberland, Cumberland and Westmorland*

Barnwell, P S 1993. The National Farm Survey. *Journal of the Historic Farm Buildings Group*, **7**, 12–19

— forthcoming 1998. An Extra Dimension: Lincolnshire Farm Buildings as Historical Evidence. *Agricultural History Reveiw*

Barnwell, P S and Adams, A T 1994. Recording for the Archive: Field Survey and the Public Record. In Giles and Wade Martins 1994, 34–9

Beacham, P (ed) 1990. *Devon Building: An Introduction to Local Traditions*

Beatson, R 1797. On Farm Buildings in General. *Communications to the Board of Agriculture; On Subjects Relative to the Husbandry and Internal Improvements of the Country* **1**, 1–57

Beckett, J V 1990. *The Agricultural Revolution*

Brassley, P 1985. *The Agricultural Economy of Northumberland and Durham in the period 1640–1750*

Brown, J 1991. *The Horse in Husbandry*

Caird, J 1852. *English Agriculture* in 1850–51. Repr 1968

Carrington, W T 1865. On Dairy Farming. *JRASE* **2nd ser 1**, 244–54

Cheke, V 1959. *The Story of Cheese-Making in Britain*

Chesher, V M and Chesher, F J 1968. *The Cornishman's House*

Child, P 1990. Farm Buildings. In Beacham 1990, 61–94

Clarke, J A 1847. On the Great Level of the Fens, Including the Fens of South Lincolnshire. *JRASE* **8**, 80–113

— 1851. On the Farming of Lincolnshire. *JRASE* **12**, 259–414

Colbeck, T L 1847. On the Agriculture of Northumberland. *JRASE* **8**, 422–37

Collins, E J T 1972. The Diffusion of the Threshing Machine in Britain. *Tools and Tillage* **2**, 16–33

Davies, C S 1960. *The Agricultural History of Cheshire, 1750–1850* (Chetham Society 3rd ser 10)

Dean, G 1850. On the Cost of Agricultural Buildings. *JRASE* **11**, 558–73

de Figuerido, P and Treuherz, J 1988. *Cheshire Country Houses*

Defoe, D 1724–6. *A Tour Through the Whole Island of Great Britain.* Repr 1971 (Penguin)

Denton, A B 1866. On the Comparative Cheapness and Advantages of Iron and Wood in the Construction of Roofs for Farm-Buildings. *JRASE* **2nd ser 2**, 116–39

Denton, J B 1865. *The Farm Homesteads of England.* 2nd edn; 1st edn, 1863

— 1879. Report of the Judges of Farm Plans sent in for the Competition at the London International Exhibition, 1879. *JRASE* **2nd ser 15**, 774–831

Denyer, S 1991. *Traditional Buildings and Life in the Lake District*

Ewart, J 1850. On the Construction of Farm-Buildings. *JRASE* **11**, 215–70

Fowler, P J 1983. *Farms in England: Prehistoric to Present*

Fraser, R 1794. *General View of the Agriculture of the County of Cornwall*

Fussell, G E 1954. Four Centuries of Cheshire Farming Systems, 1500–1900. *Transactions of the Historic Society of Lancashire and Cheshire* **106**, 57–77

— 1960. Cornish Farming, AD 1500–1900. *Amateur Historian* **4 no. 8**, 338–45

Garret, D 1747. *Designs and Estimates of Farmhouses etc for the County of York, Northumberland, Cumberland, Westmorland and the Bishopric of Durham*

Giles, C and Wade Martins, S (eds) 1994. *Recording Historic Farm Buildings: Proceedings of a One-day Conference Held on January 15th 1994 at the King's Manor, University of York*

Goddard, N 1991. Information and Innovation in Early-Victorian Farming Systems. In Holderness and Turner 1991, 165–90

Grey, J 1841. A View of the Past and Present State of Agriculture in Northumberland. *JRASE* **2**, 151–92

— 1843. On Farm Buildings. *JRASE* **4**, 1–16

Grigg, D B 1966. *The Agricultural Revolution in South Lincolnshire*

— 1989. *English Agriculture: A Historical Perspective*

Grigson, G 1948. *An English Farmhouse*

Harvey, N 1984. *A History of Farm Buildings in England and Wales* 2nd edn; 1st edn, 1970

— 1985. *Historic Farm Buildings Study. Sources of Information* (MAFF, CBA)

— 1987. *Old Farm Buildings* 3rd edn; 1st edn, 1975

Hayfield, C 1991. Manure Factories? The Post-Enclosure High Barns of the Yorkshire Wolds. *Landscape History* **13**, 33–45

Hellen, J A 1972. Agricultural Innovation and Detectable Landscape Margins: The Case of Wheelhouses in Northumberland. *Agricultural History Review* **20**, 140–54

Hepple, L W 1976. *A History of Northumberland and Newcastle upon Tyne*

Hobsbawm, E and Rudé, G 1973. *Captain Swing*

Holderness, B A and Turner, M (eds) 1991. *Land, Labour and Agriculture: Essays for Gordon Mingay*

Holland, H 1813. *General View of the Agriculture of Cheshire*

Johnson, N and Rose, P 1994. *Bodmin Moor: An Archaeological survey, Vol 1: The Human Landscape to c 1800*

Kain, R J P 1986. *An Atlas and Index of the Tithe Files*

Kain, R J P and Holt, H M E 1981. Agriculture and Land Use in Cornwall, c 1840. *Southern History* **3**, 139–81

— 1983. Farming in Cheshire circa 1840: Some Evidence from the Tithe Files. *Transactions of the Lancashire and Cheshire Antiquarian Society* **82**, 22–57

Kain, R J P and Prince, H C 1985. *The Tithe Surveys of England and Wales*

Karkeek, W F 1845. On the Farming of Cornwall. *JRASE* **6**, 400–62

Kelly 1855. *Post Office Directory of Lincolnshire*

— 1869. *Directory of Berkshire*

Laithwaite, M 1989. Devon Farmsteads: A preliminary Survey. Typescript Report for Devon County Council

— 1990. Dartmoor Farmstead Survey. Typescript Report for Devon County Council

Lake, J J 1989. *Historic Farm Buildings*

Little, W C 1887. Report on the Farm-Prize Competition in Northumberland and Durham in 1887; Classes 1, 2 and 3. *JRASE* **2nd ser 23**, 583–660

McCord, N 1979. *North East England: An Economic and Social History*

MacDonald, S 1978. The Early Threshing Machine in Northumberland. *Tools and Tillage* **3**, 168–84

MacKenzie, E 1825. *An Historical, Topographical and Descriptive View of the County of Northumberland.* 2 vols

Marshall, W 1796a. *The Rural Economy of the Midland Counties*
1796b. *The Rural Economy of the West of England*
1818. *Review and Abstract of the County Reports to the Board of Agriculture.* 5 vols

Martin, D and Martin, B 1982. *Old Farm Buildings in Eastern Sussex, 1450–1750* (*Historic Buildings of Eastern Sussex*, **3**)

Mavor, W 1813. *General View of the Agriculture of Berkshire*

Mercer, W B 1963. *A Survey of the Agriculture of Cheshire*

Mingay, G E (ed) 1989a. *The Agrarian History of England and Wales, vol 6: 1750–1850*
1989b. Conclusion: The Progress of Agriculture, 1750–1850. In Mingay 1989a, 938–91

Moscrop, W J 1865. Covered Cattle Yards. *JRASE* **2nd ser 1**, 88–99
1890. Covered Cattle Yards. *JRASE* **3rd ser 1**, 473–90

Orr, J 1918. *Agriculture in Berkshire*

Palin, W 1845. The Farming of Cheshire. *JRASE* **5**, 57–111

Pawson, H C 1961. *A Survey of the Agriculture of Northumberland*

Pearce, W 1794. *General View of the Agriculture in Berkshire*

Peters, J E C 1969. *The Development of Farm Buildings in Western Lowland Staffordshire up to 1880*
1991. *Discovering Traditional Farm Buildings.* Rev edn; 1st edn, 1981

Pevsner, N 1966. *The Buildings of England: Berkshire*

Phillips, A D M 1987. Agricultural Land Use and Cropping in Cheshire around 1840: Some Evidence from Cropping Books. *Transactions of the Lancashire and Cheshire Antiquarian Society* **84**, 46–63

Porter, R E 1976. The Marketing of Agricultural Produce in Cheshire during the 19th century. *Transactions of the Historic Society of Lancashire and Cheshire* **126**, 139–95

Punchard, F 1890a. Farming in Devon and Cornwall. *JRASE* **3rd ser 1**, 511–36
1890b. The Farm Prize Competition of 1890. *JRASE* **3rd ser 1**, 776–823

Pusey, P 1843. On the Agricultural Improvements of Lincolnshire. *JRASE* **4**, 287–316

Rees, A D 1950. *Life in the Welsh Countryside*
Return of Owners of Land, England and Wales, 1873. 2 vols (PP (HC) 1874 (C.1097) LXXII)

Robertson, R and Gilbert, G 1979. *Some Aspects of the Domestic Archaeology of Cornwall* (Institute of Cornish Studies, Special Report no. 6)

Robinson, J M 1983. *Model Farms – A Study of Decorative and Model Farm Buildings in the Age of Improvement, 1700–1846*

Rowe, D J 1971. The Culleys: Northumberland Farmers, 1767–1813. *Agricultural History Review* **19**, 42–64

Scard, G 1981. *Squire and Tenant: Rural Life in Cheshire, 1760–1900*

Sharpe, A 1993. *Minions: An Archaeological Survey of the Caradon Mining District*

Short, B 1989. *The Geography of England and Wales in 1910: An Evaluation of Lloyd George's 'Domesday' of landownership* (Historical Geography Research Group, Publication 22)

Short, B and Watkins, C 1994. The National Farm Survey of England and Wales 1941–3. *Area* **26**, 288–93

Spearing, J B 1860. On the Agriculture of Berkshire. *JRASE* **21**, 1–46

Squires, S E 1987. *The Lincolnshire Potato Railways*

Sturgess, T 1850. Farm Buildings. *JRASE* **11**, 288–99

Sylvester, D and Nulty, G 1958. *The Historical Atlas of Cheshire*

Tancred, T 1850. Essay on the Construction of Farm Buildings. *JRASE* **11**, 192–214

Taylor, D 1987. Growth and Structural Change in the English Dairy Industry, *c*1860–1930. *Agricultural History Review* **35**, 47–64

Thirsk, J 1957. *English Peasant Farming: The Agrarian History of Lincolnshire from Tudor to Recent Times*

Thirsk, J (ed) 1967a. *The Agrarian History of England and Wales, vol 4: 1500–1640*
1967b. The Farming Regions of England. In Thirsk 1967a, 1–112

Thompson, F M L 1971. *English Landed Society in the 19th Century*

Thompson, H S 1850. Farm Buildings. *JRASE* **11**, 186–92

Tuckett, P D 1866. On the Comparative Cheapness and Advantages of Iron and Wood in the Construction of Roofs for Farm-Buildings. *JRASE* **2nd ser 2**, 140–8

Wade Martins, S 1980. *A Great Estate at Work: The Holkham Estate and its Inhabitants in the Nineteenth Century*
1991. *Historic Farm Buildings, Including a Norfolk Survey*

Wedge, T 1794. *General View of the Agriculture of the County Palatine of Chester*

Whitley, N 1861. *On the Development of the Agricultural Resources of Cornwall*, repr from *The Bath and West of England Agricultural Journal* **9 pt 2**

Wiliam, E 1982. *Traditional Farm Buildings in North-East Wales, 1550–1900*
1986. *The Historic Farm Buildings of Wales*

Wilkinson, P 1987. *Alternative Uses for Redundant Farm Buildings*

Wilmot, S 1990. '*The Business of Improvement': Agriculture and Scientific Culture in Britain, c1700–c1870* (Historical Geography Research Group, Publication 24)

Worgan, G B 1811. *General View of the Agriculture of Cornwall*

Young, A 1771. *A Six Months' Tour through the North of England*. 6 vols. 2nd edn; 1st edn, 1770
1799. *General View of the County of Lincoln*

Young, T J 1915. Dairy Husbandry in Lancashire and Cheshire. *JRASE* **76**, 97–110
1924. Agriculture in the County of Chester. *JRASE* **85**, 160–75

LIST OF SITES RECORDED

The sites to which reference is made in the following list were recorded during the course of the Royal Commission's Farmsteads survey. Sites are listed by county, within which those lying in each modern civil parish are gathered together; where detached groups of parishes were surveyed, the parishes are listed by survey area within each county. At the end of the lists for Cheshire, Lincolnshire and Northumberland are listed sites outside the survey areas which were recorded during the survey. Other sites mentioned in the text but not listed here are known only from documents, and no architectural record of these sites was produced by this survey.

The list gives the name of each farm recorded, followed by the national grid reference and the Buildings Index number of the file in the National Monuments Record. Each file in the Record contains an analytical report, including a historical account and architectural survey, mostly made to Level 3 as defined in the RCHME's *Recording Historic Buildings: A Descriptive Specification* (2nd edn, 1991). In addition, there is a block plan for all but a handful of sites, together with 35 mm and aerial photographs; selected files also contain large-format photographs. The record of sites whose names are followed by an asterisk contains further drawings, which may include measured plans and sections, elevations, bird's-eye views and both measured and unmeasured drawings of selected details.

The archive which results from the survey is available for consultation at the Royal Commission's National Monuments Record, which is held in the National Monuments Record Centre, Kemble Drive, Swindon SN2 2GZ.

WEST BERKSHIRE

Beedon
Manor Farm	SU 4830 7815	32953
North Stanmore Farm*	SU 4744 7904	91640
South Stanmore Farm	SU 4790 7879	91641

Boxford
Boxford Farm	SU 4347 7150	87501
Hunt's Green Farm	SU 4311 6982	91633
Rowbury Farm	SU 4380 7504	91653

Catmore
Catmore Farm	SU 4530 8020	32956

Chaddleworth
Manor Farm	SU 4062 7868	91642

Combe
Manor Farm	SU 3683 6080	91617

Enborne
Church Farm	SU 4344 6569	91656

Hamstead Marshall
Elm Farm	SU 4137 6540	91630
Hamstead Holt Farm*	SU 3959 6622	83862
Little Farm	SU 4185 6424	91652
Plumb Farm	SU 4131 6528	91654

Hungerford
Folly Farm, Eddington	SU 3465 6944	91614
Great Hidden Farm	SU 3525 7008	91636
Little Hidden Farm	SU 3514 7122	91615

Inkpen
Belvedere, Lower Green	SU 3606 6418	91638
Inkpen House	SU 3577 6374	82359
Kirby Farm, Upper Green	SU 3709 6330	91619
Rolf's Farm, Upper Green	SU 3713 6358	91643

Kintbury
Clapton Farm	SU 3826 7002	91655
Denford Manor Farm	SU 3512 6858	91637
Holt Lodge	SU 3890 6465	91621
Holt Manor Farm	SU 4010 6453	91627
Kintbury Farm*	SU 3738 6683	91618
Mason's Farm*	SU 4031 6571	91649
Orpenham Farm*	SU 3890 7062	91620
Waterman's Farm	SU 4065 6450	91628
Wawcott Farm	SU 3903 6784	91625

Peasemore
Prince's Farm	SU 4570 7707	91658
Prior's Farm*	SU 4601 7690	87045
Widow's Farm*	SU 4600 7695	91657

Speen
Benham Marsh Farm	SU 4243 6707	91632
Bradford's Farm*	SU 4197 6813	91629
Stud Farm, Marsh Benham	SU 4299 6749	91631

Welford
Easton Farm*	SU 4190 7236	91651
Elton Farm	SU 3972 7418	91644
Halfway Farm	SU 4045 6843	91648
Home Farm	SU 4097 7288	91646
Tullock Farm*	SU 4083 7217	91647
Welford Farm	SU 4111 7330	91650
Wickham Green Farm	SU 3976 7185	91645

West Ilsley
Rowles Farm	SU 4718 8261	91639

West Woodhay
Bricklayer's Farm	SU 3888 6377	91622
Great Farm	SU 3847 6335	91623
Highwood Farm	SU 3895 6234	91624

CENTRAL CHESHIRE

Baddiley
Baddiley Farm	SJ 6184 5147	91586

Brindley
Ash House Farm	SJ 5846 5423	91598
Brindley Hall Farm*	SJ 5900 5477	91678
Brindley Lea Hall Farm	SJ 5903 5355	91579
Clay Fields Farm	SJ 5881 5422	91577
High Ash Farm	SJ 5769 5439	91597

Burland
Burland Farm	SJ 6036 5341	91583
Burland Hall Farm	SJ 6054 5378	91581
Green Farm	SJ 6044 5368	91582
Longlane Farm	SJ 6012 5391	91580
Pear Tree Farm	SJ 6161 5176	91585
Swanley Hall Farm	SJ 6163 5264	91584

Edleston
Edleston Farm	SJ 6294 5101	91587

Haughton
Dairy Farm	SJ 5859 5585	91576

Peckforton
Hill Side Farm*	SJ 5331 5560	91549
Manor Farm	SJ 5404 5649	91594
Peckforton Hall Farm*	SJ 5452 5657	71093
Stonehouse Farm	SJ 5349 5589	91593

Spurstow
Bath House Farm	SJ 5698 5535	71060
Capper's Lane Farm	SJ 5785 5544	91575
Green Butts Farm	SJ 5617 5703	91561
Haycroft Farm*	SJ 5538 5721	91595
Lower Hall	SJ 5653 5522	91563
Newhall Farm	SJ 5745 5600	91566
Pear Tree Farm	SJ 5773 5563	91574
Sunnyside Farm*	SJ 5568 5703	91557

Eaton (Congleton)

Field's Farm*	SJ 8646 6642	91603
Gorseymoor	SJ 8602 6649	91601
Jack Field's Farm	SJ 8609 6668	91603

Marton

Moss Bank Farm*	SJ 8674 6708	91604

North Rode

Bank Farm	SJ 8789 6614	91605
Bell Farm*	SJ 8979 6722	91612
Bramhallhill Farm	SJ 8815 6668	91606
Cloud View Farm*	SJ 8846 6642	91611
Dobford*	SJ 8945 6773	91613
Ethel's Green Farm	SJ 8938 6613	91610
Rode Green Farm	SJ 8875 6769	91608
Rode Hall Farm	SJ 8910 6624	91609
Yew Tree Farm	SJ 8896 6657	91607

Swettenham

Brook Farm	SJ 7961 6755	91588
Cloud Hill Farm	SJ 8070 6743	91592
Folly Farm*	SJ 8042 6730	91600
Fox Hall Farm	SJ 8015 6732	91589
Home Farm	SJ 8079 6718	91591
West Farm	SJ 7976 6735	91599

Doddington

Demesne Farm*	SJ 7043 4729	91745

Moston

Bridge Farm, Tetton*	SJ 7225 6370	91565

Tattenhall

Tattenhall Farm	SJ 4865 5814	91596

EAST CORNWALL

Altarnun

Dryworks	SX 1942 7674	91726
Goodaver	SX 2054 7454	91710

Linkinhorne

Darley*	SX 2764 7329	91738
Knowle Farm*	SX 2704 7263	91720
North Wardbrook	SX 2543 7316	91733

North Hill

Botternell	SX 2787 7460	91739
East Castick Farm*	SX 2648 7846	91744
East Tremollett	SX 2991 7566	91743
Glubhole	SX 2752 7702	91717
Landreyne*	SX 2868 7602	91712
Lower Penhole	SX 2890 7626	91740
Lynher*	SX 2778 7528	91746
Middle Tremollett	SX 2982 7589	91719
Nine Tors	SX 2398 7718	91732
Nodmans Bowda	SX 2675 7524	91734

North Bowda*	SX 2483 7738	91718
South Trewithey	SX 2803 7684	91747
Trebartha	SX 2641 7729	91736
Trebartha Barton*	SX 2647 7784	91737
Trefuge*	SX 2876 7725	91711
Tressellern	SX 2362 7689	91716
Trewithey	SX 2807 7689	91713
Upper Penhole	SX 2884 7630	91741
West Castick Farm	SX 2616 7682	91735
West Tremollett*	SX 2931 7581	91742

St Cleer

Carkeet*	SX 2198 7329	91730
Hopsland	SX 2428 6943	91714
Siblyback	SX 2348 7261	91709
South Trekeive	SX 2350 6948	91715
Wimbleford	SX 2138 7364	91731

St Neot

Berrydown Farm	SX 1932 6894	91723
Dozmaryhill	SX 1982 7543	91721
Dozmaryhill Cottage	SX 1989 7539	91724
Great Hammett*	SX 1888 6968	91706
Great Treverbyn*	SX 2306 6786	91727
Harrowbridge	SX 2059 7438	91729
Lamelgate	SX 2193 7078	91707
Littleworth*	SX 1960 7560	29916
Lower Bowden*	SX 2022 6881	91728
Lower Trenant	SX 2103 6836	91708
St Lukes Farm	SX 1944 7642	91725
Toddy Park*	SX 1878 7605	91722

SOUTH LINCOLNSHIRE

Great Hale

Crow Lane Farm*	TF 1606 4256	91532
Farm, Great Hale Fen	TF 1718 4344	91541
Hall Farm	TF 1515 4262	91521
Manor Farm*	TF 1496 4309	91516
Mastins Farm	TF 1793 4228	91539
Parks Farm*	TF 1995 4321	91544
Poplar Farm*	TF 1753 4333	91540
Rookery Farm*	TF 1520 4319	91522
Shepherd's Top Farm*	TF 1701 4206	91537
White House Farm	TF 1696 4365	91542

Helpringham

Devonport Farm	TF 1682 3862	91527
Eau End Farm	TF 1789 3830	91533
Farm, Helpringham Fen*	TF 1467 3927	91511
Farm, Helpringham Fen	TF 1614 3824	91526
Farm, Helpringham Fen	TF 1665 3883	91529
Manor Farm	TF 1405 4073	32221
Park House	TF 1563 3997	91519
Poplar Farm	TF 1661 3879	91528
Red Roof Stud	TF 1554 3872	91518
South Drove Farm	TF 1680 3772	91524
South View	TF 1542 3879	91573

Little Hale

Broadhurst Farm	TF 1743 4140	91536
Car Dike Farm	TF 1558 4126	91520
Drove Farm	TF 1803 3980	91543
Fen Farm	TF 1611 4083	91531
Grange Farm*	TF 1441 4165	91514
Home Farm	TF 1679 4002	91530
Johnson's Farm*	TF 1461 4161	91513
Lawnfield Farm	TF 1437 4184	91515
Middleyard Farm	TF 1738 3923	91535
Stennet's Farm	TF 1777 3868	91534

Swaton

Bridge Farm	TF 1318 3731	91505
Cardyke Farm	TF 1461 3730	91510
Chestnut House	TF 1337 3777	91567
Church Farm	TF 1336 3774	91506
Eau Farm	TF 1287 3752	91502
Farm, Swaton Common	TF 1151 3727	91572
Farm, Swaton Common*	TF 1161 3859	91571
Farm, Swaton Fen*	TF 1689 3631	91570
Forty Foot Farm	TF 1625 3628	91532
Grove Farm	TF 1261 3763	91503
Manor Farm	TF 1326 3801	91508
North Drove Farm	TF 1511 3768	91517
Smithy Farm	TF 1304 3737	91504
Village Farm	TF 1335 3786	91507

Braceby and Sapperton

Chestnuts Farm, Sapperton	TF 0198 3388	91480
Church Farm, Braceby	TF 0152 3530	14915
Manor Farm, Sapperton	TF 0193 3395	14917
Old Manor Farm, Braceby	TF 0158 3543	14912

Folkingham

Low Farm	TF 0699 3348	39808
Owens Barn Farm	TF 0565 3250	91494
Spring Farm	TF 0711 3344	91569

Lenton, Keisby and Osgodby

Grange Farm, Hanby*	TF 0319 3126	91486
Hanby Grange Farm, Hanby*	TF 0290 3175	91483
Hanby Lodge Farm, Hanby*	TF 0218 3208	91484

Newton and Haceby

Farm, Haceby	TF 0296 3600	91496
Haceby Lodge, Haceby	TF 0257 3675	91485
Moat Farm, Haceby*	TF 0302 3596	91488
Moat Farm, Newton*	TF 0483 3612	91493
Newton Grange Farm, Newton	TF 0712 3616	90501
Woodside Farm, Newton*	TF 0439 3614	91492

Pickworth

Laurel Farm	TF 0406 3367	91491

Lodge Farm	TF 0425 3189	91489
Manor Farm	TF 0432 3370	14950
Old Hall Farm	TF 0389 3371	14954
Pickworth Lodge Farm	TF 0450 3210	91490

Walcot (nr Folkingham)

Grange Farm	TF 0622 3516	91499
Manor Farm	TF 0595 3508	91497
Red House Farm	TF 0607 3504	91498
Walcot Lodge Farm	TF 0504 3500	91495

Bolingbroke

Hareby Farm, Hareby*	TF 3365 6573	91551
Highfield Farm	TF 3559 6565	91558

East Keal

Glebe Farm*	TF 3785 6495	91564

East Kirkby

Home Farm, Hagnaby*	TF 3428 6307	91554
Hungry Hill	TF 3354 6419	91550

Lusby with Winceby

Asgarby House Farm, Asgarby*	TF 3347 6685	91552
Hall Farm, Asgarby	TF 3271 6703	91548
Ivy House Farm, Lusby	TF 3376 6777	91553
Manor Farm, Lusby	TF 3411 6776	91555

Mavis Enderby

Northfield Farm	TF 3571 6766	91560

Revesby

Manor Farm, Miningsby	TF 3232 6416	91546
Minningsby House Farm, Miningsby	TF 3221 6395	91547

West Keal

High Barn	TF 3621 6426	91562
Laythorpe Farm	TF 3520 6299	91556

NORTH NORTHUMBERLAND

Branxton

Branxtonhill	NT 8934 3648	91703
Branxtonmoor	NT 8984 3598	91693

Carham

Downham	NT 8653 3394	91686
East Moneylaws	NT 8781 3600	91688
Mindrum	NT 8415 3274	91684
West Moneylaws*	NT 8730 3552	91687

Ewart

Lanton*	NT 9264 3120	91672

Ford

Cookstead	NT 8902 3885	91694

Crookham Eastfield	NT 9074 3904	91696
Crookham Westfield*	NT 8875 3834	91691
Mardon	NT 9044 3759	91695

Kilham

Elsdonburn Shank	NT 8622 2925	91685
Housdenhaugh	NT 8963 3232	91669
Kilham*	NT 8849 3247	91689
Reedsford	NT 8933 3247	91692
Thompson's Walls	NT 8676 3041	91659
Thornington	NT 8845 3355	91690

Kirknewton

Coldburn	NT 8925 2404	91667
Crookhouse*	NT 9055 3176	91670
Dunsdale	NT 8990 2315	91666
Elsdonburn	NT 8738 2838	91661
Fleehope*	NT 8840 2364	91663
Goldscleugh	NT 9136 2334	91671
Hethpool*	NT 8960 2840	91668
Mounthooly*	NT 8814 2256	91662
Southernknowe	NT 8891 2457	91664
Trowupburn*	NT 8765 2652	91660
Westnewton*	NT 9034 3028	91704
Whitehall	NT 8885 2604	91665

Ancroft

Brockmill Farm	NU 0597 4358	91677
Cheswick Buildings	NU 0210 4582	91673
Cheswick Cottage	NU 0404 4644	91676
East House	NU 0315 4664	91674
Goswick	NU 0071 4519	91678
Inland Pasture*	NU 0142 4904	91705
Scremerston Town Farm	NU 0156 4791	91697
Windmill Hill Farm	NU 0405 4566	91675

Easington

Easington	NU 1250 3482	91682
Easington Demesne*	NU 1250 3534	91683

Kyloe

Beal Farm	NU 0660 4272	91679
Buckton	NU 0834 3831	91680
Fenwick Granary*	NU 0705 4042	91699
Fenwick Stead	NU 0794 3952	91698
Mounthooly	NU 0543 4142	91700

Lowick

Black Heddon No. 2*	NU 0355 4000	91702

Middleton

Low Middleton*	NU 1080 3681	91701

Chollerton

Chollerton Steading*	NY 9332 7204	91681

INDEX

Page references in bold refer to illustrations. Endnotes are indicated by n and nn after page references.